CONTENTS ✔ KU-545-461

A FAIR TEST?

ASSESSMENT, ACHIEVEMENT AND EQUITY

Caroline Gipps and
Patricia Murphy

Open University Press
Buckingham · Philadelphia

Open University Press
Celtic Court
22 Ballmoor
Buckingham
MK18 1XW

and
1900 Frost Road, Suite 101
Bristol, PA 19007, USA

First Published 1994

A catalogue record of this book is available from the British Library

ISBN 0 335 15673 8 (pbk)   0 335 15674 6 (hbk)

Library of Congress Cataloging-in-Publication Data

Gipps, C.V.
    A fair test? : assessment, achievement and equity / Caroline Gipps
and Patricia Murphy.
        p.   cm. — (Assessing assessment)
    Includes bibliographical references (p.   ) and index.
    ISBN 0–335–15674–6. — ISBN 0–335–15673–8 (pbk.)
    1. Test bias—Great Britain. 2. Examinations—Great Britain—
Validity. 3. Sexism in educational tests—Great Britain.
    4. Educational tests and measurements—Great Britain. I. Murphy,
Patricia, 1952–   . II. Title. III. Series.
    LB3060.62.G57   1994
    371.2'6'013—dc20   93–23368
                                                                  CIP

Typeset by Colset Pte Ltd, Singapore
Printed in Great Britain by St Edmundsbury Press Ltd,
Bury St Edmunds, Suffolk

SERIES EDITOR'S INTRODUCTION

Changing theories and methods of assessment have been the focus of significant attention for some years now, not only in the United Kingdom, but also in many other western industrial countries and many developing countries. Curriculum developers have realized that real change will not take place in schools if traditional paper-and-pencil tests, be they essay or multiple choice, remain unchanged to exert a constraining influence on how teachers and pupils approach new curricula. Similarly, examiners have been concerned to develop more valid and 'authentic' (to use the American parlance) ways of assessing the changes which have been introduced into school syllabuses over recent years – more practical work, oral work, problem solving and so forth. In turn psychologists and sociologists have become concerned with the impact of assessment on learning and motivation, and how that impact can be developed more positively. This has led to a myriad of developments in the field of assessment, often involving an increasing role for the teacher in school-based assessment, as more relevant and challenging tasks are devised by examination agencies for administration by teachers in schools, and as the role and status of more routine teacher assessment of coursework, practical work, groupwork and so forth has become enhanced.

However, educationists have not been the only ones to focus much more closely on the inter-relation of curriculum, pedagogy and assessment. Governments around the world, but particularly in the United Kingdom, have also begun to take a close interest in the ways in which assessment can influence and even control teaching, and in the changes in curriculum and teaching which could be brought about by changes in assessment. This interest has not been wholly coherent. Government intervention in the UK has sometimes initiated, sometimes reinforced the move towards a more practical and vocationally oriented curriculum and thus the move towards more practical, school-based assessment. But government has also been concerned with issues of accountability and with what it sees as the maintenance of traditional academic standards through the use of externally set tests.

It is precisely because of this complexity and confusion that the present series of books on assessment has been developed. Many claims are being made with respect to the efficacy of new approaches to assessment which require careful review and investigation. Likewise many changes are being required by government intervention which may lead to hurried and poorly understood developments being implemented in schools. The aim of this series is to take a longer term view of the changes which are occurring, to move beyond the immediate problems of implementation and to interrogate the claims and the changes in terms of broader research evidence which derives from both theoretical and empirical work. In reviewing the field in this way the intention of the series is thus to highlight relevant research evidence, identify key factors and principles which should underpin the developments taking place, and provide teachers and administrators with a basis for informed decision-making which takes the educational issues seriously and goes beyond simply accommodating the latest policy imperative.

With these intentions in mind, Caroline Gipps and Patricia Murphy's book is a particularly timely and important one. While much debate about external testing versus school-based assessment is ostensibly concerned with the fairness and objectivity of assessment, and while much policy rhetoric encompasses a commitment to 'equal opportunities', what is actually meant by these terms, and what is accomplished in practice, is seldom subject to rigorous scrutiny. Gipps and Murphy marshal and review a wealth of international evidence on the topic and address vitally important questions concerning both the measurement of achievement and the explanations of differences in measured achievement. They set out 'to examine the extent of observed group differences . . . and to understand what these might reflect'. They raise key questions of validity and ask to what extent are apparent differences in achievement created by particular approaches to subject knowledge and the way in which it is tested: can changing the structure and content of the test change the pattern of results? In the case of boys and girls in particular, the answer seems to be 'yes', though such research evidence is also relevant within groups as well as across groups and can vary across cultures.

Thus Gipps and Murphy review definitions of equity, what various studies of achievement tell us about how different groups perform and what sorts of explanations (biological and social) have been offered to account for such differences. But they also go on to ask questions of the assessment process itself and consider how our definitions of achievement are constructed and built into the assumptions we make about tests and testing. They provide the first accessible and comparative review of major international studies of achievement and those of the British Assessment of Performance Unit (APU) and the American National Assessment of Educational Progress (NAEP). They also look at UK examination performance and recent evidence from National Curriculum assessment.

The book is consistently impressive in its scope and in its intellectual achievement of synthesizing and critically examining such a wide range of evidence. It is also important politically since it reminds us that assessment not only carries social and economic consequences but is a social as well as a technical endeavour. Measuring achievement depends on how we define achievement as well as how we design and structure assessment instruments. The authors have made an extremely significant contribution to what should be a continuing and increasingly important debate about how we construe and construct the process of assessment in a pluralist society.

Harry Torrance

ACKNOWLEDGEMENTS

We should like to thank Harry Torrance for his patience and careful editing, Harvey Goldstein, Gordon Stobart and Janette Ellwood for their comments, and also Joan Mason for her helpful insights.

Caroline Gipps would like to thank the Nuffield Foundation for the fellowship which provided her with the time to write.

Patricia's thanks go to Daniel, Siobhan and James.

Finally our thanks to Anne Swan, Louise Jordan and Amanda Claremont for surviving and transforming numerous draft stages of the text.

INTRODUCTION

Assessment has long been part of the educational system. In recent years, however, its importance has increased; not only is there more assessment in schools, but it is also of more significance for pupils and the educational system as a whole. In the UK, the General Certificate of Secondary Education (or GCSE, the 16 + exam) is now aimed at all ability groups, unlike its predecessors, the O Level/CSE exams; informal assessment for Records of Achievement is commonplace; national curriculum assessment provides a comprehensive formal and informal assessment at ages 7, 11 and 14. In the UK as in other countries, we are also seeing an element of qualification inflation which means that the level of qualifications required for various jobs has risen so that exams are more important for more pupils than they used to be; with the new emphasis on 'choice' at secondary school level selection by attainment (to over-subscribed schools at least) is re-entering the arena; national curriculum assessment results are being used increasingly to group pupils by attainment at all levels of schooling. It is clear, therefore, that assessment now plays an enhanced role in education at all phases. Because of this, it is crucially important that assessment is considered in terms of its fairness for all as a measure of achievement.

We approach the issues of equity and fairness through a focus on the outcomes of various assessments in order to examine the extent of observed group differences in performance and to understand what these might reflect. Our central concern in our examination of assessment practice is validity, using here the general dictionary definition of valid as 'sound'. The question we address, therefore, is whether assessment practice is equally fair and sound for all groups. If this is not the case, how can we interpret the results and in particular any group differences in performance?

An example will help to set the scene and explain what we are trying to do: The following piece comes from the *Times Educational Supplement* (TES, 6 September 1991) under the headline: 'No brakes to halt test score slide'. It is an article about a standardized multiple-choice exam in the USA called the Scholastic Aptitude Test (SAT). This is a voluntary exam but is taken by most students who aim to go to college, since there are no national school leaving exams. The results for 1991 were the fourth year running to show a decline:

> The SAT has been consistently criticised for being unfair to girls and (ethnic) minority students, and once again both have made a poor showing. Girls averaged 44 points fewer than boys in the maths section, and six points fewer in the verbal part.
>
> Apologists for this year's results note that the SAT is being taken by more and more pupils, thereby diluting the pool. This year it was taken by 1,032,685 seniors, an increase of 7,162 over 1990. Others point out that more minorities, girls and non-English speakers are now taking the test.
>
> Elsewhere, blame is being placed on less rigorous academic standards, too little reading and too much television.
>
> Not all the high school seniors are doing badly. Analysis of the results shows that those bound for highly-selective colleges, most of whom go to good schools in wealthy residential areas, scored nearly 100 points higher on each section of the test than their less privileged peers.

What are we to make of this piece? What does it mean to say the test is unfair to girls and minority students? Why should scores drop if more girls and ethnic minorities are included in the test population? What pre-conceptions lie behind such explanations? Does the style and content of the test itself have anything to do with the pattern of results?

We could equally well have included an article from the TES about girls' improved performance in GCSE and the extent to which this is due to course-work assessment. Does this mean that course-work assessment is unfair to boys? (And is the recent decision to reduce the amount of course-work assessment a consequence of the perceived advantage which it gives to girls?)

Questions such as these have to be considered if we are to delve into the meaning of fairness in assessment. They relate to the interpretation of assessment results as much as to technical issues to do with reducing bias and designing fairer tests. At this point we are using bias in its non-technical sense of 'prejudice' or 'slant', although it has specific technical definitions which we consider in Chapter 1.

It is not just a question of looking at equity in the context of assessment but also within the curriculum, as the two are intimately related. The way in which a subject is defined, for a syllabus and for an exam, is crucial: if a subject is defined by one group according to their background and interests, it is likely that it will be less meaningful to other groups. Bias in the curriculum (which we do not address specifically) and equal access to learning, both of which interact with teacher expectation, are crucial to how an individual (or group) achieves.

For example, international studies show that in most countries girls are less likely to study maths and science to an advanced level. In population surveys, therefore, they would perform less well than boys simply because fewer of them would have had the chance to learn advanced maths and science. Unless this is made clear, however, such surveys may be interpreted as showing that girls are less good at maths or science than boys. In studies which control for curriculum background, the pattern of performance appears much more similar. To take another example, one of the reasons for differential success in public exams in the UK is different entry patterns. Girls tend to be allocated to easier routes in maths than their ability warrants because they are seen as hard working rather than bright (Walden and Walkerdine 1985) and because they may be felt to be anxious about failure (Elwood 1992). Conversely, low-ability boys may not be put in for maths GCSE at all, which denies them the opportunity to achieve success.

There is evidence, too, that ethnic minority pupils are more likely to be allocated to lower-level exam routes (Eggleston *et al.*, 1986; Smith and Tomlinson 1989). The case-study work of Cecile Wright showed that Afro-Caribbean students were likely to be placed in bands and examination sets well below their actual academic ability. Her evidence suggested that the teachers' assessment of these students was influenced more by behavioural criteria than cognitive ones (Wright 1987). This was a result of the teachers' 'adverse relationship' with these students and the outcome was the limiting of their educational opportunities. Schools admitted on several occasions that this was an allocation based not only on ability, but also on 'social factors': they were not prepared to put Afro-Caribbean children into the academic/examination streams in case they were disruptive or unrealistically ambitious (Eggleston 1988).

Teacher expectation is a powerful factor mediating children's school experience at all levels of schooling. In the Inner London Education Authority's (ILEA) Junior School study, there was a tendency for some Afro-Caribbean children to be allocated by their teachers to the middle verbal reasoning ability band when in fact their test scores showed them to be in the top band (Mortimore *et al.* 1988). A study of black and working-class white children in London infant schools (Tizard *et al.* 1988) showed that, overall, teachers did not have lower expectations of black children: in maths they tended to overestimate black boys (because they were black and teachers did not want to appear biased and because they were boys) and underestimate white girls (because they were white and girls). What they did show, however, was a relationship between teacher expectation and the curriculum offered the child, and this in turn had an effect on the child's progress.

The picture is therefore a complex one, and not just to do with the design of tests and assessment material. Our criticism of the traditional psychometric approach to testing is that it operates on the assumption that technical solutions can be found to solve problems of equity with the emphasis on using elaborate techniques to eliminate biased items (Murphy 1990; Goldstein 1993). The limitation of this approach is that it does not look at the way in which the subject is defined (i.e. the overall domain from which test items are to be chosen), nor at the initial choice of items from the thus-defined pool, nor does it question what counts as achievement. It simply 'tinkers' with an established selection of items.

Given the complexity of the area we shall attempt to be as clear as possible about the terms we are using (for example, why we use the term equity rather than equal opportunities), our definitions and the parameters of the debate. We start by looking at some of the definitions used by researchers and educationists in relation to bias and equal opportunities and the concepts and hypotheses underlying these definitions. This is important because studies in this area and interpretations of, for example, examination results, depend on people's underlying – even unacknowledged – concepts and assumptions. Our intention is to uncover the underlying concepts and assumptions about achievement and how these are translated into assessment practice.

We then go on to look at the ways in which information has been collected about the performance of different groups of pupils, at national and international level, and how these are interpreted. Along the way we visit studies of sex differences in intellectual performance and the vexed area of intelligence testing and its carry-over, the 11 +. We shall keep returning to the underlying concepts/hypotheses in the work we review and comment on the interpretations given. In conclusion, we shall indicate where we see the field of knowledge now and the ways in which we think future research and policy should go forward.

We focus on gender, ethnic group and social class differences where ever such evidence is available; data on differences in performance in relation to all three types is generally not available and thus we cannot always deal with them all. It is of course highly likely that gender, social class and ethnic group interact and so we are missing some of the picture. But even to begin to consider for example gender and ethnic group together represents progress on much of the work that has gone before.

Finally, a brief introduction to the sources of differential performance: most of the hypotheses relating to sources of group differences in performance will be dealt with in Chapter 2 where we review studies of sex differences in intellectual abilities, but we foreshadow these here in order to provide the reader with a map of the terrain. Biological hypotheses for differences in group performance suggest that there are underlying physiological differences between groups, whether these differences are genetic, hormonal or due to differences in the structure of the brain. Interestingly, these factors are no longer used to account for differences in performance between ethnic groups, since this approach has been discredited, but are still used to account for differences between the sexes.

Environmental hypotheses include cultural, social and psychological influences (sometimes called 'psycho-social' variables) that affect the development of individuals within specific groups. For example, parents expect different behaviours from boys and girls and consequently they try to provide different activities and toys for them and provide different types of feedback. Thus boys and girls come to attend to different features of the environment and make sense of the world in different ways. This can affect their learning and performance in school through a variety of processes: different out-of-school experiences, different within-school experiences, perceived male and female domains, attitude, self-image and expectations of success. These environmental hypotheses, though mostly developed in relation to gender differences, are also useful in considering differences in performance between ethnic/cultural groups. In the environmental group of factors for differential performance we must also place equality of opportunity, that is equal access to schooling and curriculum, both formal and actual (which we discuss in Chapter 1), for without this there are bound to be group differences in performance.

Both biological and environmental hypotheses imply that the differences in performance are real. Differential performance, however, may be due to the test itself; in other words, groups (or individuals) may have an equal level of knowledge or skill but be unable to show it to the same extent because the test is unfair to one group. This might be because of the language used or artefacts in the illustrations or text which make the task meaningful to one group but less meaningful to another.

There is also, however, another possibility – that the test itself is not unfair, but something about the administration of the test produces poor performance in one group of candidates who may/ do have a similar level of knowledge or skill but again are unable to show it. An example of this is lowered performance in black children tested by white psychologists.

Having set the scene, we now turn to some definitions.

1

DEFINING EQUITY

Equal opportunities

This book and the arguments contained within it are inextricably linked with the notion of equal opportunities in education. However, simple though this term might at first seem to be, it is in fact highly contentious, as are the social and political arguments which surround it. It is important, therefore, to spend a little time going through various definitions of equal opportunities and to relate them to our definition of equity and the theoretical position on which our discussion of the literature is based.

Wood (1987) discusses various definitions of equal opportunities and lists them as being to do with:

1 Equal life chances
2 Open competition for scarce opportunities
3 Equal cultivation of different capacities
4 Independence of educational attainment from social origins.

Offering equal life chances is clearly impossible: even if one ensures that schools give the same advantages to everyone, one would have to 'equalize' for homes and parents, and then there are still

the differences in physiological make-up. In relation to open competition, Wood makes the point that although this seems appeal-
ing at first glance, the question is why something which is acquired
accidentally (i.e. ability, intelligence, aptitude or talent) is used as
a basis for allocating reward. However, as we shall see, this is the
direction in which policy on equal opportunities has moved in the
late 1980s and early 1990s.

The classic expression of Wood's third item is the 11 + examination, which, in the UK, selected for different forms of secondary
schooling; the different capacities were to be dealt with or nurtured
in different settings, from grammar school through technical to
secondary modern school, each group of children being thought to
be most able to profit from the type of school to which they were
allocated. The problem with this version is that only the high-
status, academic school is seen as being prestigious and actually
offering equal – that is, 'good' – life chances. The last item in his
list, Wood concludes, is the most attractive but the one which is
the most difficult to attain.

Wood quotes Dore as saying that the only way to promote
equality of educational opportunity is to make inequality so
apparent that the introduction of a compensatory measure (i.e.
to compensate to equalize) is made to seem imperative (Dore 1976)
and this was the basis of much of the equal opportunities policy-
making in the 1970s.

Wood turns to what he calls social engineering views of equal
opportunities and gives us the one which he feels would probably command most popular support: equal cultivation of different
capacities (the ideology underpinning the 11 + examination). What
equal cultivation means and how it is to be organized is the difficulty. Where capacity is not yet manifest, but may become so
in the future, the difficulty of implementing equal opportunities
becomes most severe. Wood asks 'how do we cultivate something
that is yet to be, let alone cultivate it equally across all persons?'
(1987: 6), and cites the case of the 11 + where local education
authorities supported their provision of different numbers of grammar school places for boys and girls on the grounds that although
the boys were manifesting less potential at the time, they actually
have more potential for the future than do girls.

Equality of opportunity, as the section on the 11 + makes clear,
was a feature of the 1944 Education Act. At this time, the focus

was upon inequalities of circumstance which might present real barriers to some individuals. Thus the provision of free education for all in the 1944 Act was an important move towards greater equality of opportunity. Halsey *et al.* (1980) refer to access and participation in relation to the *formal* opportunities which are open to members of different social groups, and it is true that in the UK we do have equal opportunities in the sense that there is formal equal opportunity for access to and participation in education. During the 1960s, however, understanding of this formal notion of equality shifted with the realization that educational opportunities were not *actually* equally accessible to all groups. In investigating educational access, Halsey and colleagues turned instead to look at educational outcomes in order to assess actual opportunities, i.e. those available and taken up. They focused on 'the relative chances of access to schools and qualifications which were, substantively as distinct from formally, open to the children of different social classes. In effect, taking the word "equality" to have its normal meaning in common speech, the definition now shifts from equality of opportunity to equality of outcome' (Halsey *et al.* 1980: 202). This definition of equal opportunities, which focuses on equality of *outcome*, is the one underlying discussions of group performance at public examination level.

Gillborn (1990) reviews the literature on equal opportunities in relation to ethnic minorities. On the one hand, writers such as Jeffcote criticize the 1970s view of equal opportunities as narrow and elitist (because it emphasizes the high status of academic performance); it is essentially conservative in concept because the gross disparities in wealth, power and status which characterize our society remain unchallenged. On the other hand, equal opportunities is seen by the extreme Right as a revolutionary device which would disturb the 'natural' social order and as an attempt to attack White British society. For example, Flew argues that differences in outcome performance do not necessarily demonstrate differences in opportunity; groups compared may indeed not be equally able, equally eager and equally well qualified (Flew 1986, quoted in Gillborn 1990) and those who espouse this argument recognize only the formal equality of opportunity and/or treatment. This argument is often linked with discussions of competition arguing that if competitions are held fairly, then clearly the best person wins. The point which Gillborn makes is that education is not a competition but that it is an attempt to provide the best possible educational provision, support and opportunities for all groups.

Early attempts to achieve equality of opportunity for girls and boys focused in the main on equality of resources and access to curriculum offerings. In a review of this approach in various countries, Yates (1985) concludes that a simple policy of equal offerings was a naive approach to social equality given the very different out-of-school experiences of girls and boys. In Yates' view, the fundamental problem is that this policy focus reflects a deficit model approach to inequality: girls are 'blamed' for behaving like girls and encouraged to behave more like boys. This model implies the possibility of overcoming disadvantage through the acquisition of what is lacking. This approach leaves the *status quo* essentially unchanged, since girls are unlikely to achieve parity through equality of resources and formal equality of access alone. As Yates puts it: 'where the criteria of success and the norms of teaching and curriculum are still defined in terms of the already dominant group, that group is always likely to remain one step ahead' (Yates 1985: 212). What is needed, rather, is a quite different experience of education. In this vein, Thelin (1990) argues that equal opportunities should address jobs, power, authority, family life and child care. Girls and women are entitled to be equal on their own terms and according to their own needs, they should not be limited to the agenda set by boys and men: the interests, strategies and plans of girls and young women should be as important as those of their male peers.

Weiner (1990) identifies two distinct feminist perspectives that emerged in the early 1980s, that of equal opportunities and that of anti-sexist initiatives. These hinge on different interpretations of equality that correspond to the definitions which emerged in the debate about multicultural as opposed to anti-racist approaches to education. The equal opportunities perspective and the multicultural perspective operate within existing educational structures, while the anti-sexist and anti-racist perspectives challenge the unequal power relations between the sexes and ethnic groups and aim to transform the patriarchal and ethnocentric nature of school structures and curricula. The latter group moves beyond looking at resources and access (as described by Yates) to develop strategies for challenging white male domination of schooling both in terms of what is learnt and how it is learnt and valued. Weiner (1990) points out, however, that in recent years the experience of trying to implement change has brought the two approaches closer together; new strategies which combine features of both are being sought to achieve feasible and practical reform rather than radical change.

In the UK, the Equal Opportunities Commission (EOC) does not generally define equal opportunities in education, but simply uses the term in relation to sex discrimination. In their leaflet 'Do You Provide Equal Educational Opportunities?' (EOC 1982), they define discriminatory practices which may be found unlawful in a court of law. These include the use of separate tests for boys and girls, the use of different sex norms in the calculation of scores, the operation of a quota system based on pupils' sex, the exclusion of pupils from a course of study solely on the grounds of sex, the exclusion of pupils from courses as a result of single-sex schooling, and sex discrimination in careers guidance. They then offer guidelines for good practice in schools which really focus on not discriminating between boys and girls, i.e. offering actual as well as formal equality of opportunity. This includes examining the curriculum, looking at the content of reading schemes and books and considering the hidden curriculum. In a leaflet produced in 1991 entitled 'Equal Opportunities in Schools', the EOC goes further in giving advice to school governors. Although they talk largely about sex stereotyping and discrimination, they do by implication outline their notion of equality of opportunity, again linking it to sex discrimination. Discrimination means less favourable treatment, of which there may be two kinds: (1) direct discrimination where a person of one sex is treated less favourably because of his or her sex, and (2) indirect discrimination where a conditional requirement is applied to both sexes but disproportionately few people of one sex can comply with it and the inability to comply is to the disadvantage of the individual concerned. The EOC makes the point that even nearly 20 years after the passing of the Sex Discrimination Act 1975, there is still a problem in securing equal educational chances for girls and boys. It is not just a matter of unequal access to facilities but that many teachers have different expectations of girls and boys. Boys generally receive more teacher attention and dominate in the use of equipment in science, technology and computer studies, while girls are frequently subjected to verbal and sometimes physical abuse by the boys.

Perspectives on equality in the USA are rather different and it is here that the concept of equity emerges. The key document is the influential and controversial Coleman Report (Coleman *et al.* 1966). This was based on the survey of Equality of Educational Opportunity asked for by Congress in 1964 to study the lack of availability of equal educational opportunities for individuals by reason of 'race, colour, religion or national origin'. The survey was designed around five concepts of inequality:

1 Differences in input characteristics (in schools), such as income, quality of staffing and other resources.
2 Differences in social and racial composition of the school population.
3 Inequality arising from intangible characteristics of schools, such as teacher morale, teacher expectation of students, student motivation, etc.
4 Inequality in terms of the effects of the school for individuals with equal backgrounds and ability, i.e. equality of results given the same individual input.
5 Equality of results given unequal individual inputs.

This survey has been widely criticized, not least for the very narrow measure of achievement used. However, the Report and the debate it fuelled have been influential in determining what is meant by equity in education and the relationship of this to equality of educational opportunity. Coleman's perspective is on equality of outcomes (for groups rather than individuals); he concludes that the extent to which this can be achieved depends not only on the equality of educational input but also on the effectiveness of the school's influence relative to the external divergent influences in bringing about achievement. In this perspective, the responsibility to create achievement rests with the institution not the student; equality of output is determined not by the resource inputs alone but by the power of those resources to bring about achievement (i.e. resources and effective use of resources). This is in contrast to the policy approach described by Yates (see above), which focuses simply on offering resources.

Fennema (1990), writing about equity in maths education nearly 25 years after the Coleman Report, considers similar alternative

definitions of equity to Wood (1987), but concludes that 'the definition of equity as the achievement of equal outcomes offers the
greatest promise for achieving true justice . . . justice will not be
achieved until the goals of education are met equally by both sexes'
(Fennema 1990: 5). It is worth noting that Fennema refers to equity
rather than equal opportunities as Wood does, even though the
definitions they consider are similar. What marks Fennema's use
of the term equity is her focus on justice. Secada (1989: 69) makes
the following distinction between equity and equality: 'educational
equity should be construed as a check on the justice of specific
actions that are carried out within the educational arena and the
arrangements that result from those actions. Equality is defined
implicitly as the absence of differences (between groups)'. He goes
on to suggest that equality studies focus on quantitative differences
between groups and cannot address those qualitative issues related
to the curriculum against which that equality is assessed. Secada
sees these issues as the ones that need to be tackled if any attempt
is to be made to ensure educational equity.

National policy is clearly influential in determining how definitions of equity and equality of opportunity are translated into
educational practice. Coleman's (1968) concept of effective equality of opportunity, that is, equality in those elements that are effective for learning, did dominate action in the USA and similar
perceptions of equality are evident in British and European policy.
Such a concept led to the notion of compensatory education and
a concern largely with the plight of minority groups rather than
with individual rights and freedoms. Apple's (1989) review of
recent public policy in the USA, Britain and Australia leads him to
conclude that equality has now been redefined. It is no longer
linked to group oppression and disadvantage but is concerned to
ensure individual choice within a 'free-market' perception of the
educational community. In Apple's view, this redefinition has re-
instated the disadvantage model that Yates referred to in educational policy. Underachievement is once again the responsibility of
the individual rather than the educational institution. Apple is at
pains to point out that educators must not collude in allowing this
'even more limited vision of equality on the social and educational
agenda' or forget 'the reality of the oppressive conditions that exist
for so many (people)' (p. 23). He argues that attention must be
refocused on important curricular questions, to which we add

Table 1.1 Curriculum and assessment questions in relation to equity

Curricular questions	Assessment questions
Whose knowledge is taught?	What knowledge is assessed and equated with achievement?
Why is it taught in a particular way to this particular group?	Are the form, content and mode of assessment appropriate for different groups and individuals?
How do we enable the histories and cultures of people of colour, and of women, to be taught in responsible and responsive ways?	Is this range of cultural knowledge reflected in definitions of achievement? How does cultural knowledge mediate individuals' responses to assessments in ways which alter the construct being assessed?

Source: After Apple (1989)

assessment questions (see Table 1.1) where we list the important curriculum and assessment questions to be asked in relation to equity.

The goal of equal outcomes (or equality of output as Coleman puts it) must, according to Levine (1975), be seen as distinct from, and partially conflicting with, the goal of equal opportunity. Individual outcomes in a competitive system will be unequal; only when the barriers that comprise *un*equal opportunity have been eliminated so that the rules of the competition are fair will 'intragroup differences and equality of results take precedence over intergroup differences and equality of opportunity' (Levine 1975: 319). A redefinition of equality to be concerned with equality of outcomes would in any case have, in the context of assessment, major implications for the way our society functions to filter students into certain life and career patterns.

Assessment and equal opportunities

Assessment is intimately linked with the whole area of equality and equity, since our measure of achievement depends almost uniquely on some form of assessment; formal assessment is the 'objective' quantitative indicator used in virtually all studies of equality of educational opportunity. Assessment is therefore as important to the equity debate as equity issues are to assessment.

Wood (1987) makes the telling point that assessment has been seen at various times both to promote equal opportunities and to militate against them. Originally, exams were seen as a way of encouraging advancement through talent rather than social connections and the classic example given is the introduction of the civil service exams in Britain in the 1850s. Later, in the UK with the 11 + and in the USA post-1965 era of civil rights legislation, exams and tests were seen as denying opportunity, since formal equal opportunity to sit a test does not offer equal opportunity for continuing education. Wood points out that the crucial distinction between the two points of argument is that advancement through talent *as measured by tests and exams* is disputed: critics were saying that the opportunity to acquire talent or at least to be able to show it to sufficient effect were not equally distributed and that black and/or working-class children were the losers. However, the notion of assessment as promoting equal opportunities still carries much weight. Most people, Wood imagines, would say that public examinations offer a necessary corrective to progress through social connections and they function to identify talent which might otherwise remain hidden. The notion of the standard test as a way of offering impartial assessment is of course a powerful one, though if there is not equality of educational opportunity preceding the test, then the 'fairness' of this approach is called into question.

Scarr (1984), however, argues that in the absence of tests other less objective assessments will be found and used; abandoning tests cannot make society more pluralistic, ensure equal rights or redistribute social and economic benefits. The use of standardized tests to give all children the same chance to compete is a case of equal opportunity construed as identical treatment for all regardless of their initial differences in preparation. Scarr accepts that minority children are not equally prepared to compete (relating to actual equality of opportunity as opposed to *formal* equality of opportunity), but she argues that opponents of the use of standardized tests with minority children are objecting primarily to the negative social outcomes of testing, or side-effects (e.g. labelling) for which they blame bias in the tests and testing procedures.

Scarr has an entirely benevolent view of testing, however, and operates on the assumption that testing should inform instruction and that tests should be used appropriately in the best interests of the child. The problem with this assumption is, of course, that testing can and does have negative effects. Scarr concludes that equal opportunity must not be construed as equal treatment for all. Because if it is, it ignores the large individual differences in learning rates and does nothing to remedy performance gaps between groups. 'To give more minority children an equal opportunity we will have to give them more time and instruction in the school skills that will make them literate citizens in the majority culture' (Scarr 1984: 9). This, of course, is what the Head Start Programme set out to do.

In a study of GCSE examination performance at 16 in English and mathematics, Stobart *et al.* (1992a) review some British work on assessment and equal opportunities. They point out that much of the research in this area assumes an agreed meaning in terms of absence of bias, but tends to duck the issue of whether one should be looking for equality of access and/or equality of outcomes. The first question they raise is 'to what extent should we expect similar performances from girls and boys in public exams?' Similar performances occur in standardized intelligence tests because the selection of items ensures that both groups get the same mean IQ; should we therefore not also expect it for public examinations?

Their view is that enough is known about the way in which the design of examinations affects outcomes that to look only at equality of treatment (in terms of entry patterns and marking) would be naive. However, they do not encourage the development of assessment schemes which would ensure equal outcomes. This is because relying on manipulating the style of assessment would mask the important contributions of pupil perceptions of subjects, the experiences they bring to a subject and the type of demands a subject makes. Thus, while not making equal outcomes a direct goal, neither are they satisfied with the current imbalances in both entries and results in public examinations at 16 and 18. 'From an equal opportunities viewpoint all is not well – particularly in such central subjects as mathematics, English, sciences and modern languages. The problem is to determine how much of the problem lies in the pupils' perceptions and outside experiences and how much in the structure and assessment of the subjects' (Stobart *et al.* 1992a: 262). Their view is that the examination boards have a requirement to pursue equal opportunities actively, not simply by avoiding insensitivity in question papers, but by active investigation of the demands which syllabuses make in relation to gender, cultural and class differences.

One problem, they maintain, is that we are unlikely to know that we have provided equal opportunities until we get equal outcomes. But, if equal opportunities relates to not putting obstacles in the way of particular groups, it does not follow necessarily that factors such as interest, diligence or relevant experience will be equal among groups. The example they give is if a particular ethnic group strives much harder on average than other groups for good examination results and by dint of hard work achieves them, should an attempt be made to level those scores to bring them into line with other groups? The authors accept that by engineering the assessment they could bring male and female performance nearer into line. The issue then becomes a question of the extent of this alignment and whether we are then treating gender differences merely 'as artefacts of test items rather than indicative of a particular view of educational achievement' (Murphy 1990: 1). This, of course, links with the notion of the subject's validity. To what extent should we 'distort' a subject in order to produce a test which provides equal outcomes? For example, bringing multiple-choice papers into English to improve the relative performance of boys or introducing essay questions into mathematics to improve the relative performance of girls would both pose acute validity problems as we explain in the next section.

To sum up, the definitions of equal opportunities vary and have shifted over the years. Despite a lack of consensus, there seems to be a general understanding that formal equality of opportunity is not sufficient to ensure fairness. Our view is that while one must strive for actual equality of opportunity, equality of outcomes is not an appropriate goal. The focus on equality of outcomes is, we feel, unsound, since different groups may indeed have different qualities and abilities and certainly experiences: manipulating test items and procedures in order to produce equal outcomes may be doing violence to the construct or skill being assessed and certainly camouflaging genuine group differences. Furthermore, equal opportunities is not only a contested but also a deeply confusing concept, generally ill-defined in the public mind. We therefore use the concept of *equity,* which is defined in the dictionary as moral justice, or the spirit of justice. Equity does not imply equality of outcome and does not presume identical experiences for all – both of these are unrealistic. The concept of equity in assessment as we use it implies that assessment practice and interpretation of results are fair and just for all groups. Our focus on equity and assessment will therefore consider not only the practices of assessment but also the definition of achievement, while at the same time recognizing that other factors (e.g. pupil motivation and esteem, teacher behaviour and expectation) also come into play in determining achievement.

Bias

Bias is defined in the dictionary as prejudice; Goldstein (1993) refers to 'slant'; Shepard *et al.* (1981) describe a test as biased if 'two individuals with equal ability but from different groups do not have the same probability of success'. The term ability is used here presumably to denote ability in the subject or skill being tested, rather than a general ability.

Bias in relation to assessment is generally taken to mean that the assessment is unfair to one particular group or another. This rather simple definition, however, belies the complexity of the underlying situation. Differential performance on a test, i.e. where different groups get different score levels, may not be the result of bias in the assessment; it may be due to real differences in performance among groups, which may in turn be due to differing access to learning, as we have discussed, or it may be due to real differences in the group's attainment in the topic under consideration. The question of whether a test is biased or whether the group in question has a different underlying level of attainment is actually extremely difficult to answer. Wood (1987) describes these different factors as the opportunity to acquire talent (access issues) and the opportunity to show talent to good effect (fairness in the assessment).

The existence of group differences in average performance on tests is often taken to imply that the tests are biased, the assumption being that one group is not inherently less able than the other. However, the two groups may well have been subject to different environmental experiences or unequal access to the curriculum. This difference will be reflected in average test scores, but a test that reflects such unequal opportunity in its scores is not strictly speaking biased, though it could be said to be invalid.

As the chapter on IQ testing will make clear, it is common for IQ tests to be constructed so as to remove items which show gender differences and for there to be separate norms for boys and girls for verbal and non-verbal reasoning tests used in the 11 +. But Goldstein (1986) asks the question why should one stop at adjusting for gender differences? Since this is commonly justified as being due to different maturity levels, why then not adjust also for household size, there being evidence that children in larger households mature earlier? But the main factor causing differential performance is of course social class; therefore, the argument goes why not adjust for social class as well?

In the USA, there have been attempts to devise tests which favour blacks over whites. Goldstein (1986), however, points out that this kind of manipulation of test items is quite different from procedures which are aimed at producing sex- and race-fair tests by eliminating negative stereotypes, derogatory references, etc. Goldstein's paper is largely about the issue of designing tests specifically to favour one gender or the other, i.e. manipulating the overall test bias. His point is that *if* we accept that equality of outcome is both legitimate and desirable, so that we wish to produce exams or tests which have equal score distributions for boys and girls, then we could achieve this through careful choice of format, content, etc. Goldstein suggests the resulting examinations might do much to encourage the sexes to participate more equally in certain subjects and the resulting effects on teaching and the curriculum would be a rather interesting example of an assessment-led pedagogy. However, having said that it would be feasible to carry out such a procedure, in order to eliminate ethnic group differences (as indeed has been done with gender differences in IQ tests) it is difficult to imagine a consensus about the desirability of such an attempt, since as we have pointed out, 'equality of outcome' is highly contentious.

The situation is complicated by the fact that since differences in interest and motivation are considered to be biasing factors, all tests or assessment methods may be said to have a certain amount of bias. A particular reading passage might be more interesting and motivating to a girl than a boy even when overtly gender-related material is removed, or for one who is sports-minded or for someone who is interested in science as opposed to someone who is interested in literature (Wood 1991). This, of course, means that all tests are likely to be biased against particular interest groups and the issue then is how far to take this particular form of reasoning. Indeed, removing particular types of items because they are biased in favour of one gender can cause problems if the topic being assessed is an important part of the syllabus. In this situation, it may be necessary to leave in some items assessing this topic but to make sure that they are not over-represented in the assessment as a whole. Including a variety of assessment techniques may be the best way of reducing biases associated with certain techniques of assessment, e.g. in relation to girls' poorer showing on multiple-choice type questions and boys' poorer showing on essay-type questions (Murphy 1980, 1982).

Wood's view is that genuine differences between groups should be allowed to reveal themselves, the important point being that test developers have a water-tight defence for including items in a test, i.e. in relation to the definition of the domain being assessed. What we know about gender differences in performance for example can and should inform the final composition of the paper, not by veto to prevent particular items from being put into a test, but as a moderating influence. Furthermore, 'group differences . . . should always be looked at for what they might say about the teaching of the subject or test construction strategies' (Wood 1991: 171).

Goldstein (1993) recognizes that group differences arise not just from the type of instrument used but from the construction of the assessment itself and the interaction between the assessment and the groups tested. His conclusion is that bias is not a useful term because it is simplistic and 'its use can result in a subtle obfuscation of important issues' (p. 8). He prefers instead to use the term differential performance and suggests that we investigate differences at the level of the construct being assessed, rather than through statistical manipulation of items.

An alternative viewpoint, in the traditional psychometric model, is (as we outlined in the Introduction) that it is possible to identify bias in test items through statistical procedures. These procedures determine whether any questions in a test or exam are particularly difficult for a certain group once that group's overall test performance is taken into account. This particular form of item analysis is referred to as 'differential item functioning' (see p. 112).

Smith and Whetton (1988) distinguish between item bias and test bias. The former relates to *questions* which favour one or other group disproportionately, whereas the latter relates to *average test scores* for various groups. To reduce test bias (i.e. to reduce any overall mean score differences between groups) would require loading a test with items that are biased against higher scoring groups. For example, if girls score higher on a verbal test, then to reduce test bias one would have to include several items using vocabulary from traditionally male pursuits. Smith and Whetton view this approach to removing overall test bias as unsound. They argue that since the purpose of, for example, a verbal reasoning test is to measure reasoning processes using word knowledge as the medium for these processes, test developers should ensure that the word knowledge is common to all test takers. Deliberately using words known by only one group would, they argue, increase rather than decrease the test bias even if the end result was an equal mean score for all groups. The reduction of *item* bias, on the other hand, they view as enhancing the test's construct validity.

Our view is that statistical procedures for determining item bias tell us only about the difficulty levels of the items for different groups, as Goldstein (1993) also points out; they tell us nothing about the construct being assessed. Thus we do not agree with Smith and Whetton's view that reducing item bias can enhance the test's construct validity; we may simply be disadvantaging another group unless we understand what is happening at the construct level. Items may have different meanings for different groups and items which do not fit a common pattern of responses may simply be assessing a different attribute.

In the USA, there is a 'Code of Fair Testing Practices in Education', which requires test agencies to indicate for all tests and assessments 'the nature of the evidence obtained concerning the appropriateness of each test for groups of different racial, ethnic or linguistic backgrounds' (JCTP 1988), and demands that 'Test developers should strive to make tests that are as fair as possible for test takers of different races, gender, ethnic backgrounds, or handicapping conditions'. The code has met with a certain amount of scepticism in America, largely because of the lack of any measures for enforcement. As a former Assistant Secretary of Education put it:

If all the maxims are followed I have no doubt the overall quotient of goodness and virtue should be raised. Like Moses, the test-makers have laid down ten commandments they hope everyone will obey. That doesn't work very well in religion – adultery continues.

(Times Educational Supplement, 25 November 1988)

However, there *has* been litigation over assessment in the USA, the most relevant being the suit the Golden Rule Insurance Company brought against Educational Testing Services (ETS; the equivalent of Britain's National Foundation for Educational Research) which develops, among other things, insurance licensing exams. The Golden Rule Company alleged that these licensing exams were discriminatory to Blacks. The case was settled out of court in 1984 by an agreement, the key provision of which was that preference should be given in test construction to items that showed smaller differences in black and white performance. This has come to be called the Golden Rule Strategy, and the Golden Rule Bias Reduction Principle (Weiss 1987) states that 'among questions of equal difficulty and validity in each content area, questions which display the least differences in passing rates between majority and minority test takers should be used first'. However, by 1987, the ETS president recanted on the 1984 agreement and the issue is now hotly disputed. The contention centres around the point that relying on group differences in performance on test questions as indicators of 'bias' ignores the possibility that such differences may validly reflect real differences in knowledge or skill (Faggen 1987).

According to Goldstein (1986), the psychometricians' view is that technical criteria *alone* should determine test content, while an alternative view is that political and social desiderata may also be used. He suggests that Golden Rule-type strategies could usefully be incorporated into standard assessment construction techniques, there being nothing wrong with the principle of trying to equalize (or otherwise constrain) group differences.

Linn (1989) traces the treatment of bias in testing in the USA through the American Standards and Guidelines for Educational and Psychological Testing. The early technical recommendations were targeted towards the test developer and test publisher. However, more recently the focus has included the responsibilities of test users. For example, by 1974 test users were urged to avoid bias in selection, administration and interpretation of the tests and to avoid even the appearance of discriminatory practice. Here we see a shift in the notion of bias from the technical to the social based on use; this shift mirrors the changes in our understandings of validity in assessment. As Linn (1982) points out, tests may be differentially valid for members of different groups and they may thus have different meanings for these groups. In this sense, bias refers to a particular use of a test not to the test itself.

Bias and validity

As we have already intimated, bias and validity issues are linked. The dictionary definition of valid, as we have pointed out, is 'sound'; in assessment, validity has traditionally meant the extent to which a test measures what it claims to measure. Recently, the notion of a unitary concept of validity has been put forward by among others Cronbach (1980) and Messick (1989), moving away from the traditional model of validity. Three broad categories – content validation, criterion validation and construct validation – are viewed as types of *evidence about* validity rather than types of validity. Cronbach and Messick identify construct validity as the unifying concept underlying all validity. Their argument is that no criterion or universe of content is ever entirely adequate to define the quality being measured and that a variety of types of logical and empirical evidence is necessary to support a given interpretation (for a concise and readable summary of the issues, see Nuttall 1987; Moss 1992). Cole and Moss (1989) conclude that an integrated conception of validity in which multiple types of evidence are considered is essential to judging the appropriateness of a test score interpretation, especially in relation to issues of bias. The construct is, for most educational measurement purposes, of interest primarily as a way of understanding the score and its appropriateness for use and is therefore the fundamental issue with regard to assessment and equity.

Although measurement theory has emphasized the importance of appropriateness for use, it has not focused on the way use influences the meaning constructed for the test score. 'We wish to emphasise the importance of the context of use in influencing the meaning given to the score and thus the need for context based construct validation' (Cole and Moss 1989: 203). Cole and Moss conclude that an inference from a test score is biased when it is not equally valid for different groups. Bias is present when a test score has meanings or implications for a relevant sub-group of test takers that are different from the meanings or implications for the remainder of the test takers. Thus 'bias is differential validity for a given interpretation of a test score for any definable relevant sub-group of test takers' (p. 205). For example, a word problem arithmetic addition test is used to measure children's addition skills. If, however, it is used to identify children with difficulties in arithmetic in a group of primarily Spanish-speaking children, low scores might indicate that they had difficulty reading the questions in English rather than difficulty with addition. If so, we would say that the use of this test is biased with respect to such Spanish-speaking children. By contrast, had a test of reading comprehension in English been used to identify children with reading problems for additional instruction, the inability of the Spanish-speaking children to do well on the test would not necessarily indicate bias for this use. On the other hand, if the same reading test was used as a measure of intelligence or learning potential, it would be biased with respect to the Spanish-speaking group for that use. 'So, the desired interpretation in the context of use determines what is, or is not, evidence of bias' (Cole and Moss 1989: 205).

The American Education of all Handicapped Children Act 1975 (PL 94–142) also relates bias to validity. It requires that tests used to make placement decisions for children be 'validated for intended use, given in the child's native language and administered by trained personnel'. In addition, reliance on a single source of information as the only basis for a placement decision is prohibited (quoted by Linn 1989: 9). This is echoed in the 1985 Standards for Educational and Psychological Testing: 'when a test is used to make decisions about students' promotion or graduation, there should be evidence that the test covers only the specific or generalised knowledge, skills and abilities that students have had an opportunity to learn' (APA 1985: 53, Standard 8.7, quoted in Linn 1989: 8).

When proposed uses can result in decisions that have significant consequences for individuals or for systems, issues of bias become particularly salient. Then we must ask whether the construct specification implies some skills or knowledge that are irrelevant to the intended interpretation and use, suggesting that the test is less valid for students not possessing those abilities, e.g. a test of analogical reasoning that requires students to know certain facts to answer the questions will be less valid for students who lack the necessary knowledge.

Sources of unfairness (or invalidity)

One source of poor performance on a test can be the test material itself, e.g. the inadequate or stereotyped representation of some groups or language use which has emotional overtones for one group. In the USA, this is referred to as facial bias (Cole and Moss 1989), defined as when particular words or item formats appear to disfavour one group whether or not they have that effect. For example, using the male pronoun 'he' throughout or involving only male figures in the items would count as facial bias whether or not this affects the scores of women. The conclusion of Cole and Moss is that test content should include balanced representation of the least advantaged groups.

The Fawcett Society (1987) examined a range of exam papers in order to look at the gender roles as reflected in the papers. The Society carried out a detailed analysis of 1986 examination papers from the English and Welsh Examination Boards and identified seven types of discrimination:

1 The overall effect of a paper can be biased because reference is made predominately to one sex.
2 The presentation of men and women in the paper is stereotyped: men are admirable, women frivolous.
3 The questions are about subjects of interest only to boys.
4 The assumption that people are male and so is the genotype, girls and feminine pronouns go into brackets if they appear at all.
5 The authors of texts studied are almost exclusively male.
6 Passages chosen for criticism and comment have a strong male bias.
7 An opportunity to mention eminent women has been missed.

The authors make a distinction between explicit and non-explicit sexism. In explicit sexism, men or boys make most of the appearances in the paper or are the ones shown using maths in an intelligent way, while women and girls appear in frivolous or stereotyped roles. To counteract non-explicit sexism, examiners have tried to use more gender-neutral terms. However, recent changes in GCSE practice to broaden the range of texts used to include female writers and those from ethnic minorities, as well as writing which is more accessible to pupils, has been highly contentious because it brings up the issue of what it is 'valuable' to learn.

There are a number of ways in which the content can influence performance on a test: it can alienate some individuals (as described above); familiarity with content can enhance confidence, which in turn influences success; alternatively, where some pupils have met the content before, they are likely to define the task purpose in relation to past experience, and hence the construct alters for them. This may result in a lower score because of a different perception of purpose. The format of the task can also influence performance; format includes how the task is presented, and how the response is recorded. Issues to do with format (e.g. multiple-choice and essay-type questions) will be addressed in Chapter 8.

Administration and scoring are also important issues. Standardization of testing conditions leads to a specified test administration process and is thought to be most fair. However, any test administration conditions that affect groups differently can produce bias. For example, the race or sex of the test administrator, the extent to which the directions motivate different groups, the interpretation of directions about how to take the test, all affect performance. Marking is also an area in which bias may appear. Although open-ended responses offer greater scope for biased marking and are thought to be least fair since markers are given more latitude, a multiple-choice format, while offering no latitude to the marker, allows the assessor to become the marker and his or her biases are then built into the alternatives offered. Concerns over reliability between markers become concerns of bias whenever markers are influenced by group-related characteristics of an examinee that are irrelevant to the construct and purposes of the test. In some situations, markers might either know an examinee personally or be able to infer group membership on the basis of the examinee's name, school designation or aspects of the response such as handwriting or characteristic surface errors. Here the danger is that the assigned score may be influenced by the marker's conscious or unconscious expectations about an examinee based upon sex, ethnic origin, ability level, social class, etc., as with teacher expectation.

Another way in which bias can arise is when valued responses reflect skills, knowledge or values irrelevant to the construct of interest; for example, content knowledge (when a test is intended to measure writing skill) or writing skill or spelling (when a test is intended to measure content knowledge) are all potentially irrelevant influences on the scores. In these cases, the groups of concern could be examinees with poor handwriting, inadequate knowledge of an arbitrary topic, or limited facility with standard written English. Subjective judgements can be particularly difficult when the examinee and the raters do not share a common cultural heritage and hence common values about what constitutes competent performance. Although training and monitoring of markers can help minimize threats of bias resulting from the influence of irrelevant factors, where cultural value differences between markers and examinees are present, it becomes especially important to guard against this and to specify the scoring criteria in relation to the construct being assessed.

To sum up, bias is a difficult concept in relation to assessment and, as with equal opportunities, often poorly defined. We intend, therefore, to use the term as little as possible, mostly when it is used by other researchers; for our own arguments our use of the term will be in its general sense of prejudice or slant, and we will where possible use invalidity or differential performance instead. We feel strongly that focusing on 'bias' in the test itself has distracted attention from wider equity issues. As we pointed out in the Introduction, differences in group performance may be due to any of the environmental, psycho-social factors which impinge on groups of pupils or to the content, format, administration and scoring of the test.

In the next chapter, we begin our review of differential performance by looking at sex differences in intellectual abilities.

2

SEX DIFFERENCES IN INTELLECTUAL ABILITIES

Introduction

The study of observed differences between the sexes has a long history. During the nineteenth and twentieth centuries, a great deal of research was carried out with the expressed aim of revealing the nature of differences between the sexes. Typically, researchers assumed that sex differences in intellectual abilities existed and were motivated to provide an appropriate explanation for them. The explanations that emerged tended to be polarized, relying on either biological or environmental factors to account for individual differences. The current social and political climate of opinion helped determine which type of explanation prevailed.

For example, research in the latter half of the nineteenth century was much influenced by the development of evolutionary theory. Darwin, however, was a product of the Victorian era and not immune to its values. He considered that intellectually males attained higher excellence than females in whatever they undertook 'whether requiring deep thought, reason or imagination or merely the use of the senses and hands' (Darwin 1871). His explanation for the evolutionary origins of males' superior intellectual powers was based on the contentious belief that men had always provided for, and defended, women. In Shields' view, nineteenth-century researchers sought justification for their society and found it in evolutionary theory. She saw this as a 'natural consequence of their attempt at objectivity', and comments, 'So ingrained was the need for justification that scientists' observations were sometimes blatantly guided by their expectations . . . The "natural" woman, as described by scientists of that time bore an uncanny resemblance to the "ideal" woman of Victorian society' (Shields 1978: 754). Hence nineteenth-century woman was depicted by male scientists as 'biologically conservative, less variable, neurally underdeveloped, and physiologically vulnerable. She was also genteel, unimaginative, perceptive, modest, emotional, coy, dependent, and above all, maternal' (Shields 1978).

The wider social context in which research is conducted influences the theoretical perspectives adopted and the manner of their application. Archer (1978) argues that the focus on simple biological explanations for sex differences that characterized much of the research in the 1960s and 1970s, was a direct consequence of an earlier predominance of environmental explanations. This predominance was explained by Crook (1970) in relation to the social and political climate of North America in the early part of the twentieth century, when behaviourism was so popular among American psychologists. There is recognition in the research community of the need to consider the interaction between biological and environmental factors when generating explanations for behaviour; however, in practice researchers continue to search for the most significant source of influence. The concern to reveal sex differences in order to explain the 'natural order' and hence inform social policy of the day has had serious implications for the nature and quality of research findings. Similar problems have arisen with research into other aspects of individual differences, an example being the race and IQ debate.

Some methodological problems

The primary aim of most studies into sex differences has been to *demonstrate* differences in performance which are then used to justify a preconceived causal explanation. To interpret findings appropriately, it is therefore essential to understand the theoretical perspective of the researcher. However, all too often this perspective is not articulated in the reports of studies and this has led to problems with the use of data. For example, one has to be aware of the way researchers define the constructs upon which measures are based. Their conceptualization of constructs reveal aspects of their theoretical position with regard to the nature of human beings and sex differences between them.

The use of animal samples has been an area of particular concern in research into sex differences among humans. As Archer (1976) observes, the correspondence between animal and human tests is not satisfactory. In particular, the measures defined as representative of the constructs being researched necessarily vary between animal and human samples. In a study of aggression in animals (Gray 1971), the measures developed to represent the construct included 'threat displays', 'duration of fighting', 'outcome of fights', etc. Human studies in the same field (Garai and Scheinfeld 1968) refer to rather different measures, for example 'verbal aggression', and teacher ratings of 'impulsivity' and 'assertiveness'. It is clear that the measured characteristics are not comparable. Given this difficulty, one would expect limited and very careful references to studies using animal samples. Unfortunately, this is often not the case. For example, research on the effect of testosterone on young male chicks (Andrew and Rogers 1972) was quoted by Hutt (1972a) in support of her neurochemical theory to explain sex differences in people without reference to the nature of the sample used.

Another related problem is that terms such as 'aggression' typically represent a heterogeneous array of measures linked by the researcher and reflect his or her particular theoretical viewpoint. Again it is difficult to extract this information from the generalizations reported by the research. In some cases, generalizations are taken a step further. For example, Witkin *et al.* (1962) generalized from tests involving visual–spatial tasks to more general sex differences in cognitive style. A consequence of this is that the suggested sex difference appears to be more wide-ranging than the evidence justifies.

Value judgements and beliefs about stereotypes also affect how terms are described and interpreted. Again we can find an example in the work of Witkin *et al.* (1962; Witkin 1967). Some of the tasks where they identified a male superiority involved separating the stimulus from the background – a simple geometric form hidden in a complex design. This sex difference in performance was characterized by Witkin *et al.* as 'field independence' in the male and 'field dependence' in the female. A description which corresponds well with the prevailing stereotypes of the passive, dependent female and the active, independent male.

In reviewing research findings, it is also important to look critically at the sampling strategy employed. Stein and Bailey (1973) pointed out that many of the psychological theories used as baselines in sex differences studies were developed from all-male samples. The implication of this distorted sampling is that female behaviour may automatically become 'deviant' and any sex differences so demonstrated would be questionable. The sample selected must attempt to be representative. If not, then interpretations of findings must reflect the inadequacies of the sampling strategy. Some research (e.g. Conel 1963, on eight children), though very interesting, cannot be regarded as indicative or predictive of any sex differences in the population. Similarly, a failure to observe any differences when small samples are used may indicate a failure on the behalf of the researcher to consider 'effect size'. A major criticism of Maccoby and Jacklin's (1974) review was their use of research studies using young children to generate conclusions about overall sex differences. Generalizations about sex differences in adolescence may not hold for adults, for example. Fairweather (1976) also comments on the 'possible sex biases in the constitution of student populations and the volunteering patterns within those populations'.

In this review of the literature on sex differences in intellectual abilities, the many emotional and social variables which have been studied will not be considered. It would seem obvious that 'abilities' cannot be separated from personality factors, etc., but this interaction is rarely taken into account in sex differences studies. It is important at this point to state clearly what is meant by ability. Archer (1971) notes that it is a misleading term as it presupposes the existence of some innate fixed capacity. Sherman (1977) suggests that it should be replaced with more neutral terms such as skills or performance. What is measured, and then equated with ability, is performance on a particular task. This performance is correlated to intellectual achievement but is not predictive of intellectual ability. When the term ability is used here, it does not imply that the difference being discussed is biologically determined.

The choice of terminology is significant as it reflects our own biases as well as others. Sex is typically used to denote *biological* distinctions between males and females. Gender, on the other hand, is often used to refer to societal definitions of female and male traits, that is, 'feminine' and 'masculine' characteristics. We have used the term 'sex differences' in the title to this chapter because our aim is to explore the possibility of cognitive differences between males and females; we use the term 'gender' in this chapter when this is the term used by the particular author under consideration. In the other chapters of the book we will use the term gender to indicate that we are concerned with both biological and environmental hypotheses. In so doing, we are recognizing that while biological variables may be significant, these are undoubtedly confounded with psychosocial variables.

Research evidence up to the 1970s

Variability within and between the sexes

We referred earlier to nineteenth-century scientists' view of women as 'less variable'. Evolutionary theory considered the male to have been shaped for thought and creativity, the female for reproduction. Noddings makes the point that observed variance between the sexes explains nothing, only when the 'biological suggestion is attached does it become an explanation. In point of historical fact, the biological explanation of observed variances is the variability hypothesis' (Noddings 1992: 88).

We discuss IQ fully in the next chapter but it is also relevant to this discussion. The questions for an IQ test are selected on the basis that approximately the same proportion of each sex responds correctly. The standardization of the Wechsler Intelligence Scale for Children (WISC-R) has achieved almost perfect parity between the sexes from the age of 6 to 16 (Kaufman and Doppelt 1976). Although intelligence tests are constructed so that overall there are no sex differences, the tests do reveal differences in the pattern of intellectual abilities for males and females. Hutt (1972b) takes the evidence from selected items as support for her view that men think differently from women. She also argues that the advanced maturation of girls does not allow a fair comparison to be made. Maccoby and Jacklin (1974) reviewed studies investigating sex differences which were published in American journals during a 10-year period preceding 1974. They found that the sexes did not differ consistently in tests of composite abilities. Girls appeared to have a slight advantage on tests up to the age of 7 years. Maccoby and Jacklin speculate that this could be seen as evidence in support of the different maturation rates of boys and girls. However, Bayley (1956) has shown that the rate of intellectual development is not connected to indexes of physical growth such as height or bone development. Fairweather (1976) quotes the results of Ingram (1975) for young children and Barnsley and Rabinovitch (1970) for adults which indicate no relationship between muscular development and IQ, to challenge the hypothesis that 'maturation lags' hide a male superiority in intellectual abilities. Kipinis (1976), in looking at Wechsler's findings, reported that educational attainment correlates well with tested intelligence in the adult population and concludes that whichever sex is afforded the greater educational advantage is likely to prove the more intelligent (in society's terms). This is a key issue in relation to teacher expectation and equal access to learning.

Consideration of the variability within the sexes showed initially more boys than girls to be gifted (Terman *et al.* 1925). In Terman's study of large samples, no sex differences were found between mean IQ scores but more males were found to have unusually high and low scores. Hutt quotes Tyler (1965) to show that though average scores in IQ tests are similar, the scores of males will spread more across the range. She sees this as a further example of the 'tendency for a more conservative expression of characteristics in females' and gives support to Heim's hypothesis of the 'mediocrity of women' (Heim 1970). Hutt concludes that the male domination of the 'intellectual and creative echelons seems to have a basis other than masculine privilege' (Hutt 1972a: 89–90). Miles (1954) pointed out that the selection of Terman's sample, by teacher judgement of giftedness and children volunteering, makes interpretation of the results difficult if not impossible.

Both Miles (1954) and Terman and Tyler (1954) reviewed a number of studies to find out whether one sex was more variable in intelligence than the other. They concluded that there appeared to be no consistent tendency towards a higher incidence of gifted boys and that the sex ratios in the gifted range depended on the content of the test.

Maccoby and Jacklin (1974) reviewed the literature to consider variability in specific abilities. With regard to verbal ability they found no firm support that males are more variable, although they noted a trend in this direction for subjects of 12 years and older. The evidence for greater male variability in numerical and spatial abilities was more consistent, though very few studies had been carried out, especially in spatial abilities. Maccoby and Jacklin discuss the nature of this variability in terms of score distributions. The higher average scores of girls in the verbal domain reflect a distribution where girls achieve more very high scores and fewer very low scores than boys. In contrast, Gates (1961) found that boys outnumbered girls among the lowest scores by about 2:1 in reading tests. Keating (1972) found the standard deviations of boys' scores were higher than those of the girls and considerably more boys scored at the top of the range in tests of mathematical ability. Maccoby and Jacklin (1974) conclude from Keating's work and previous reports on retardation that the greater variability in maths scores reflects a greater representation of males at both the high and low ends of the distribution.

Intelligence is not a single homogeneous mental ability and IQ tests reflect this. The Wechsler tests are composed of sub-scales of items which represent different types of tasks. The main evidence for sex differences in intellectual abilities arises from such sub-scales. Males and females typically differ in the sub-test scales in which their best scores are obtained.

Sex differences in specific abilities

Verbal ability

Hutt (1972a) selects for consideration those studies of verbal ability that support her initial preconception of sex differences. That is that female skills are in accord with the female role of nurture and correlate with other primate species. The implication of this hypothesis is that female superiority in 'communicative' verbal skills alone is consistent with their nurturant role. She refers to the study by Bennett *et al.* (1959) to make the point that while females may be 'verbally fluent or precocious in tests of verbal reasoning and comprehension they score lower than males' (Hutt 1972c: 107). Bennett *et al.* used the Differential Aptitude Test, which showed that girls score higher on language usage tasks but boys score higher than girls on verbal reasoning tasks. Hutt quotes Tyler (1965) that most of the available evidence seems to indicate '. . . that it is verbal fluency rather than in the grasp of verbal meanings where females are superior'. In contrast, Miner's (1957) review of evidence concluded that in all components of intelligence tests vocabulary sub-tests are the best predictors of total scores. Goslin (1963) was also of the view that verbal ability was of critical importance in the performance of virtually every task requiring high intelligence. Moore (1967) conducted a longitudinal study of a small sample of children ($N = 76$) and measured their IQ and linguistic development regularly from 6 months to 8 years of age. He concluded, 'in general ability the sexes started virtually equal, the girls scored a little higher during the period of acquisition of language and were then overtaken and surpassed by the boys'. Moore like Hutt links girls' early focus on developing linguistic skills to their need to communicate because of their greater interest in personal relationships and predilection for nurturant roles.

Buffery and Gray (1972) quoted Guilford's (1967) summary of sex differences which shows that on the ten tests on which females are superior, seven involved verbal ability and at least one of these tests was of verbal reasoning. They conclude that women are clearly superior to men on tests of verbal fluency and possibly on other kinds of linguistic skills. Sex differences in verbal abilities are thought to begin very early; small-scale studies (e.g. Moore 1967; Lewis and Freedle 1972; Clarke-Stewart 1973) found that girls between the ages of 0 and 18 months might be ahead in 'speech quotients', response to vocal stimulation, comprehension and vocabulary. However, Maccoby and Jacklin (1974) found that for eight other studies of infants up to the age of 2 years and thirteen studies involving children of pre-school age, no sex differences in verbal skills were demonstrated. Exceptions to this have been found by two major studies (Shipman 1971, Stanford Research Institute 1972). These studies looked at large samples of pre-school children and found girls clearly ahead on a number of language measures. They were, however, selected from impoverished or disadvantaged families.

In the early school years, very few differences in verbal ability have been demonstrated. Brimer (1969) found that on receptive vocabulary tests using very large samples of children between the ages of 6 and 11, boys actually obtained higher average scores than girls; although it is worth noting that a casual look at the test reveals a predominance of 'male-orientated' pictures. Most studies of children in this age range found no consistent sex differences, the notable exception being the Stanford Research Institute's (1972) study of disadvantaged children. In this study, girls scored higher than boys on a range of language skills. Maccoby and Jacklin (1974: 84) conclude from their review that it is at the 'age of 10 or 11 that girls begin to come into their own in verbal performance'. Their review of the studies involving high school and college students revealed that although sex differences were not always found, when they did occur they showed girls outperforming boys at a variety of verbal skills. The observed difference or lack of it appeared to depend on the type of test used.

By considering only the studies that involved large samples not selected so as to result in distortion or perspective bias, one can generalize to the extent that any pre-school differences in verbal ability have not been conclusively proven. There is therefore no support for the view that girls develop early linguistic skills in order to communicate, nor that there is such a link with nurturant roles. During the school years of 4–11, the two sexes perform very similarly on verbal tasks. Any sex differences that do occur favour girls, especially from underprivileged backgrounds. From adolescence onwards, female superiority in a variety of verbal abilities occurs and continues into adulthood. One must treat this statement with caution; verbal ability covers a wide range of tasks and overall performance does not give insight into specific abilities. As Fairweather (1976: 262) comments: 'viewed critically . . . the evidence is not compelling'.

In attempting to look at specific verbal abilities, tasks are used which of necessity depend on additional verbal skills. A verbal reasoning task will also involve reading and comprehension, for example, to varying degrees. Consequently, there is always overlap between the specific and composite tasks. This inability to isolate tasks has meant that very little has been established about male and female performance on specific verbal abilities.

Reading is often cited in the context of sex differences in verbal skills. Fairweather (1976) refers to Thompson's (1975) review of reading achievement to highlight the significance of cultural factors on achievement measures. Thompson found significant sex differences in American studies but not in studies conducted in England and Scotland. Fairweather also points to evidence that suggests the influence of sex roles on achievement domains. Asher and Gottmann (1973) reported a highly significant female superiority for reading comprehension and in a follow-up study it was noted that both boys and girls perceive reading as a feminine activity (Asher and Markell 1974). When test scores were linked to level of interest in the material to be read, boys appeared to be poorly motivated on low-interest material whereas girls performed equally well across all material. Dwyer (1974) performed a multiple-regression analysis for such factors as IQ, sex role standards and sex role preference for children between the ages of 7 and 18 ($N = 385$) and concluded:

> The results suggest that reading and arithmetic sex differences are more a function of the child's perception of these areas as sex appropriate or sex inappropriate than the child's biological sex, individual preference for masculine or feminine sex role, or liking or disliking of reading or arithmetic.
> (Dwyer 1974, quoted in Fairweather 1976: 259)

Evidence of this kind is particularly pertinent when we consider the outcomes of national surveys of achievements in later chapters.

Mathematical ability

A review of the performance of the sexes on mathematical tests shows that before the age of 3 years, there appear to be no sex differences on tasks of number conservation and enumeration. However, it must be noted that sample sizes are small and such studies are rare. Shipman's (1971) work on a large sample of underprivileged children found girls to be superior on enumeration tasks between the ages of 3 and 4 years. In the early school years, large studies of disadvantaged children, including the Stanford Research Institute (1972) study, show girls to be ahead of boys on tests of quantitative ability. Other studies with more representative samples show no differences in the early years. Between the ages of 9 and 13, most studies indicate that the sexes perform similarly, though differences in favour of boys have been demonstrated by Hilton and Berglund (1971), Keating and Stanley (1972) and Svensson (1971). During adolescence and later there is a consistent trend in male superiority in quantitative ability, but it should be noted that the magnitude of the sex differences varies from study to study.

Quantitative ability like verbal ability is a heterogeneous concept. When studies look for sex differences in specific mathematical abilities, they use measures which demand a range of different abilities. The problem of 'purity' of task, referred to in the previous section on verbal ability performance, arises again in this area.

Visual–spatial ability

In an attempt to look at specific quantitative abilities, the notion of a visual–spatial skill was defined. Unfortunately, this is again a composite skill and such measures offer little help in understanding the formal processes in operation when students undertake such tasks. Coltheart *et al.* (1975) point out that tasks described as 'spatial' could be carried out by verbal processing and vice versa. Another argument suggests that females use language adaptively to solve spatial problems. In other words, they perform spatial tasks in a qualitatively different fashion than males. Saraga (1975) reviewed the evidence on 'spatial' skills and commented that performance could only be considered in the context of the specific tasks undertaken.

In her review of the literature, Hutt (1972a) assumes a continuous male superiority on tests of 'perceptual field dependence'. This provides support for her theory of the genetic control of abilities. In a similar vein, Buffery and Gray (1972) review the data on the existence of sex differences in the perception and use of spatial relationship in man [*sic*] and supportive evidence from animal studies to make their case for male superiority in this ability. However, comparing such measures as maze running in rats with human performance on Thurstone's Primary Mental Abilities Test is clearly questionable. Buffery and Gray (1972: 123) justify their approach in the following way: 'The sex differences in emotional and cognitive behaviour among mammalian species are all remote but necessary consequences of the same overriding fact: the division of labour between the sexes in reproductive behaviour.'

On the basis of the evidence and their own studies, Buffery and Gray developed a neuropsychological theory to explain sex differences in spatial and linguistic abilities. They conclude that the female and male brains are differentially lateralized. The female brain has a high degree of lateralization which promotes better overall linguistic performance, whereas the male brain is ambilateral which is conducive to better visual–spatial functioning. In Fairweather's view, this theory was not well supported by the experimental data.

Studies have rarely demonstrated significant findings of sex differences in spatial abilities in early childhood. Fairweather's (1976) review of the research took note of the Scottish standardization of WISC (Scottish Council for Research in Education 1967), which found boys at 13 years of age to be superior on picture completion and block design tasks. The emergence of male superiority in the defined spatial scales coincides with adolescence (Meyer and Bendig 1961; Bennett *et al.* 1966), which corresponds with Maccoby and Jacklin's conclusions. Fairweather suggests on the basis of his review, that the male advantage appears to be confined to the transformation of visual stimuli in three dimensions. When tasks do not demand 'performance' in three dimensions, the evidence is much less consistent.

An area often related to spatial skills is that of field dependence. Field dependence measures require the subject to separate an element from its background. The tasks most frequently cited as measures of field dependence–independence are the Embedded Figures Test (where simple patterns have to be isolated from complex backgrounds), the Rod and Frame Test (in which a rod has to be adjusted to the vertical in a tilted frame) and the Tilted Room Test. We referred earlier to problems associated with terms such as field dependence. It is more helpful to consider the abilities demanded by the tasks. Three visual–spatial abilities are commonly identified: *spatial perception*, which involves subjects in locating the horizontal or the vertical while rejecting distracting information (the Rod and Frame Test is an example of this); *mental rotation*, which involves the ability to imagine objects when they are rotated, folded or in the case of solid objects unfolded; and *spatial visualization*, which requires complex analytic processing of spatial information (the Embedded Figures Test demands abilities of this kind).

Modifications of the original Witkin Embedded Figures Test have been given to pre-school children in various studies (e.g. Shipman 1971; Sitkei and Meyers 1969; Coates 1972). These studies revealed either no sex differences or, as in the case of Coates, a difference in favour of girls. It is only after the age of 8 that sex differences across studies have been found, though not consistently. Where they do occur (Keogh and Ryan 1971, Rod and Frame test; Wapner 1968, Body adjustment test; Corah 1965), they favour males.

The issue of sex differences in spatial abilities is further confused by the studies of Kagan and Kogan (1970), Berry (1966) and Dawson (1967), who found that cultural differences affected spatial performance. For example, Berry found no sex differences in an Eskimo sample of men and women but did find a male superiority in spatial performances when the sample was selected from the Temne tribe from Sierra Leone. The explanation for this cultural difference was posited in relation to the social roles accorded to women and children. Goldstein and Chance (1965) also found that, with training on the Embedded Figures Test, women's scores increased and eventually no differences were noted in further trials. However, Yen's (1975) study of a large sample of high school students in San Francisco demonstrated highly significant differences which favoured males on the spatial sub-test of the Primary Mental Abilities Test, Spatial Relations Test, Form Board Test and Mental Rotations Test.

Maccoby and Jacklin (1974), in their review, conclude that no sex differences in spatial abilities are found until adolescence (an exception being Keogh's 1971 study). After adolescence the trend is in favour of male superiority. They quote two studies (Droege 1967; Flanagan *et al.* 1961) which used space-factor tests with high school students. Both studies found that boys' superiority on spatial skills increases through high school. Bearing in mind the need to define spatial skills in terms of task performance, there appears to be a clear male superiority on a narrow range of spatial skills. The evidence suggests that this superiority does not exist before adolescence, only after it and into adulthood. Such evidence calls into question theories about brain differentiation between the sexes and other genetically determined hypotheses relating to spatial abilities, pointing instead to a developing difference as males and females respond to their environment and the expectations of significant others.

Analytical ability

Witkin *et al.* (1967) have assumed that male superiority on visual–spatial tasks is indicative of some general intellectual capacity in males for analytic thought. Witkin regarded the Embedded Figures Test and the Rod and Frame Test as demanding analytical rather than spatial abilities. Sherman (1967) disputes this interpretation, regarding it as similar to concluding that women are more analytic than men based on findings of superior female ability to decontextualize the red and green figures on the Isihara Colour Blindness Test. The majority of studies into sex differences in analytic ability have a similar failing, that is they discuss analytic ability irrespective of the content of the task. The tests used to monitor analytic ability range across verbal, numerical and spatial tasks. Comparability of performance across such a range is therefore immediately contentious. The analytic *attitude* of males is referred to by Garai and Scheinfeld (1968): men ask 'why' and 'how' questions, while women are interested in finding out the social mores that apply.

In her study of sex differences in perception and cognition, McGuinness (1976: 146) provides a quite different interpretation of the data. She argues that:

> . . . woman who is more communicative and whose interest is more social would use both direct, perceptual and abstract linguistic cues to enable her to form judgements of intent. She would thus seek the internal aspects of personal and social situations asking 'why' questions, rather than 'what' questions . . . her type of thinking could thus be described as 'analytic', the capacity to both interpret intention and to abstract the constituent elements from any type of verbal or non-verbal communication.

Other research has focused on tasks involving set breaking or restructuring as an important dimension of analytic ability or problem-solving abilities. Set breaking or restructuring refers to the ability, when faced with a set of problems, to reject an initial cumbersome but successful problem-solving approach and to use a simpler more direct approach to solve future problems when the initial approach fails to work. Male superiority on such tasks has been shown by Milton (1959), Guetzkow (1951) and Sweeney (1953), and lends some support to Broverman and co-workers' (1968) hormonal theory of the skill dichotomy between males and females. However, other tests which obviously display some elements of analytic thought processes (e.g. the Stroop Colour–Word Test, where the subject is given a set of colour names printed in the wrong colour ink and must state the colour of the ink rather than read the printed word), show contradictory findings as the sexes perform very similarly on this instance of set breaking. Maccoby and Jacklin (1974) in their review of the range of studies said to relate to analytic style, conclude that Broverman and co-workers' view that boys are more able than girls to inhibit a dominant response in problem-solving situations is not well founded. Furthermore the sex difference appears to be confined to visual–spatial tasks alone. To draw any conclusion on sex differences in analytic ability would be unwise. The constructs are too vaguely defined to ensure that the tasks are comparable and the influence of motivation and personality is too large. There is no conclusive evidence to show that field independence in males reflects greater analytic ability or that one sex is superior at analytic re-grouping or set breaking.

Creativity

An area of cognitive styles where many assumptions of sex stereotyped behaviour abound is that of 'creativity'. No measures exist which can be equated with 'creativity' as we understand it. By the very nature of the attribute, it is a composite of many variables, thus making it impossible to define uniquely. The Piagetian logical reasoning tasks which call for hypothesis generation and therefore some measure of creativity revealed no consistent sex differences in Maccoby and Jacklin's (1974) review. In most work on creativity, two measures are used: the *number* of different ideas and the *uniqueness* of ideas produced. Such measures tend to be verbal and Hutt (1972c) equates them with verbal fluency (number of responses) and originality (uniqueness of responses). She concludes from research that girls show greater fluency (Bhavani and Hutt, in Hutt 1972c) and no sex differences are found on the number of unique responses. Maccoby and Jacklin (1974) review the measures related to the variety and range of ideas and hypotheses. They also distinguish verbal from non-verbal measures. They found that verbal tests of creativity show no sex differences in the pre-school and early school years. From the age of 7 onwards, however, girls show an advantage in a majority of studies. On non-verbal measures, no clear trends towards superiority of either sex can be discerned.

Differences in auditory skills

McGuinness' (1976) findings led her to conclude that females are more sensitive than males to auditory stimuli and that males have significantly greater visual acuity. She judged these results to be demonstrative of a reliable difference in central neural organiza-tion between males and females. Once again, the difficulty of considering a variety of measures under the umbrella heading of 'audition' arises. McGuinness quotes studies involving response to intensity as the most consistent in demonstrating sex differ-ences (e.g. Elliott 1971 on children; McGuinness 1972 on adults). Maccoby and Jacklin (1974) considered eleven related studies of audition, many of which involved response to intensity, though the method of measuring response varied considerably from cardiac response, motor response through to galvanic skin response, and found no consistent sex differences in neonatals and pre-school children. They summarize that there may be some evidence, though not conclusive, that infant girls in a very narrow age range show a greater responsiveness to sounds on some measures. The majority of studies during the compulsory school years, however, have demonstrated no consistent sex differences in auditory response.

Visual ability

The notion that males are predisposed to visual stimuli was sup-ported to some extent by Maccoby and Jacklin's (1974) review. They found no sex differences in habituation (decrement in looking-time over a period) during the first few days of life. After this the results are inconsistent but show a slight trend in the direc-tion of male superiority. Fairweather (1976) quotes Caron and co-workers' (1973) study on 586 children between the ages of 16 and 18 weeks; they found boys looked longer than girls in all phases (pre-habituation, habituation and recovery). Other studies (e.g. Banikiotes *et al.* 1972; Vietze *et al.* 1974) have failed to find clear interpretable sex differences. In considering visual stimuli response as a whole regardless of the measure, though this is of debatable validity, one finds a very inconsistent picture of sex differences. From first birthday to adulthood, the majority of studies reveal no sex differences in visual perception. Some interesting exceptions are studies involving autokinetic effects to apparent motion where males were found to be more susceptible (McKitrick 1965). Maccoby and Jacklin (1974: 35) conclude that the sexes are 'very similar in their interest in, and utilization of, information that comes to them via hearing and vision'.

Perceptual motor skills
Sex differences in perceptual motor skills have often been quoted in support of the hypothesis that males and females 'learn' differently. Summarizing early work on sex differences, Anastasi (1958), concludes that boys show greater speed and coordination of gross bodily movements, whereas girls excel in manual dexterity, but there have been very few studies able to add to Anastasi's summary. Other research has not supported the hypothesis that girls are superior in fine muscle movements (Kinsbourne and McMurray 1975; Ingram 1975). What has been shown is that girls are superior to boys on more complex tasks and are faster (Denckla 1973). When speed measures of manual dexterity are used, girls tend to score higher than boys (Laosa and Brophy 1972; Droege 1967; Very 1967; Backman 1972; Strutl *et al.* 1973).

In considering simple reaction time tests, Garai and Scheinfeld's (1968) review concludes that overall males are superior. However, the literature is not unequivocal. Fairweather (1976) suggests that on the basis of consistent evidence over a substantial range males only appear to have an advantage after puberty. For example, Fulton and Hubbard (1975) find no sex differences in reaction time between 9 and 17 years of age. Other studies have found that sex differences disappear with practice and what differences do exist are exceedingly small. In terms of choice reaction time, there is little evidence for consistent sex differences. Maccoby and Jacklin (1974) considered a whole range of studies using discrimination learning tasks and found overall no consistent sex differences. There is clearly insufficient evidence from such studies to support any theory of differential learning among the sexes.

Summary

In summarizing the early evidence of sex differences in cognitive abilities, the following caveats need to be borne in mind:

- The problem of task 'impurity', that is, the tasks are assumed to represent a unitary homogeneous construct which is rarely the case.
- Construct definition – constructs are often quite general and vaguely defined. For example, one researcher's problem-solving skill is another researcher's verbal ability skill.
- Test context and content are rarely considered either in defining the construct or in interpreting performance.
- The interdependence of affective and cognitive abilities is not considered in defining the measures or in attributing meaning to scores.

These issues bring into question all of the findings in this area of study, be they of differences or similarities between the sexes. However, reviewing those studies with reasonable samples and looking for consistent trends in the findings, the following points can be made. From adolescence onwards, there is an indication of female superiority in a variety of *verbal abilities* which continues into adulthood. There is, however, evidence in terms of the numbers of boys and girls with similar test scores, which suggests that performance differences may be minimal. The various studies looking at the *quantitative* ability of males and females have shown conflicting results. After the age of 13, there is a consistent trend in male superiority in quantitative ability. The magnitude of the difference between the sexes does vary from study to study.

Visual–spatial ability was identified as a component of mathematical ability. In general, differences on such tasks do not emerge until adolescence when the trend is for males to out-perform females on a narrow range of spatial skills. These differences continue into adulthood. Differences between the *analytical abilities* of the sexes have been studied but no conclusive evidence has been established because of the very different content of the tests used.

Tests of *creativity* invariably involve other cognitive abilities. Studies involving verbal tests tend to show girls with an advantage, whereas on non-verbal measures no sex differences in performance have been noted. Studies of *modality preference*, auditory versus visual, have been carried out because of their implications for learning. The research methods used, however, have not revealed sex differences in audition and vision. *Perceptual motor* skills have been investigated to explore the hypothesis that males and females 'learn' differently. A very wide range of tests have been included in numerous studies. These studies have provided insufficient evidence to support any theory of differential learning among the sexes.

Some recent developments

Fairweather (1976) concluded from his review of sex differences in cognition that there was insufficient evidence of differences between the sexes to allow theories to be developed to account for them. He also commented that given there are so few differences, it is questionable why researchers seek to explain the very large differences in sex roles and expectations by such means as 'masculine' and 'feminine' theories of development, be they innate or social.

Views such as Fairweather's have fuelled the debate about whether sex differences research should be carried out at all. Certain researchers, for example, feel strongly that between-sex comparisons should not be reported (Baumeister 1988). This reflects their view that sex differences research and the reporting of findings by sex is an inherently sexist practice (McHugh *et al.* 1986). It is worth bearing this perspective in mind when reading some of the later chapters which review the findings from international surveys of achievement. On the other hand, there are researchers who believe that findings which manifest sex differences should always be reported. The reasons given for this position are numerous but essentially the view is held that only through research can it be established whether beliefs and stereotypes about males and females have any validity.

Recent critiques of Maccoby and Jacklin's (1974) review have cited the following factors as sources of invalidity: large discrepancies between studies; unrepresentative samples; the small size of some of the differences; and the statistical approach which involves a simple count of studies with particular findings. To counter some of these criticisms, more recent reviews have employed meta-analytic techniques. Such techniques focus on estimating the size of effect being investigated across studies that meet specified criteria. This method also has its critics, as it remains questionable whether it is valid to aggregate across studies of varying quality. For further information about the technique, Halpern (1992) provides a useful and simple discussion and more detailed accounts can be found in Orwin and Cordray (1985) and Hyde and Linn (1986).

Wilder and Powell (1989) carried out a survey of the literature on sex differences in test performance. They quote Hyde and Linn's (1988) meta-analysis of research into verbal differences, which concluded that no gender difference in verbal ability had been found. They also refer to the research of Benbow and Stanley (1980, 1981, 1983) and their study of 'mathematically precocious youth'. This research has accummulated data since 1972 for a very large sample of students aged between 12 and 13 years. The study was extended to include verbally precocious students in 1980. The findings of this study revealed no mean gender differences in verbal ability. However, the sample has been criticized for being unrepresentative, comprising predominantly white, middle-class students (Wilder *et al.* 1988). In the same study, consistent differences on the mathematical sections of the Scholastic Aptitude Test (SAT) were found in favour of males.

With regard to spatial abilities, Linn and Peterson (1986) found that males out-performed females on tests of spatial perception at ages 7 and 8. This performance gap increased with age. Gender differences in favour of males were also found for mental rotation tasks from childhood (age 10) through to adulthood. No gender differences in performance were established for tasks requiring spatial visualization. Wilder and Powell (1989: 9) conclude that:

> . . . there is evidence of differences in the test performance of males and females on some tasks on some tests. These differences are quite small in the verbal domain and larger in quantitative areas. The quantitative differences seem to appear or increase during the high school years.

Wilder and Powell also looked at trends in sex differences. They refer to Feingold's conclusion that females had narrowed the gender gap in quantitative performance on nationally normed tests over the past 20–40 years (Wilder and Powell 1989: 14). This overall narrowing of performance between the two sexes was accompanied by an increase in the gender difference in favour of males at the higher levels of mathematical ability. Feingold attributes this trend to the greater variability in male performance which cancels gender differences in the low scoring area of the scale and magnifies them at the high end. Feingold's findings were corroborated by Benbow and Stanley's data (Benbow 1988). Benbow considered the evidence gave support to the possibility of differential biological mechanisms to explain the phenomenon. In Benbow's review of her longitudinal study of mathematically precocious youth, she considered the conventional environmental explanations for gender differences in test performance in maths. She showed for each explanation that either the predicted difference was not observed or was much smaller than for other populations studied. The psychosocial explanations she considered included negative attitudes to maths, level of confidence in maths ability, maths anxiety, parental and teacher encouragement in maths, and previous course experience. Benbow concluded that for her high-ability sample a primarily environmental explanation was inadequate. However, the self-selected nature of Benbow and Stanley's sample makes it difficult to evaluate such conclusions. Of interest here is the criticism that followed the publication of Benbow's findings. This indicated that despite espousing interactional views, many researchers still assume that any identification of biological causal factors automatically suggests that one sex (usually female) is deficient in some significant way. Others have interpreted the results as further evidence of the 'masculine' nature of the mathematical domain (Halpern 1988).

The apparent trend in narrowing the gap between male and female test performance is also evident in the verbal domain. The small female advantage noted by Maccoby and Jacklin (1974) appears in more recent studies to have been eliminated or in some cases reversed (Wilder and Powell 1989). It is important to consider overall performance effects in the context of how that overall performance was achieved. The apparent elimination of differences between males and females may mask other trends in performance, a point we return to in discussions of particular assessment practices.

Feingold (1992) summarizes the evidence concerning differences between the sexes from recent meta-analytic reviews and the analysis of norms from standardized tests. He suggests that on average males score higher than females on tests of general knowledge, mechanical reasoning and mental rotations; females score higher than males on tests of language usage (spelling, grammar) and perceptual speed; and that there are no measurable differences in general verbal ability, arithmetic, abstract reasoning, spatial visualization and memory span (Jacklin 1989; Kimball 1989; Linn and Hyde 1989; Wilder and Powell 1989). Feingold also notes the trend analyses which have demonstrated that sex differences between adolescent males and females have been considerably reduced over the last 20 years (Feingold 1988, 1991a; Hyde and Linn 1988).

Feingold goes on to focus on the issue of sex differences in variability which, in his view, has been neglected in the studies that postdate Maccoby and Jacklin's (1974) review. The findings of Rosenthal and Rubin (1982) and Becker and Hedges (1984) indicated that cognitive gender differences have decreased over time and suggest, in Feingold's view, that sex differences are affected by social factors. He goes on to hypothesize that if 'cultural factors contribute to a greater male variability in test performance, sex differences in variability may also have decreased' (Feingold 1992: 68). To establish whether this was the case, Feingold assessed the effect sizes (male and female variance ratios) of sex differences in variability in the national norms of the Differential Aptitude Test (DAT), the Primary Scholastic Aptitude Test (PSAT), the Weschler Adult Intelligence Scale (WAIS), and the California Achievement Test (CAT). The results showed that males were more variable than females in general knowledge, mechanical reasoning, quantitative ability, spatial visualization and spelling. Homogeneity of variance was found for most verbal tests, short-term memory, abstract reasoning and perceptual speed. Gender difference decreases were found for some of the DAT and WAIS sub-tests; however, general sex differences in variability remained fairly stable over the last generation. Critics of Feingold's use of averaged untransformed variance ratios while supporting his conclusions suggest that his method might have exaggerated the differences in male and female variability (Katzman and Alliger 1992).

Feingold's results could be seen to support those proponents of greater male variability who typically favour biological explanations for sex differences (see Noddings 1992). However, Feingold argues that sex differences in variability 'may be attributable to cultural factors'. In support of this, he quotes studies which reveal cross-cultural variations in sex differences in variability (Feingold 1991b). The data from his study do not, in his view, support a purely cultural hypothesis. However, his concern is to highlight the possible interactions between biological and cultural factors and to demonstrate the inadequacy of previous research into intellectual sex differences, which focused on sex differences in means alone.

The earlier discussion about creativity referred to the performance on Piagetian logical reasoning tasks. These tasks demand hypothesis generation and as such were seen to tap an aspect of 'creativity'. Earlier studies revealed no consistent sex differences in tests involving these tasks. A long-term study by Adey and Shayer (in press) is of interest here, not so much with regard to creativity but more generally in terms of the nature of measured sex differences in performance and current explanations for them. Shayer and Adey investigated the possibility of promoting formal operational thinking in 11- to 14-year-olds. Their interventions were based on a set of activities designed to address all ten of Piaget's schemata of formal operations (Adey *et al.* 1989). Students undertook a pre-test before the 2-year intervention, a post-test immediately after the intervention, a delayed post-test 1 year later and then public external examinations (GCSE) which take place 2–3 years after the end of the intervention.

GCSE results for science revealed that the study group of boys aged 12 plus at the start of the project showed significant gains over the control group, on average obtaining a grade higher once individual pre-test differences were taken into account. The 11 plus girls (i.e. girls aged 11 at the start of the programme) did show a significant effect. Their science grades were enhanced in comparison to the control group (two-thirds of a standard deviation). A similar pattern was found for mathematics. The boys aged 12 plus at the start of the programme improved their mathematical performance in comparison with the control group, though not to the same extent as in science. For the 11 plus group of girls, the effect in mathematics was stronger than for science (over 0.7 of a standard deviation). The GCSE English data showed significant effects in three out of the four groups. There were effects for the 12 plus boys and 11 plus girls as before, although weaker for the boys in this domain compared with science and mathematics. There was in addition an effect for the group of girls who started the programme at 12 years of age.

Adey and Shayer consider various explanations for their results. They conclude that the overall results are best explained in terms of a general intellectual development, taking into account 'the long-established evidence on the faster intellectual development of girls over boys at this age'. For Adey and Shayer, this explanation explains satisfactorily the age differences, as the 11 plus boys' group is still at the stage of concrete operational reasoning, whereas the 12 plus group has reached the emergent phase. The girls at 11 correspond to this stage of intellectual development because of earlier intellectual maturation, whereas at 12 plus girls seemed to have passed the period of most effective intervention. Adey and Shayer claim to be unconfident about age and gender differences in their results and their explanation does assume differential intellectual maturation, which is contentious.

In seeking other explanations for the results, Adey and Shayer consider the possible effect of affective disillusion on girls, which is commonly noted in the domains of science and mathematics, a concern we will address briefly at the end of this chapter and later in our review of international surveys of achievement. Adey and Shayer remain speculative about the possible interpretations of their results, that is, whether the influence of the intervention is domain-specific acting independently on two intellectual structures (they suggest a spatial-numerical one and a linguistic one) or domain-independent enabling development in learning in all academic domains. They recognize the need for considerable further research but are confident that their findings with regard to enhancement can be replicated across a range of subject areas.

Halpern (1992) recently conducted a review of sex difference research for a second time and provides a picture of differences that complements the one provided by Maccoby and Jacklin (1974) while taking account of methodological critiques of their work. Halpern focuses on the three cognitive abilities – verbal, quantitative and visual–spatial – that Maccoby and Jacklin found differ by sex.

Verbal abilities
Halpern (1992) looks at the effect size for verbal abilities and raises the problem of the inclusion or exclusion of studies which find null results. She explains that meta-analyses always include studies that report no differences and consequently yield smaller estimates of differences compared with data summary techniques which focus only on those studies that are statistically significant. Halpern challenges Hyde and Linn's (1988) conclusion (referred to earlier) that 'gender differences in verbal abilities no longer exist'. She rather interprets their findings as indicating a mixed pattern of outcomes. Some studies revealed no sex differences for certain verbal abilities, whereas others showed small differences (sometimes in favour of males) and others moderate differences for 'at least one component of verbal ability'. She also suggests that the size of effect in favour of females would have been much larger if the samples used had included more subjects from the low end of the abilities distribution.

Halpern also raises the problem of how to define constructs adequately and develop tests that validly assess performance on them. She quotes evidence from newly developed tests to highlight the problem of looking at trends over time on data derived from studies whose instruments are non-comparable. For example, Hines (1990) found very large differences in favour of females on tests requiring students to generate synonyms. Block *et al.* (1989) found similar large effect sizes in favour of females for consonant–vowel matching tests. Halpern concludes that there are many types of verbal abilities that show no sex differences but there are some consistent sex differences. She lists these as fluent speech production, anagrams, and general and mixed tests of verbal abilities where females outperform males; and solving analogies and the verbal part of the SAT where the reverse obtains.

In Halpern's view, most literature reviews underestimate the female advantage in verbal ability as so few studies include low verbal ability samples which are predominantly male. Halpern is also critical of reviews that focus on trends in sex differences but take no account of other variables that change over the years in addition to the effect under consideration. These include the nature of the sample – there are now far more women going on to higher education than hitherto, for example. The tests themselves have changed (a point to consider when looking at international survey findings), as have the nature of studies which are funded and published. These variables in Halpern's view bring into question the apparent trend in SAT-V (Scholastic Aptitude Test – Verbal) performance that has shown the female advantage established in the late 1960s and early 1970s to have been reversed. The sizeable male advantage in verbal SAT scores cannot, Halpern argues, be explained by females apparently 'losing' their verbal ability relative to males. She identifies various factors which could account for the performance shift between males and females. Low-ability males tend not to enter for the SAT (see later discussion about differential exam performance in the UK at 16 plus); SAT-V items are biased in terms of vocabulary and content (we discuss this point further at the end of the chapter); the tests do not include items testing the verbal abilities that females excel on, whereas they are heavily weighted with verbal tasks where the largest male advantage is found.

Halpern's review reopens the debate about the nature of verbal abilities and the constructs that define them. She also extends the debate to include a critical focus on the nature of the samples used and the characteristics of the assessment instruments employed. These are two areas of concern we pursue in later chapters.

Quantitative ability

In looking at this domain of achievement, Halpern (1992) refers to the study by Stones *et al.* (1982). They gave tests covering ten different mathematical categories to students at ten different colleges. No overall differences were found using multivariate analysis but significant differences did emerge on the individual tests. Females out-performed males on tests of mathematical sentences and mathematical reasoning. Males scored significantly higher than females in geometry, measurement, probability and statistics. These findings are also replicated in various national surveys, which we discuss later. Halpern considers the evidence from many large-scale studies and concludes that sex differences in some aspects of quantitative ability are well-founded. She does, however, point out that when previous mathematical experience (i.e. number of prior courses taken) is controlled for, the sex differences are substantially reduced if not eliminated (Meece *et al.* 1982).

In her review of trends in quantitative abilities, Halpern cites Hyde and co-workers' (1990) meta-analytic review of 110 studies as the most reliable. They concluded that the most dramatic age trend was on tests of mathematical problem-solving, slightly favouring females in primary and middle schools, but showing a moderate male advantage in high school and college. The findings were confirmed by Aiken (1986–87) and Marshall and Smith (1987). No trends in sex differences in mathematical performance are revealed by the SAT-Maths scores or by Benbow's (1988) study of intellectually precocious youth, both showing relatively stable patterns of performance for males and females.

Visual–spatial abilities

We referred to three visual–spatial factors earlier in the chapter. Halpern adds a fourth for consideration, that is, *spatio-temporal ability*. This involves judgement about, and responses to, dynamic visual displays. Halpern begins her review of this domain with the caution that many studies reveal conflicting findings. She considers that such findings reflect the multidimensional complexity of visual–spatial abilities. She refers to Caplan and co-workers' (1985) critique, which questioned whether construct 'spatial abilities' exist and which also suggested that valid tests of this ability should involve real-world tasks. While agreeing with these latter points, Halpern nevertheless concludes that evidence of male superiority is consistently found on spatial perception and mental rotation tasks (Linn and Peterson 1986) and spatio-temporal tasks (Schiff and Oldak 1990; Smith and McPhee 1987). She also refers to the greater variability in male test scores on tests of visual–spatial abilities (Kail *et al.* 1979). Halpern sees these findings as indicative of a possible difference in the way men and women perform spatial tasks, a point we commented on in the earlier discussion of visual–spatial tasks. She follows up this line of speculation when she attempts to make sense of the female superiority in language. Referring to Sherman's (1967) hypothesis, Halpern (1992: 224) considers whether 'each sex develops somewhat fixed patterns or preferences for interacting with the result that early developmental differences guide later actions. In this way a small critical difference in ability between the sexes grows larger over time.'

If this is the case, females may prefer verbal strategies which advantage them in some domains and disadvantage them in others (for example, when performing spatial tasks). Sex differences in visual–spatial ability are perhaps one of the most consistent findings in this area of research. The differences measured also appear to be the largest. Halpern reports on the substantial effect size established for tests of mental rotation (Sanders *et al.* 1982; Petersen and Crockett 1985). Meta-analyses on spatial abilities have not explored whether effect sizes have changed over time. Halpern challenges Feingold's findings that sex differences in spatial abilities are decreasing on the grounds that his use of a test of spatial visualization, a factor for which no consistent sex differences in performance have been demonstrated, invalidates his conclusions.

Summary

The literature on sex differences continues to grow, particularly in recent years. In Halpern's (1992) review, she comments that much of this more recent research is well considered and of high quality. There nevertheless remain those studies whose quality is questionable. Before we summarize the findings, we will highlight the additional caveats that have been identified in this section of the chapter:

- Sampling should take account of the distribution of the population on a particular ability, since the portion of the distribution studied will affect the findings and the conclusions which can be derived from them.
- The age range of the sample will influence the data and needs to be considered when making interpretations or reviewing conclusions.
- Analyses which look at changes in differential performance over time need to recognize the changing nature of certain related variables, e.g. the constitution of samples, the assessment tasks (e.g. their focus and content) and the test context (e.g. laboratory or naturalistic).

The findings of new studies and re-analyses of prior ones continue to show a female superiority on certain verbal abilities. The female advantage is largest for pre-school and adult samples. There is evidence that the gap between males and females on verbal ability tests has decreased, although there are conflicting results regarding this. Males have been shown to excel at solving verbal analogies and appear to be disproportionately represented in the lower end of the verbal abilities scale, while the SAT-V results show a steady decline in female scores relative to male scores with males now out-performing females.

In the mathematical domain, the results indicate a male superiority which emerges in adolescence and appears to increase particularly on tests of mathematical problem-solving. Males predominate in the highest ability end of the mathematical ability distribution. The similarity in the performance of the majority of the population on tests of qualitative ability has been noted, suggesting that it is among the more gifted student samples that differences begin to emerge. (Females continue to excel at computational tasks in the primary school years.)

There continues to be a consistent male advantage on tests of spatial perception, spatio-temporal tasks and mental rotation, with large effects being observed for the latter. This effect appears to emerge towards the end of the primary phase of schooling.

Again we have to note that the list of intellectual differences is small in comparison to the similarities that exist between the sexes. Recent studies show a continued interest in the possibility of the existence of differential biological mechanisms to account for different skills or approaches to tasks. The interest in psychosocial variables also remains. This has led to a focus on the nature of the instruments themselves and the age, make-up and experience of the study samples where effects are observed. The development of analytical methods to explore the interaction between biological and psychosocial influences has marked much of the work over the last decade. The value of this recent research for us is not primarily in identifying differences between the sexes but in uncovering the way that people perceive and respond to various tasks and test contexts. Understanding how people make sense of tasks lies at the heart of developing valid assessment measures and interpretations of their outcomes. It is therefore essential to identify those variables that mediate students' achievements in their responses to tasks.

Throughout the chapter, we have briefly noted where particular biological theories have driven research or have been developed as a consequence of it. We have also identified various social or psychological factors that have been used to interpret and explain findings. To close the chapter, we summarize these to provide a framework for looking in more detail at specific assessment practices in subsequent chapters of the book.

Sources of group differences in performance: Some hypotheses

Biological hypotheses

Three biological systems feature in theories developed to account for sex differences in cognitive abilities. These are genetic or chromosomal differences, hormonal differences and brain differences. As Halpern (1992) notes, the systems are not separate, which makes it difficult to determine the contribution each makes within any one individual. We describe the various theories associated with each system and briefly indicate their present status in research.

Genetic theories

The extent to which intelligence is inherited remains an unanswered question. With regard to sex differences in intellectual abilities, one popular theory considers that spatial ability is inherited and determined by a genetic code on the X-chromosome. Some early studies found support for this hypothesis (Stafford 1961, 1963); however, later studies failed to replicate the findings. Such a theory is no longer viewed to have validity given the complex multidimensional nature of cognitive abilities, which are considered unlikely to be determined by a single gene. Furthermore, the fact that all individuals exhibit spatial abilities to varying degrees is seen to conflict with such a hypothesis.

Hormonal differences

Various studies have been conducted to determine the role played by prenatal sex hormones on the normal development of cognitive abilities. While there is evidence of a link between sex hormones and cognitive development, the effects are neither simple nor well understood.

Other researchers have explored the influence of hormonal changes at puberty on the development of sex differences in cognition. Two theories have focused on girls' earlier physical maturation compared to boys. One theory links early physical maturation with intellectual development in order to explain girls' assumed superiority in early language-related skills. However, such a theory assumes different biological mechanisms are responsible for verbal abilities and spatial abilities and that it is only the former that are advantaged by early maturation.

Another weakness of this theory is that the underlying cognitive mechanisms that are thought to vary as a function of maturation are unspecified (Halpern 1992). This theory nevertheless remains attractive when explanations are sought for observed age-related differences between boys' and girls' performance.

The second theory looks specifically at sex differences in cognition in relation to maturation rates at puberty. The hypothesis is that late maturers (typically males) exhibit more highly developed spatial skills than verbal skills, whereas for early maturers (typically females) the converse is true. While some research findings have been seen to support this hypothesis, more recent reviews have revealed only a limited association between spatial abilities and age at puberty and some research has found no association between the two. Reviews indicate that sex differences on measures of certain spatial abilities emerge before puberty, suggesting that maturation rate at puberty does not directly influence the development of spatial skills.

Halpern (1992) refers to two other hormone-related theories which consider the level and balance of the sex hormones and their influence on spatial skill development. Hier and Crowley (1982) proposed that a minimal level of androgen is needed at puberty for spatial skills to develop. However, their sample was small and selected because of their androgen deficiency. The other theory developed by Petersen (1976) and elaborated by Nyborg (1984, 1988, 1990) is that an optimum concentration of some hormones is needed for the expression of spatial ability to be realized. All theories that rely on changes that occur at puberty are brought into question by findings which reveal sex differences in cognition emerging in pre-adolescents.

Brain differences
The third category of theories relate to the structure, organization and function of the brain, which it is suggested vary between males

and females. Much research has indicated that the different hemispheres of the brain are dominant for different cognitive functions. Halpern (1992) quotes five reviews in the literature which conclude that males and females differ in brain organization for intellectual behaviours, the female brain being more symmetrically organized than the male brain. While there are studies that fail to find such differences, where differences are found they consistently reveal female brains to be less lateralized than male brains. The hypothesis is that women have language functions represented in both cerebral hemispheres. Conversely, men are more lateralized for language, hence the non-dominant hemisphere for language is more specialized for spatial tasks. The evidence that strong lateralization leads to highly developed spatial skills and weak lateralization advantages verbal abilities is not very strong. Halpern (1992) also points out that there are methodological problems with the research studies used to develop the theory, particularly with regard to the methods used for measuring lateralization.

Other theories regarding differential brain structure and function have focused on differences within the hemispheres rather than between them, and differences in the central neural fibres that connect the two hemispheres. In the first case, there is little research to report on; in the second, there are findings that parts of the central neural fibres are larger in females than in males, but again only a small amount of research evidence is available and the implications of this have not been explored. A review of the biological hypotheses and research evidence to support or refute them indicate again that similarities between males and females far outweigh any differences observed. While there is evidence of differences, the research remains incomplete and various methodological problems remain to be addressed. The potential for sex differentiated biological influences on cognitive development still exists but they are as yet not proven.

Environmental hypotheses

A wide range of social and psychological factors have been identified in hypotheses developed to explain differences in performance between males and females. Our intention here is to refer to the most commonly cited factors and to indicate how their hypothesized influence is characterized in terms of differential performance. They are related more directly to research evidence in subsequent chapters.

In their summary of sex role development research, Wilder and Powell (1989) comment on the different ways parents respond to boys and girls and encourage them to interact with the environment and other people. Parents expect different behaviours from boys and girls and these expectations are reflected in the activities, toys and home environments they provide for them and in the different types of feedback they typically mete out. Boys and girls have also been found to partake in different hobbies and pastimes from an early age. A consequence of these differences is that children develop different ways of responding to the world and making sense of it, ways which influence how they learn and what they learn. Children imbue from these different treatments ideas about what constitutes appropriate behaviours for them and come to understand what others' expectations of them are.

In similar ways, boys and girls experience schooling differently and are treated differently by teachers depending on whether they are girls or boys. For example, the interactions between teachers and boys and between teachers and girls have been found to vary in frequency, duration and content. Consequently, boys and girls develop different perceptions of their abilities and relationships with academic disciplines. Teachers' judgements of girls' and boys' achievements and needs have also been found to vary in stereotypical ways, as do their expectations of them. Children's judgements closely reflect those of their teachers and are again domain-dependent. Thus there are expectations that girls perform better in language domains than quantitative domains, are more conformist and less prepared to take risks intellectually. Very often these assumed differences in intellectual functioning are based on behavioural differences rather than observed differences in pupils' actual achievements. The question we need to ask now is how might such a picture of socialization processes influence cognition?

Self-image
One hypothesis suggests that students will perform better on tasks where there is a close correspondence between their self-image and the gender stereotyping of the task. Males would therefore be expected to out-perform females on certain spatial and mathema-

tical tasks and there is evidence that this is the case. This hypothesis would extend to cover not only the construct assessed by the task, but the type of language used to convey the task, the specific content involved in the task and the setting for this. Wilder and Powell (1989) quote a variety of sources of evidence that indicate that item content is a source of differential performance.

Differential out-of-school experiences

One explanation for why item content appears to differentially influence males' and females' performance is that it reflects the different life-experiences of males and females. Some studies, for example, have established a relationship between participation in certain spatial activities and spatial abilities. If this hypothesis is valid, it follows that training in, say, spatial skills will alter levels of performance. Again various studies have demonstrated that spatial ability can be improved by training and that this improvement occurs for both males and females.

Attitudes

We have mentioned that one consequence of socialization is that girls and boys develop different attitudes to certain academic disciplines. There is evidence, for example, that females have more negative attitudes to mathematics and science than males. It is hypothesized that these negative attitudes will influence whether students will feel able to engage with certain tasks and the subsequent quality of their engagement. The prediction is that negative attitudes will result in lower performance.

Another related hypothesis concerns students' perceptions of the value of certain subjects for themselves and their future lives. Boys tend to see mathematics and science as important for their future careers whatever these may be, whereas both girls and boys agree that these are of less value for girls' lives and careers. Such perceptions it is hypothesized will affect students' motivation, which will again influence their engagement with domain-specific tasks. One consequence predicted is that students' performance may be affected and their potential learning either limited or enhanced, depending on their view of the appropriateness of the activities they are expected to engage with.

Expectations of success

Halpern (1992) refers to the hypothesized relationship between levels of confidence and measured performance. Males are said to be more confident about their abilities than females and this is seen to advantage them and disadvantage females in tests. That this confidence may be misplaced is irrelevant, as the hypothesis is that it is the belief in one's ability which influences the quality of the interaction with the task. Hence females' purported lack of confidence, it is suggested, will limit their ability to demonstrate their achievements.

Various terms have been coined by researchers to describe the differences in males' and females' achievement motivation. Females' 'fear of success' (Horner 1969) or 'learned helplessness' (Licht and Dweck 1983) are typical examples of this. Wilder and Powell (1989) comment on the meta-analysis of studies that examined sex differences in attributions related to success and failure, conducted by Whitley and Frieze (1985). The constant difference that emerged from this analysis was that 'men are more likely than women to attribute their outcomes to their ability, regardless of outcome, and that men are less likely than women to attribute their successes or failures to luck' (Wilder and Powell 1989: 19). However, the study concluded that these differences were insufficient to explain male and female performance patterns.

Differential within-school experiences

It has been suggested that females and minorities typically receive different educational experiences to white middle-class males, the latter being encouraged to function in a non-conformist way and rewarded for independent, self-confident behaviour. Females and minorities, on the other hand, are expected to operate within the dominant classroom ethos. Independent behaviour by these latter groups is interpreted as deviant, rather than as evidence of initiative or creativity. It is hypothesized that these different approaches to the teaching of sub-groups encourages differential skill development. In particular, it is suggested that teachers encourage males to develop those attributes required for future achievement in mathematics and science. There is evidence that classroom dynamics influence achievement but the effects are not simple or well understood.

A further related hypothesis is that male and female patterns of performance reflect the different patterns of courses experienced in schools and colleges. Controlling for curriculum experience has been found to reduce the differences between male and female performance. However, achievement differences are not solely a function of differences in curriculum experience as many studies have demonstrated.

Masculine and feminine domains

In this hypothesis it is the actual structure of the domain which is seen to be biased against certain groups; the bias being evidenced in the learning styles preferred, the modes and styles of expression selected and the achievements that are valued. This bias becomes part of a domain because of the over-representation of members of a particular sub-group within it. Hence maths and science are denoted as 'masculine'. It is predicted that while there may be merit in the other group's response to tasks in terms of specific achievements, this merit is not recognized and hence overall performance for this group appears to be inferior.

We have listed some of the main psychosocial variables. However, it is clear that many of these variables are interdependent. Sex differences in intellectual abilities are likely to arise from a complex pattern of influences. Researchers have focused in recent years on developing models to account for sex differences in cognition which recognize the complexity of the process, the interdependence of the influences and the simultaneous or sequential contributions of biological and psychosocial factors to the measured outcomes. Wilder and Powell (1989) make reference to numerous examples of these models and provide helpful schematic representations of some to indicate their interactive nature and their potential for informing the development of new hypotheses and ameliorating strategies.

The interest in psychosocial explanations is related to their implications for change, hence evidence of empirical trends in cognitive sex differences provides support for these hypotheses. However, the question of whether effect sizes are decreasing remains unresolved. It is clear that there are no biological or environmental theories that explain all of the evidence emerging about sex differences in intellectual abilities. Halpern's conclusion after her detailed review of the field seems particularly pertinent to our concerns:

> For the vast majority of the population – that is, most of us in the middle range of abilities – I am convinced that psychosocial explanations are much more powerful than biological ones. Sex differences for the middle range of the abilities distribution tend to be smaller and more fragile than those at the extremes. Thus the kind of answer that I am willing to accept as an explanation of cognitive sex differences will be one of degree, and it will differ for various portions of the abilities distribution and for type of test.
>
> (Halpern 1992: 246)

She continues:

> . . . because the nature–nurture controversy has been found to be of limited usefulness researchers need to construct new frameworks and new paradigms to answer old questions . . . instead of arguing about the size of the sex difference . . . or whether it is better explained by biological or psychosocial explanations, researchers could be exploring the *nature* of the sex difference.
>
> (Halpern 1992: 250, our emphasis)

This emphasis is one we share, hence our intent to document evidence of differences in assessment outcomes and to then explore them in relation to various assessment practices. What is missing from the work described is any critique of the assessment used and it is to this that we now turn our attention.

3

INTELLIGENCE AND INTELLIGENCE TESTING

Introduction

Having looked at some of the evidence for differences in intellectual abilities, we now move on to consider how these are assessed. Here we focus on intelligence testing, in later chapters on international and national surveys of achievement and examinations. First, we shall look at the development of intelligence tests, then at the uses of these tests, including the 11+. Of the hypotheses referred to in the Introduction and Chapter 2, we shall see that biological factors were widely used to account for the differences in group perfor-mance; later, environmental factors were seen to be important, while critical analyses show that many of the tests themselves are culturally 'biased' or slanted.

The development of intelligence tests

Definitions of intelligence abound: 'innate, general cognitive ability' (Burt); 'to judge well, to comprehend well, to reason well, these are the essential activities of intelligence' (Binet and Simon);

the ability 'to carry out abstract thinking' (Terman, quoted in Ryan 1972). Most definitions emphasize abstract reasoning ability and this is what many tests emphasize. Those who feel that intelligence is too complicated to define precisely, maintain that it is what IQ tests test.

In fact, the tests which we now call IQ tests were developed before rather than following a theory of intelligence. In 1905 Binet, a French psychologist, published the first intelligence test, which was for identifying children with special educational needs. His approach to the development of the test was a practical, even pragmatic, one: items of an educational nature were chosen for their effectiveness in distinguishing between children who were judged by their teachers to be 'bright' or 'dull'. At the same time, psychologists were working on the theory of intelligence – trying to define 'the essence of intelligence'. In 1904, a year before Binet's test appeared, Charles Spearman published a classic paper on general intelligence. Binet and Spearman were critical of each other's work but the serendipitous timing of developments in the measurement and theory of intelligence gave IQ testing considerable appeal. Theoretical developments generated the concept of 'general intelligence', a cognitive quality which these tests were then assumed to measure. However, it is now clear that success at school depends on more than cognitive ability: it is also determined by motivational and social factors within and outside the school (the psychosocial factors we explored in Chapter 2).

Binet was commissioned in 1904 to develop techniques for identifying those children whose poor performance in school suggested the need for special education. Binet decided not to assess learnt skills like reading, but tasks related to everyday life involving basic reasoning processes of ordering, comprehension, invention and correction (Gould 1981). Binet's conscious decision to use a large series of diverse activities, a 'hodge-podge' of tasks, was based on the hope that by mixing together enough tests of different abilities, he would be able to get at the child's general potential: 'One might almost say, "It matters very little what the tests are so long as they are numerous" ' (quoted in Gould 1981: 149). Binet attempted to separate out 'natural intelligence' and instruction in his scale, by using nothing that required reading or writing or in which the child could succeed by means of rote learning. But beyond this Binet did not define the meaning of the score he assigned to each child, nor did he give any theoretical interpretation to his scale of intelligence. This was not because Binet was a-theoretical, far from it, but because he thought intelligence was too complex to capture with a single number and because intellectual qualities could not be measured in the same way as linear surfaces or height. In fact, 'The scale, properly speaking, does not permit the measure of the intelligence . . .' (quoted in Gould 1981: 151). The score was an empirical guide for a specific practical purpose, and Binet was careful to make clear that the figure should not be given more credence than this since it was unwarranted and dangerous. Although Binet did not believe in a single underlying general ability which could be measured on a scale, others did. Binet's notion of mental age (the level on the developmental scale that the testee reached) suited very well those who supported the notion of 'g' or general intelligence. A German psychologist, William Stern, took the process a stage further. He divided mental age by chronological age, multiplied by 100 and rounded off; the result was the intelligence quotient and the IQ score was born. Thus it became possible to describe the abilities of a child through a simple number.

As Gould points out, Binet was also cautious about his tests and the use made of the results, because he was afraid that rather than simply helping to identify children for special educational provision, they would also be used to label children and to set limits on their potential (and, of course, he was right). Binet mentioned specifically teachers using IQ as a convenient way to get rid of troublesome children and what we know as the self-fulfilling prophecy: it is only too easy to notice signs of backwardness when one is forewarned. The aim of Binet's scale was to identify children in order to help and improve them, not to label them in order to limit them. Some children might not reach normal levels of achievement, but all could improve with special help. With his special classes and programmes of 'mental orthopaedics', his pupils benefited and in this sense he felt their intelligence had increased, that is their capacity to learn and to assimilate instruction.

Binet's intentions and actions were, we would say, educationally and socially sound. He is often referred to as the father of IQ testing, but given his views and the misuse of IQ tests since, in particular to segregate, allocate, stream and generally limit opportunities for some children, this hardly seems fair.

What happened in the USA, Gould argues, was that Binet's test was 'hijacked' by American psychologists who espoused a hereditarian theory of intelligence. They took Binet's scores as measures of an entity called intelligence. They assumed that intelligence was largely inherited, they confused cultural and environmental differences with innate properties, and they believed that inherited IQ marked people and groups for life and assigned them to an inevitable station.

For example, H. H. Goddard, who was a keen user of Binet's scales in America, used the test to identify the feeble-minded so as to limit their reproduction and also to prevent their immigration into the USA. On one of his early visits to Ellis Island (where immigrants waited to be processed), Goddard picked out a young man whom he thought was clearly defective. Using an interpreter, this young man was given the Binet scale and he came out as having a mental age of 8. The interpreter, however, told Goddard that he himself could not have done the test when he first came to the country and for this reason the test was unfair. Unconvinced, Goddard persuaded the interpreter that the boy was indeed defective (Goddard 1913, quoted in Gould 1981).

Although Goddard himself changed his views by 1928, his ideas were widely taken up and the IQ/heredity lobby has had a continuing presence in the USA, to a greater extent than in the UK. Gould makes an authoritative and meticulously researched critique of intelligence and intelligence testing in his book. The fervour of his critique is perhaps explained by the more extreme use of the hereditarian and IQ argument in the USA. Sterilization of low IQ women and girls was widespread: over 7500 females were sterilized in Virginia alone between 1924 and 1972, a fact which in the UK we find startling. Although Gould's book has been criticized for not dealing adequately with recent history in this area, or indeed recent critique of the IQ and heredity argument, its relevance to our theme is for highlighting the purpose of Binet's original scales and their clear misuse when they 'identified' low scoring groups and individuals whose lives were then profoundly affected.

An American psychologist, Terman, who was a firm believer in the influence of heredity on intelligence, was actually the main popularizer of intelligence testing in California and subsequently throughout the USA. He, like Binet, first used IQ tests to identify individual children with special educational needs, both subnormal and gifted. Terman's contribution to the debate was to suggest that pupils could be grouped according to their ability and follow different courses of study. Binet's test was an ideal tool for identifying 'feeble-minded' children and other group tests were later developed by English psychologists – notably Cyril Burt and Charles Spearman as well as by Godfrey Thomson, later, at Moray House in Scotland – for identifying children of different abilities.

The notion of innate ability or potential is one which suggests that ability is a characteristic of an individual prior to, and independent of, any interaction with the environment and any specific social or educational influences. Thus Burt asserted that this innate potential set an upper limit to what could be achieved at school. Yet as Ryan (1972: 42) points out, '. . . the notion of potential ability both as something abstracted from all interactions with the environment and at the same time as something measurable in a person's behaviour simply does not make sense'. This argument does not deny that there are genetic and environmental determinants of cognitive ability, but that it is impossible to separate out only the non-environmental determinants of ability for testing.

A further assumption of the concept of innate intelligence is that IQ scores should remain fairly constant throughout life. However, during the 1920s and 1930s, some researchers began to discover that substantial shifts in children's measured IQ, both upwards and downwards, could result from major environmental changes in their lives. Studies reviewed in the mid-1940s indicated that not only was measured IQ not constant, as was generally believed at the time, but also that IQ development was closely related to factors in the social environment (Husen and Tuijnman 1991). Indeed, Husen now argues, on the basis of a longitudinal study of males in Sweden, that formal schooling is important in enhancing what he calls the intellectual capital of a nation, by producing positive changes in adult IQ scores. Husen uses in support of his argument other research which, using survey data from 14 countries, shows that over a generation there has been an increase in measured IQ amounting to almost one standard deviation.

The hereditarian argument was sparked off again in 1969 by Jensen, an American psychometrician, and the debate was pursued on both sides of the Atlantic. The argument was to do with the nature/nurture problem, i.e. the extent to which intelligence is genetically determined or depends on upbringing and environment (for a detailed account of the debate, see Kamin 1974). Jensen's paper (Jensen 1969) argued that: the Headstart compensatory education programmes had failed to improve the educational performance of (mainly black) disadvantaged ghetto children; IQ is fundamentally important to determining educational achievement and it is genetically determined; differences in IQ between different groups (including blacks and whites) are also genetically determined and cannot be ameliorated by educational and social reforms. This line of argument was pursued by Jensen to suggest a different, more basic, education programme for blacks and by others that low IQ parents be sterilized so as to limit the number of (low IQ) children they have. Incidentally, we must point out that the design and evaluation of the Headstart programmes have been heavily criticized and that progress was initially measured by means of IQ tests, which, as we will show, are culturally biased.

Scarr (1984: 435) cuts through the notion of innate potential and states firmly that 'intelligence, as measured by IQ tests, is primarily *school-learning* ability, not general adaptation to life'. Intelligence, she argues, is the result of experience and learning: some test items call for past learning, others require the use of past learning to solve new problems, but all intelligence tests presuppose past learning. Scarr does not deny genetic differences in 'intelligence': with equal learning opportunities individuals vary enormously in what they have learned and the skills they have developed. However, without any learning opportunities, we would all be equally 'stupid and ignorant'.

Because of the definition of intelligence as potential or ability, the validation of IQ tests has been problematic. Validity, in a technical sense, generally refers to the extent to which a test measures what it was designed to measure and not some other aspect of behaviour. The standard way of calculating this aspect of validity is by correlating scores on the test with some other measure, or criterion, which represents the behaviour in question; this second measure needs to be independent of the test items, otherwise the comparison is circular. With intelligence tests, this second measure is difficult to select. Some test developers correlate scores with those from other well-established tests, thus neatly bypassing the validation issue, since the assumption that the original test is valid is accepted (and perpetuated). Other authors correlate scores on the IQ test with educational success: this assesses a particular form of validity, 'predictive validity', and it is generally accepted that IQ scores predict individuals' school performance fairly well (Richardson 1991). Validation against school performance began with Binet because he selected his items to distinguish between children who were judged to be 'bright' or 'dull' at school. But there is a problem with this form of validation: the argument is circular because IQ items are selected specifically to correlate with performance in school, and strictly speaking it makes IQ tests measures of educational competence rather than of 'intelligence'. Of course, this indicates the tautology of Husen's claim that schooling increases 'intelligence'.

Part of the attraction of IQ tests was that they were thought to measure ability independently of schooling, and that non-verbal tests were independent of culture. Evidence to contradict this began to emerge in the 1950s (Torrance 1981) and there now seems to be a fairly clear understanding that IQ tests are biased in favour of individuals from the dominant culture who designed the tests; in the UK this means those from a white, male, Anglo Saxon background and, in addition, middle class.

In order to consider whether IQ tests are culturally biased, it is important to consider their rationale and construction in detail. Difficulties over validity are exaggerated by the fact that two assumptions underlying the tests are often forgotten. The first assumption was that those being compared on the test have common experiences. We recognize now that intelligence tests are culturally specific and should not be used with culturally different populations, although we seem more inclined to see this as operating across cultures rather than within cultures. The content of IQ tests is riddled with general cultural knowledge and are just as unfair to children from minority groups within a culture as they are if used across different cultures.

The second assumption was that such tests sample intelligent behaviour. Tests cannot cover the whole domain of a skill, so they must sample from this domain; both the definition of the whole domain and the sampling of items from it are highly significant aspects of validity. The rationale is that individuals who know, for example, the capital of Greece are likely to know other similar facts; a person who can repeat six digits backwards is also likely to be able to manipulate other information in his or her head;

a person who can abstract similarities knows how to think abstractly, etc. Deciding which items to include, however, is likely to be affected by the cultural background of the test developer. As a result, many items assume certain values on the part of the child, or ask for specific information.

The cultural bias of IQ tests, particularly the traditional ones (e.g. the Stanford–Binet and the Wechsler tests), is apparent when looking at the items, particularly the verbal items. The vocabulary sub-tests ask for meanings of words like catacomb and parterre; comprehension items include 'why is it generally better to give money to an organized charity than to a street beggar?'; similarities ask 'what do the words liberty and justice have in common?' Items such as these clearly depend on knowledge and values which are culture and social-class related.

Selection of items for intelligence tests follows various criteria (Ryan 1972). One key criterion is that items become increasingly difficult, usually on the basis of age. This is calculated during the construction of the test by the proportion of children in the sample who pass the items at each age. The test items (for children's IQ tests) are chosen to reflect the abilities of children as these change with age. Another criterion is a statistical one related to the contribution that any one item makes to the total score. The aim here is to have a collection of items which correlate highly with each other and with the overall score; this results in a consistent test (but reduces the opportunity to include a range of culturally heterogeneous items). Overall parity between males and females is also sought; therefore, items which show consistent or large sex differences are removed during the development of the test. A second statistical criterion is reliability – whether individuals get the same results on re-testing after a short period of time. Although there are selection criteria like those listed above, there are no theoretically based criteria for selection of items, i.e. which relate to the definition of intelligence. As Ryan (1972: 49) puts it: 'There is no discussion in the manuals for these tests of why a scale of changes in ability with chronological age should be chosen to measure intelligence'. These tests, she maintains, are more properly called developmental scales of difficulty, and no attempt is made to explain how these relate to what the tests were designed to measure, viz. intelligence. Thus an IQ score is essentially an indication of how far up the scale of difficulty (as defined by the test constructor) an individual has got with respect to his or her chrono-logical age group.

As well as invalidity in the definition of content domain and in selection of items from it, there can also be bias in the standardization of the test. When tests such as these are developed, they are trialled on large populations in order to determine levels of performance for different groups – usually age and gender groups. Through discovering what is 'normal' or average for any one age, an individual's raw score can be transformed into a standardized score, in this case an intelligence quotient, by comparing it with the performance of others of the same age. Clearly, if the norms are being used to interpret scores in relation to average performance of particular age groups, then the make-up of the standardization sample is crucial – it effectively determines the usefulness and applicability of the test. Thus we know that tests standardized in one country cannot be transferred for use in another, without being re-standardized on a sample representative of the second country (and indeed item analysis would have to be carried out again to make sure the items were appropriate). But *within* a country the standardization sample is also very important; it must reflect the population as a whole and this is not always easy. As Ryan observes, the Wechsler scale and the Stanford–Binet were originally standardized in the USA using a population which matched the census profile. As a result, it did not include the migrant and unemployed workers who tend to be lost from a census; not only that, but these two tests were originally standardized on whites only. While more care may be taken over standardization nowadays, obtaining a fully representative sample is not always easy.

Two issues arise if the standardization sample is unrepresentative. If only a white population is used, then there are no norms for a black population. One can give the test to black children and see how well they do, but then one is seeing how they perform on a 'white' intelligence test, i.e. a test that is designed and trialled on the basis of the performance of white children, with all the cultural specificity which this implies. Furthermore, if disadvantaged groups which are likely to score low are under-represented in the standardization sample, then individuals from those groups will be underestimated on the subsequent IQ test because their lower-scoring population did not make up enough of the standardization sample. This means that disadvantaged groups will be further disadvantaged by the test.

Attempts have been made to produce non-verbal 'culture-fair' or 'culture-free' tests. The best known of these is Raven's Progressive Matrices, in which the testee has to select a figure to complete a matrix. Another is the Porteus Maze Test, which contains a series of mazes on paper and the test is to draw a route through them in pencil. These tests were validated originally by correlating scores on them with scores on traditional IQ tests. Unfortunately, it is now realized that such tests depend heavily on knowledge and skills which vary between subgroups (see Chapter 2). For example, the Matrices Test requires mathematical and spatial skills which are unlikely to be acquired by anyone who has not been to school; even among schooled populations, this test has been shown to produce, contrary to expectation, more variance across samples from different countries than did the verbal IQ tests which were expected to show such variation (Husen and Tuijnman 1991). The Porteus mazes require experience of paper and pencil work, visualization skills and understanding of mazes and cul-de-sacs as a concept – thus, for example, when they were given to Australian Aborigines who had not been to school, results were very poor. The interpretation made at the time was that the Aborigines were of exceptionally low intelligence. It is now accepted that the point at issue is unfamiliarity with the task in the test, in their case streets and cul-de-sacs in particular (we may find this example absurd, but at the time it was taken seriously and had its effect on the treatment of Aborigines).

The conclusion now is that it is not possible to devise tests which do not depend heavily on knowledge which is culture-dependent (Evans and Waites 1981) and this has profound implications for the possibility of developing tests which can be used validly across groups.

As well as macro-factors producing differential group performance on intelligence tests (e.g. lack of cultural overlap), there are more immediate micro-factors. The time of day and previous activity can affect test scores, but most importantly for our theme, in an *individual* testing situation the characteristics of the tester can affect performance. If the tester is aloof and rigid in manner, people score lower than when the behaviour is more natural and warmer. If the tester expects someone to do really well or badly, the individual usually does, rather like the self-fulfilling prophecy: subtle interpersonal cues have a powerful effect (Watson 1972). The effect of the race of the tester has been studied extensively in the USA. As early as 1936, it was known that American blacks scored on average six points lower on intelligence tests when tested by whites than by other blacks. It was not until the 1960s, however, that it came to be realized that this was caused by stress on the part of the testee. In 1968, Watson, a white educational psychologist, together with a black assistant, went to a secondary school in London where there were many West Indian pupils. They tested the West Indian pupils separately and found that not only did those tested by Watson do considerably worse than those tested by the black assistant, but also they displayed aggression and anger when they returned to the classroom. This replicated the findings of Katz in the USA (Watson 1972). Other research on stress has shown that mild levels of stress tend to improve performance on simple tasks but impair performance on more complex ones.

The British Ability Scales were developed in the 1970s in order to overcome some of the criticisms of validity and cultural bias described above. First, it was to be standardized on a British population and, second, it was to sample performance on a range of mental abilities related to 'educability': the research group considered intelligence to consist of an amalgam of special abilities. There was therefore an attempt to have a theoretical framework for the skills that were being sampled (Elliot *et al.* 1978) and the items were chosen in relation to underlying psychological constructs, although the existence of such constructs is not proven (Richardson 1991). More recent work in the field of cognition has focused on developing the theoretical basis of intelligence.

The uses of intelligence tests

It is important now to consider what IQ tests have been used for. The concept of intelligence as innate ability is a very powerful one and IQ tests have been, and still are, used to allocate children to various forms of educational provision: special education, selective schools, comprehensive schools which seek to balance their intake by ability, even to streams within schools. This allocation usually carries with it major implications for the individual's life chances and therefore IQ tests are highly significant.

Allocation to special education

As we have seen, Binet's scales were designed to be used to identify children for special education, in order to give them appropriate support. As more and more children were brought into compulsory primary education in the UK, there was concern about the increasing numbers of children who were thought to be subnormal and therefore ineducable. Sub-normality was, by the beginning of the century, seen as being distinct from lunacy, and as such, 'feeble-minded' children needed to be sifted out from the rest of the child population so that they could go to special schools. Identifying these children accurately was clearly important: children who were not feeble-minded should not be misidentified, not only because of the stigma attached to going to a special school, but also because the special schools were more expensive to run.

In 1913, Cyril Burt was installed as the first psychologist for the London County Council to help with organizing provision for sub-normal children and he used the new Stanford–Binet IQ tests to identify these children. The significance of Burt's appointment to the London County Council was that he was *not* a medical man: his post marked the beginning of the professionalization of psychology as a discipline, with its own expertise and an aura of scientific responsibility (Thompson and Sharp 1988). These factors were crucial to the acceptance of IQ testing: it was scientific, and therefore 'objective', and the figure was a useful shorthand way of describing children. Furthermore, the theory behind the tests suggested that these measures could be used to predict future academic performance. This combination of objective test score and the theory of general intelligence was a powerful one (Sutherland 1984) in the years after the First World War.

It was Cyril Burt who first suggested that an IQ of 70 be used as the cut-off point to identify sub-normal children for special schooling. It should be pointed out that he chose this number because it produced a population size that his special schools in London could cater for at the time; and because Burt used it others used it after him, without questioning.

The situation with regard to the placement of black children into special schools was investigated more than 20 years ago by Bernard Coard (1971). An Inner London Education Authority report (ILEA 1968) had shown that over 28 per cent of children in their day special schools were 'immigrant' compared with 15 per cent in the general school population; of these, 75 per cent were West Indian, while they made up only 50 per cent of the general 'immigrant' population. Furthermore, nine of the nineteen headteachers of educationally sub-normal (ESN) schools surveyed thought that 20 per cent or more of their immigrant pupils had been wrongly placed: 'where children are suspected as being wrongly placed in the ESN school, this is four times as likely in the case of immigrant pupils' (ILEA 1968: 5). The ILEA's response at the time was that 'special schools for ESN children must continue to provide for immigrant children even those of relatively high IQ, until more suitable alternative provision can be made' (ILEA 1968: 6). The ILEA's view then was that this was in the best interests of the child, whereas as Coard (1971) argued, since children rarely got transferred from special schools back to mainstream schools, it could not be in their best interests to be allocated there inappropriately.

Coard's booklet, which was widely publicized in the Caribbean community at the time, gave a comprehensive account of why these West Indian children were being inappropriately assessed and wrongly placed. First, there is a cultural difference between the white middle-class teacher and the black child not only in terms of language but also behaviour and attitude towards the teacher. The West Indian child was not expected to talk much in the classroom, nor to 'talk back' to the teacher; English teachers interpreted this unresponsiveness as hostility or low intelligence. At the time, many of these children had recently come from the West Indies, sometimes to a half-forgotten family, and were suffering from shock and emotional disturbance. They often reacted, particularly the boys, by being aggressive. Coard argues that teachers found this hard to handle: 'This accounts for the extremely large numbers of West Indian children who are submitted for assessment by the teachers, not on grounds of intellectual capacity, but because they are a "bloody nuisance" ' (Coard 1971: 15).

Second, there is the assessment process itself (as already outlined in this chapter) Coard identifies the same cultural and social biases and emotional disturbance in the testing situation as in the class-room situation. The vocabulary and style of the IQ test is white middle class; being tested is for many of these children a 'foreign' experience and the presence of the white tester may make them anxious. In addition, for an emotionally disturbed child having to sit still and answer questions and do tasks for an hour or more, can be particularly difficult and thus the child is likely to do badly. Low IQ test scores serve to confirm the teacher's suspicion, who then has 'objective' evidence that the child is of low intelligence or educationally sub-normal.

Coard was making two separate points, first that the West Indian children were more likely to be submitted for assessment and second that the IQ test would not give a fair measure of their educational ability. Among Coard's recommendations were that all children who had been assessed by white psychologists be re-assessed by blacks, that in future only black psychologists should assess black children, and that tests be designed specifically for West Indian children.

In 1970, just before Coard's booklet was published, Haringey Local Education Authority (LEA) was taken to the Race Relations Board by the North London Indian Association for similar reasons. Although the Board did not find that an unlawful act had been committed, it suggested that IQ tests might be unsuitable for assess-ing ethnic minority children (Tomlinson 1982). (This was at the same time as a Californian case which resulted in the banning of IQ tests for the purposes of assessment for special educational needs (SEN) classes.) Clearly, what is being described here is an assessment situation in which culturally inappropriate tests are being used. The assessment practice is not fair to all groups and is therefore not equitable.

Tomlinson (1982) goes further and sets the discussion in rela-tion to IQ testing and SEN allocation within a general framework of social control: particular groups are identified for special educa-tion because they are troublesome, or to maintain the social order. To support this argument, she points out that educationally sub-normal, maladjusted and disruptive children 'occur' almost exclu-sively in manual working-class families and disproportionately in black families. Indeed, she goes so far as to say that the position of West Indian children in special education is one of the clearest indications that this type of education 'does not exist solely to cater for the needs of individual children, but is related to the way particular groups are regarded as potentially troublesome to schools and society' (Tomlinson 1982: 155). In 1972 (when figures were last collected by ethnic group), Tomlinson points out that West Indian children constituted 1.1 per cent of all children in state schools but 4.9 per cent of children in ESN-Mild schools; of the total population at state schools in 1972, 0.66 per cent were in ESN-Mild schools, but for West Indian children the percentage was 2.9 per cent. Fewer Asian children are allocated to special education: in 1972, 0.5 per cent of Indian and Pakistani children were in ESN-Mild schools, compared with 0.66 per cent of the total population and 2.9 per cent of West Indian children. Tomlinson concludes that the 'problems' of this group of children are perceived differently from that of West Indians by teachers and other professionals: the Asian children are perceived to have language problems rather than behavioural problems and their parents as valuing education highly. In short, this group is *not* seen as a threat to the normal order of schools by 'bad' or disruptive behaviour. Thus they are not as likely to be put forward for allocation to special education.

Like Coard, Tomlinson identifies the assessment procedure as confirming the teachers' stereotypical beliefs about children from disadvantaged and black families. In a study of placement procedures, Tomlinson found that psychologists who relied on IQ test scores and believed West Indian children had family problems were more likely to recommend ESN-M schooling, while those who did not believe that IQ tests were valid for West Indian children, and who were dubious about the way schools treated West Indian children, were less likely to recommend placement. 'The actual referral and assessment procedures, based as they are on the cultural and racial beliefs of professionals, would certainly seem to work against the children of WI origin . . .' (Tomlinson 1982: 167). As for social class, Tomlinson points out that in the early part of this century, it was the poor who were troublesome to the state education system, starting with the 'discovery' of feebleminded children in the Board Schools for the poor in London. The 'commonsense' notion that only the lower classes produced dull children was aided by the upper and middle classes' tendency to provide privately for their dull and defective children. In the 1920s, the Eugenics Movement was at its height in Britain (Torrance

1981) and the connection was firmly made between defects, lack of intelligence, low socio-economic status, and a variety of undesirable social attributes in the 'social problem classes' (Wood Report 1929, quoted in Tomlinson 1982).

There are currently no official statistics kept on the ethnic background of pupils allocated to different schools in the UK. Although some monitoring of ethnic background began again after DES Circular 16/89, this only relates to pupils entering schools at ages 5 and 11, and does not include pupils transferred at other ages. Thus any data on the current allocation process has to come from research studies and these are consistent in suggesting that Afro-Caribbean students are over-represented in special educational provision; where this used to be to ESN-Mild schools [re-named Mild Learning Difficulty (MLD) from 1981] in the late 1970s, it was to units for behaviourally and educationally disturbed children (EBD) by the mid-to late 1980s (Ford *et al.* 1982; Wright 1986; Tomlinson 1983; ILEA 1988, 1990). There was also a corresponding increase in suspensions. In the particular case of referral to EBD schools, it seems that use of biased IQ tests is not itself the issue, but rather the subjective assessments of teachers who find the behaviour of certain groups of pupils – in particular, Afro-Caribbean boys – difficult to understand and to deal with.

The 'Larry P' case was a watershed in the history of intelligence testing in the USA. This was a test case brought in California in 1979 which sought to ban the use of IQ tests to allocate children to classes for the 'educable mentally retarded' (EMR) on the grounds that they discriminated against blacks and other minority groups. The case included expert testimony from both the defence and prosecution. The judge ruled against the Californian educational authorities on the grounds that standardized intelligence tests *are* racially and culturally biased, and have a discriminatory impact against black children. He argued that no attempt had been made to eliminate cultural bias from the tests, rather that 'experts' had been willing to tolerate, even encourage, tests that portray blacks and other minorities as intellectually inferior. In addition, he made the point that the tests had not been validated for the purpose of 'essentially permanent placement of black children into educationally dead-end, isolated and stigmatising classes' (Evans and Waites 1981).

Another major case which focused on the use of IQ tests for placing black pupils in EMR classes centred directly on issues of test bias. This second case in 1980 in Chicago found that the Weschler tests and the Stanford–Binet were substantially free of cultural bias contrary to the finding in the Larry P case. The judge examined the test item by item and decided on a commonsense basis that only nine questions were a problem. Since the test scores were interpreted by school psychologists who had reached masters level, a good number of whom were black, and since the test scores were only one of the criteria for the decision the court decided that it was unlikely that those few items would result in the misallocation of black children in the Chicago school system. The judge therefore held that the tests used in this manner did not discriminate against black children in the Chicago public schools (Wigdor and Garner 1982). However, Wigdor and Garner conclude that: '. . . school officials are on notice that they must address questions of validation and impact. The unthinking or naive use of intelligence tests or other assessment devices to place children of linguistic or racial minority status in special education programmes will be defensible in court' (p. 113).

In the USA, Shepard (1983) has reviewed the tests used to identify 'learning disabled' (LD) children (children of above average or normal intelligence with learning difficulties in a specific area) and studied the identification process. She concluded that, as well as considerable weakness in the reliability and validity of the tests, there was inadequacy in the training of the school psychologists and LD teachers: they did not understand the technical issues, nor the characteristics of the 'condition'. Furthermore, identification was often done on a 'relative' basis, with almost average children being referred in high socio-economic districts because they could not keep up with their classmates. There was also a professional concern that minority children were being 'over-identified' as with West Indian children in Britain. Shepard, accepting that in some cases identification was made as the only way of getting support for the child, suggests that improving the technical adequacy of the tests, including IQ tests, is not the real answer; the context of the decision-making process is so complex and there are underlying philosophical/educational questions which need to be addressed in relation to test use and validity.

Another important case, though not related to intelligence testing, was the 1979 'Debra P' case, which was brought in relation to minimum competency testing. A class of black Florida high school students challenged the State-mandated literacy test which students had to pass as one condition for graduating. They based their charge on the disproportionate numbers of black students who failed the test the first time compared with whites: 78 per cent of black students failed compared with 25 per cent of white students. The court did not take issue with the State's decision to tie graduation to passing a minimum competency test. However, they did look at the validity of the test. At district level, the court found that the test used was valid and reliable. However, the case went to appeal and while the Circuit Court said that the test *did* have adequate construct validity (i.e. it tested functional literacy as defined by the Florida Board of Education), and also agreed with the trial court's ruling that it was valid for the State to assess functional literacy, the appeal court did not find either of these conditions sufficient to satisfy equal protection considerations and ruled that the test was, at least as far as they could see, fundamentally unfair in that it may have covered matters not taught in the schools of the State. They sent the case back to the District Court for investigation of this issue. To be judged fair, the tests would have had to be demonstrated to be a test of material that was in fact taught in the classroom. This decision put onto the State of Florida the burden of proving what the report called the 'curricular validity' of the test (Wigdor and Garner 1982).

It is important not to oversimplify the critique of the allocation of ethnic minority pupils to special education as a mechanism for social control of particular ethnic groups who do not match the dominant middle-class culture, since some pupils clearly do need and would benefit from special help. However, when disproportionate numbers of the members of particular groups are so allocated, there is clearly a *prima facie* case to answer. Likewise, it is important not to allocate pupils wrongly to such provision if their educational interests would be better served in mainstream schools.

Ability grouping

In the USA, there has been a long history of legislation in relation to ability testing and minority groups. The situation began in the early 1950s when the US Supreme Court ruled that segregated school systems were illegal. After this, integrated schooling gradually developed; however, many formerly segregated school systems introduced testing programmes to 'track' students into ability groups. This had the effect of continuing racial patterns of segregation since, on the basis of the testing, minority groups were allocated to the bottom streams. Since the late 1960s, the use of this 'apparently neutral' mechanism to recreate all-black classes in what were formerly segregated systems has come to court several times and, at one point in the South, all testing for the purposes of ability grouping was prohibited 'until such time as meaningful integration of the schools had been achieved' (Wigdor and Garner 1982).

Streaming by ability was widespread in junior schools in the UK until the 1960s, and the stream to which a child was allocated at 7 years of age was an important determinant of success in the selection process for secondary school. This streaming has also been shown to be linked to social class (Simon 1971). Even in the grammar schools, which had already over-selected middle-class pupils, the A streams had more middle-class children in them and the C streams more working-class children. (Simon makes the point that the work of Russian psychologist Luria was important in the move away from streaming, stressing as he did the formative power of education which denied the rationale underlying streaming.) A report for the British Psychological Society on selection for secondary school underlined the dangers of streaming in junior schools, which was held to exacerbate environmentally influenced differences among children (Simon 1971).

The longitudinal study by Douglas (1964) finally showed that the process of streaming was biased in favour of middle-class children and furthermore was a self-verifying procedure:

> Streaming by ability reinforces the process of social selection . . . Children who come from well kept homes and who are themselves clean . . . stand a greater chance of being put in the upper streams than their measured ability would seem to

justify. Once there they are likely to stay and improve in performance in succeeding years. This is in striking contrast to the deterioration noticed in those children of similar measured ability who were placed in the lower streams.

(Douglas 1964)

Even in the early comprehensive schools there was rigid streaming on the basis of tests given before, or soon after, entry and the streams were found to reflect social class groupings (Ford 1969).

The 11+

In the UK, secondary education was selective up until the 1970s (and still is in a small number of LEAs); selection to 'academic' grammar schools was through an exam, the 11+. Selection was thus to schools, rather than groups, to provide the most effective education. The 1926 Hadow Report on *The Education of the Adolescent* concluded that almost all children were eligible for secondary education, but not the same secondary education: it talked about the equal cultivation of different capacity, a definition of equity which we looked at in Chapter 1. At the end of their primary school careers, at the age of 11, children were to be classified by aptitude and to go to secondary grammar schools or secondary modern schools or remain in senior classes in the primary school. As the report put it: 'all go forward, though along different paths. Selection by differentiation takes the place of selection by elimination' (Sutherland 1984). The intention was the most efficient use of educational resources and, where those resources were limited, that they be directed towards those children most able to profit from them. These suggestions were refined in the Spens Report of 1938, which proposed the (to us familiar) tripartite division of secondary education in to grammar, modern and technical schools. The aim, however, was the same: 'all go forward, though along different paths' and the IQ test was to play an important role.

Clearly, the concept of selection by differentiation required an assessment of the child's ability. Hadow and Spens, both of whom were heavily influenced by evidence from Cyril Burt, and His Majesty's Inspectorate (HMI) of Schools, suggested using examination papers in English and arithmetic and a standardized group intelligence test for those children seeking access to secondary school. By 1938, what we think of as the 11+ was largely in place. When secondary education became free after the passing of the 1944 Education Act, the pressure on the selection process increased because access to grammar school was, in theory, available to all. Within this process of selection there was evidence of concern for equality of opportunity. In 1920, Northumberland was the first LEA in England to use a group test of intelligence, and their reason for doing this was entirely concerned with equity. The LEA covered both urban and rural areas and there was a tendency for schools in the more remote districts to submit few or no candidates for the scholarship exam to secondary school at age 11. What the LEA wished to discover was whether this was due to a lack of ability on the part of the children, or a lack of resources on the part of the schools (Thompson and Sharp 1988).

Differentiated secondary education for all as we have said sees equality in terms of preventing wastage of talent or, as we put it in Chapter 1, achieving independence of educational attainment from social origins. But, Thom (1986) points out, the Mass Observation Surveys found that the assessment procedures for allocation to secondary education were seen by the general public as one of the major *barriers* to equality. Instead of exams, tests and teachers' reports it was suggested that intelligence tests and teachers' reports alone be used. This had already been suggested by R. H. Tawney as being more fair to all and a way of reducing the competitive struggle of the existing exams at age 11. The White Paper of 1943 which outlined the 1944 legislation suggested that allocation to secondary school be by teacher report, with the aid of intelligence tests if necessary. However Ernest Bevin complained that intelligence tests penalized the working class, while Cyril Burt claimed that selection by intelligence test *only* penalized the secondary schools, since children needed the right social background, as well as intelligence, to succeed there. (Burt clearly did not believe in disregarding social origins.)

In the end, the 1944 Act did not actually prescribe the method of selection and it was up to the LEAs, therefore, to decide on their own procedures. Batteries of maths, English and IQ tests such as those produced by Moray House and the NFER were popular, especially since a battery was felt to be a better predictor of success at secondary school than a single test. The group tests of verbal and non-verbal reasoning used in the 11+ were intelligence tests and the rationale for their use was that they could identify potential, or talent, somehow separated from schooling.

11+ and social class

There was in the 1920s, as articulated by Burt among others, a definite feeling that social background was a prime factor in school performance as well as intelligence and that some children, although 'intelligent', would be better off *not* going on to secondary education. But at the heart of the post-war debate was the desire to offer a decent education to poor children, and considerable efforts were made in some areas to arrive at the best method of selection. A 1931 report to the London County Council (LCC) pointed out:

> The investigation has furthermore shown that the scholarship examination selects some children of only ordinary intelligence – children who have enjoyed special advantages, among which may be mentioned good homes, ambitious parents, specially good teaching. This result also suggests that selection by means of an intelligence test plus a scholarship examination would be a fairer method than by examination alone.
>
> (quoted in Sutherland 1984: 263)

As Sutherland makes clear, a number of authorities – including the LCC (despite the report above), Hull, Blackpool and Sheffield – considered carefully the use of an intelligence test (together with English and maths tests) and decided to do without. Those authorities which had a sophisticated approach to attainment testing were less likely to be seduced by the grandiose claims made for intelligence tests: 'Being well-informed about the whole field of mental testing and examination techniques did not automatically lead to the use of an intelligence test' (Sutherland 1984: 264).

The detailed discussions of opportunities, access and fairness outlined by Sutherland that were commonplace in the 1930s and 1940s seem quite extraordinary in the 1990s of post-Thatcher Britain with the commodification of education and the emphasis on competition for scarce resources. Sutherland's point, however, is that the use of attainment and intelligence tests did little to alter the basic social structure of English society at the time. The reason was that the English educational establishment was pretty much in control and it had no special need for new tools and technology. When it did take on the new testing technology, it was exploited to serve existing elite structures and methods of selection rather than to produce a more equitable system.

During the 1950s and 1960s, evidence grew that the 11+ selection procedure (which by then almost universally employed verbal or non-verbal reasoning tests) was biased in favour of children from middle-class backgrounds, was amenable to coaching and therefore not a measure of pure 'talent'. However, despite alleged bias in the tests, one argument was that if allocation to grammar school had been based *entirely* on measured intelligence, the proportion of working-class grammar school entrants in the 1950s would have been higher than it was. Indeed, the abolition of intelligence tests in the 11+ exam by South West Herts in the mid-1950s led to a small but persistent diminution of opportunity for working-class children and a corresponding increase in opportunity for those from higher social levels (Floud and Halsey 1957).

A national study by Yates and Pidgeon (1957) investigated the efficiency and fairness of the 11+ exam. They found that the difference in social class composition between grammar and secondary modern populations was smaller when verbal reasoning tests only were used than when a battery of tests plus a primary head's 'assessment' were used. Of course, the issue here is whether social class affected the head's assessment of the pupils. Indeed, Yates and Pidgeon reported that use of primary heads' assessments was widespread and 73 per cent of the LEAs (123/146 responded) instructed teachers to take account of home background and qualities of character in making these assessments. Not surprisingly, they found a significant relationship between a child's chances of being allocated to grammar school and the amount of encouragement he or she was thought likely to receive from his or her parents. They concluded that it was certainly possible to improve the validity of the allocation procedure; however, even the most efficient system would result in approximately 10 per cent misallocation, which, given the sharply differentiated nature of the system, was not acceptable. It became clear that a large number of children were misclassified, and the transfer arrangements between grammar and secondary modern schools were unable to make up for this, particularly since teachers were (understandably) reluctant to move children from grammar to secondary modern schools. In a review of intelligence testing for the British Psychological Society, Philip Vernon accepted that the definition of intelligence was far from certain, pointed out that there was no evidence that intelligence was normally distributed in the population, and concluded as did Yates and Pidgeon, that selection for secondary school be dropped and comprehensive secondary schools be developed (Vernon 1957).

11+ and gender

The 11+ still survives in pockets of England and in Northern Ireland, and criticism of it in recent years has focused on gender rather than social class. The issue appears at first sight to be simple enough: girls at 11 score considerably better than boys on most of the tests used in the 11+, but particularly so on verbal reasoning tests, which now tend to form the backbone of the assessment. The question is, since girls do better, should they not be allocated more grammar school places? In fact, not only do they not gain more places, but in some LEAs, Birmingham for example, girls have been allocated fewer places. In Avon, the LEA used separate pass lists for boys and girls and offered equal numbers of places to each (this was the most common practice in LEAs) but this means, of course, that girls must score higher than boys in order to get a grammar school place (Goldstein 1986). This is a state of affairs which girls and their parents are becoming less inclined to accept and the Equal Opportunities Commission (EOC) has brought a number of cases to court. The first example was the Avon case in the late 1970s, but there have been a number since, notably in Birmingham and Northern Ireland. One defence used to be that boys went on to do better in public exams, but this is no longer the case. The parity situation would be that at least a common pass mark is used; without this, LEAs are in effect adjusting for sex (Goldstein 1986).

The High Court of Northern Ireland found in 1988 that the education authority for the Western and Belfast district had unlawfully discriminated against girls in the transfer procedure:

the Department of Education for Northern Ireland had decided on separate quotas for boys and girls in allocation to grammar school. Grammar school places were awarded to the top 27 per cent of both boys and girls, but this meant that the boys needed scores of 69 and 66 while girls needed to score 71 in both the tests taken. The Court decided that this did not represent equality of opportunity in education (EOC Press Notice, 1 July 1988). Allocation to secondary school in Northern Ireland using verbal reasoning (V-R) tests ceased in 1992 with the advent of national curriculum assessment procedures (see Chapter 7). However, since there are still selective grammar schools, the problems over perceived fairness of selection are unlikely to go away.

The House of Lords found in 1989 that Birmingham LEA, which actually provided more grammar school places for boys than for girls, was in breach of the Sex Discrimination Act 1975 (*Guardian Law Report*, 24 February 1989). Again, girls who scored higher than boys on the tests did not gain grammar school places and thus were denied the same opportunity as boys. (An attempt by the LEA to argue that education in their grammar schools was not 'better' than education in their other schools was dismissed!) The LEA has so far not resolved the situation: in 1992, the High Court ruled that the LEA continued to discriminate against girls and that their duty to ensure equal access continued irrespective of whether any of the grammar schools opted out of LEA control (EOC, 17 February 1992).

The grounds for defending separate lists and quotas for boys and girls in allocating grammar school places are that there is no reason to expect that girls should be able to profit more from grammar school education. Girls' superior performance at 11, on this argument, is taken to be due to earlier maturity (see Hutt's position in Chapter 2) and boys' better performance at A Level taken to clinch the argument. The LEA position on equity seems to be that, given the imponderables in the situation, the best approach is to treat the sexes as having equal potential and to adjust the cut-off scores to achieve the admission of equal numbers or equivalent proportions of each sex.

Conclusions

Intelligence testing has been a powerful tool in the measurement of intellectual ability. Differences in performance between different groups, including gender and ethnic groups, are explained by various writers as being due to biological factors, environmental factors, to factors in the tests themselves or their administration (i.e the three sets of hypotheses outlined in our Introduction). In relation to intelligence, the first argument maintains that certain groups are genetically superior and pass on their superior intellect in their genes. The second argument maintains that, potentially, groups are equally capable of high intelligence but that different environmental conditions, including cultural and educational ones, result in differing levels of measured ability. The third argument maintains that the middle class and majority ethnic group define intelligence according to their own characteristics or qualities, and are thus able to maintain their privileged position.

A critique of the psychometric approach which we referred to in the Introduction is particularly relevant here: the aura of scientific objectivity surrounding IQ tests meant that there was little attempt to question them. The emphasis on using detailed statistical techniques to produce 'reliable' tests meant that issues of validity – both in relation to the construct of intelligence and in relation to the tests' appropriateness or fairness for different groups – could be ignored.

Furthermore, the concept of a factor of general ability spawned the belief that one could measure one core ability (e.g. maths ability or reading ability) and use this to predict future performance not only in that core skill but also more widely (it is still common practice to determine academic streams in secondary school on the basis of maths performance). This argument assumes not only general ability, thus neglecting the full range of abilities and attainments an individual is likely to have, but also the notion of prediction, thus ignoring the possibility of major changes in performance as a result of environmental changes including teaching. Intelligence is deemed to be a characteristic of the individual, like height, which is observable (and therefore measurable) and unlikely to change.

In line with our theme of 'A Fair Test?' we have focused on factors within the tests and their administration which may result in differential group performance while, we hope, making clear that the situation is more complex than this. Most particularly that the cultural, social and gender group of the test developers is the one which defines what is normal and high status; those who cannot match this are *ipso facto* inferior, rather than just different. Indeed, Broadfoot (1979: 44) claims that intelligence testing was a means of control 'unsurpassed in teaching the doomed majority that their failure was the result of their own inbuilt inadequacy'. Intelligence testing legitimates the perpetuation of class inequalities and is used to obscure this perpetuation, since the power of the 'objective, scientific', numerical score is very strong in our society.

There are many examples of IQ tests (and other tests based on a similar psychometric model) being used invalidly with minority groups to allocate members of that group to educational provision which may be of a lower status, limiting, or simply inappropriate for those individuals. Use of tests in this way with this result is clearly inequitable. This is not to deny that instructional needs differ across individuals and groups, but to point out that procedures for investigating these are often unfair. It is particularly important that tests that are used for placement decisions be fair: tests which are used to band, allocate and select have a profound effect on children's lives.

We now turn to look at international studies of attainment in different school subjects, to see what they say about differential performance, what assumptions are held about achievement in these studies, and what we can draw from them.

4

INTERNATIONAL SURVEYS OF ACHIEVEMENT

A major source of evidence for differential performance in relation to gender is the international surveys carried out under the auspices of the International Association for the Evaluation of Educational Achievement (IEA) and the International Assessment of Educational Progress (IAEP). We will therefore look at these in depth and discuss their findings. In essence we shall, after reviewing their findings, ask: What evidence is there of differential performance and how can we interpret it? Do the authors or their reviewers consider the reasons for any differences in performance: are biological or environmental factors considered to be relevant? Are the assessments themselves reviewed for causes of differences or invalidity? In short, what conceptual/theoretical stance do the authors take in relation to differential performance and its causes? The same questions will be asked of the national surveys of achievement in the following two chapters.

The first surveys were carried out by the International Association for the Evaluation of Educational Achievement. The IEA was the initiator of cross-national studies in the 1960s under the direction of Torsten Husen. The surveys include two in maths and two in science which have been analysed in some detail. A third survey is being prepared in maths and science for 1993, but the Department for Education has refused to cooperate, so the UK is unlikely to be one of the 40 participating countries. The IAEP has also carried out two surveys of maths and science in 1988 and 1990.

International surveys such as these have become increasingly important at a political level: countries in the developed world want to know where they stand in relation to each other in performance in school subjects. The result is a form of international league-table and worldwide interest in these is growing. This is another aspect of the increasing significance of assessment in education to which we referred in the Introduction. Former president George Bush, in his National Goals for the year 2000 for the USA, gave coming top in international studies of performance in maths and science as one of his goals: being 'beaten' by Korea did not go down well in the USA. However, despite the interest in these cross-national surveys and the belief in their accuracy – certainly by politicians – there are some serious questions to be asked about their validity. As will by now have become clear, one of our arguments is that achievement, in its definition and its assessment, is heavily culturally and context dependent; this raises a host of questions about the comparison of performance with common assessments across a broad range of cultures. We will return to the limitations of these studies in the final section of the chapter.

Mathematics

First international mathematics study

The first international study of mathematics achievement (FIMS) was carried out in 1964 by the IEA (Husen 1967) and involved 12 countries including England, Scotland and the USA. The age groups tested were 13-year-olds, the grade or class with the highest proportion of 13-year-olds, and two groups in their final year of secondary schooling: those specializing in mathematics and those not studying mathematics. These last two groups ranged in average age from 17 years 11 months in Scotland to 19 years 10 months in Germany. The areas covered were arithmetic, algebra and geometry with calculus, analysis, sets and logic for the older sample. It is not clear what proportion of the items were in multiple-choice format.

The study found that there were clear differences in favour of boys in all four age samples when results for all the countries were combined and allowances were made for level of mathematics instruction. For individual countries, in all cases except two, boys performed better than girls, although this was less marked when level of instruction was allowed for. This difference became more marked with age: for the pre-university year populations, there was 'a marked male superiority in most countries for the population not specialising in mathematics and strong male superiority among mathematics specialists [particularly] in the countries where stringent selection procedures are at work – namely, Belgium, France and Germany' (Husen 1967: 241) The study also analysed performance by type of mathematics task, predicting that girls would do better on 'highly verbal problems', while boys would do better on computational problems. It found, however, that overall the boys out-performed the girls even on the verbal problem tasks, especially in the 13-year-old class and at the pre-university non-specialist level. In some countries, the difference in performance between the sexes was similar in the two types of task while in other countries it was not.

The report suggests that these differences could not be explained simply by sex differences in mental abilities or aptitude for mathematics (i.e. biological factors), since the results contradict those from other research which show girls to have a stronger verbal ability, while boys have stronger numerical and spatial abilities. (Although, as our Chapter 2 suggests, this picture is not quite so clear-cut.) In some countries, girls showed higher computational ability and scored 'unexpectedly' slightly better overall in maths than the boys; the differences were not the same across countries, and there were significant interactions between countries and sexes. These findings would suggest that environmental factors are coming into play and indeed the authors looked at other factors: interest in and attitude towards mathematics and single-sex versus co-educational schooling. (Nowhere, however, is there a consideration of test content or format as a cause of differences.) Boys were found to be more interested in mathematics at both ages and at the older age were more likely to plan to study maths further; there were, however, only minor differences between the sexes in their views about the difficulty of learning maths. Looking at individual countries, girls in England and France showed significantly more interest than boys in the specialist pre-university sample. The authors state that this is not surprising since the girls involved are a highly selected group: these girls' greater interest and greater achievement in maths must be what leads them to continue studying the subject, while most girls tend to cease studying maths. However, since in most countries it is less usual for girls to continue with maths to this specialist level, it is interesting to speculate why this high level of interest is only found in this sample of girls in England and France.

The findings in relation to single-sex and co-educational schooling are more interesting. In the sample as a whole, the differences between the sexes are much less in the co-educational schools. Boys in single-sex schools perform better than in co-ed schools, whereas for girls this is the case at 13, but reversed at the older level; whether this is caused by selective factors or the superiority of one type of school over the other the authors say cannot be answered by this type of study. For individual countries, only in the younger age group in Australia and Israel are the girls superior to boys; in both cases, these are in single-sex schools and the differences are not significant. In nine instances, boys were significantly superior to girls in single-sex schools, while in only four instances were the boys significantly superior to the girls in co-ed schools. Over all countries, the picture was mixed and no reason was advanced for the varied pattern.

What emerges from these analyses is that the difference in maths achievement between the sexes is considerably lower in co-ed schools. The reason advanced for this is the greater equality of opportunity for girls to learn maths in these schools. However, interest in maths showed the greatest sex differences in co-educational schools: in each instance, the difference was significant, whereas in no instance was it significant in the single-sex schools. The authors suggest that this is possibly due to the greater concern about role and self-image where the two sexes are in the same school (given that maths is perceived as a 'male' subject). The apparently contradictory findings for co-ed schools in interest and achievement are given the 'most sensible interpretation' that in single-sex schools girls are given the opportunity to take the kind of mathematics they want (and are therefore more interested in it) and their self-image as 'non-mathematicians' is not affected to the same extent as in co-ed schools by the presence of boys. However, girls in co-ed schools do better because of their greater opportunity to learn maths.

The authors generally look to the role of women in different countries and the degree of co-education to help explain differential performance in relation to gender. For example, the differences in role expectation between cultures mediated through school organization results in the ratio of male to female students varying considerably among the 12 countries: in the pre-university sample in Belgium, the Netherlands, France and England, five to seven times as many male as female students were taking maths, while the ratio was close to two to one in the USA, Finland, Japan and Scotland.

Such inequitable differences in access to advanced level work in mathematics must be a cause for concern, particularly since mathematics is required for entry to a number of university courses and careers in science, technology and computing.

Second international maths study

The IEA's second international maths study (SIMS) (Robitaille and Garden 1989) involved 20 countries. The testing was carried out between 1980 and 1982 using some of the same tests as the first study, and focusing on two of the same samples: the grade or class in which the modal number of students was aged 13 (20 countries) and students in the final year of secondary school who were specializing in maths (15 countries). The areas tested included arithmetic, algebra, geometry, measurement and descriptive statistics. All the items were multiple-choice format.

At 13, girls consistently out-performed boys in Belgium, Finland, Sweden and Thailand. The reverse was the case for Ontario, France, Hong Kong, Israel, Luxembourg, the Netherlands, New Zealand, Nigeria, Scotland and Swaziland. The authors state that there are clear between-country differences and similarities which require explanation, and here they look at some within-school factors which would affect boys and girls differentially (the same type of points are investigated in the APU and NAEP surveys discussed in Chapters 5 and 6). The authors report that, for example, in Thailand the majority of maths teachers at this stage are female, whereas in the Netherlands and Luxembourg they are predominantly male. In Nigeria, most of the teachers are male, but then so are most of the pupils (73 per cent), with selection procedures operating against girls. Looking at performance on types of task, the results showed that girls were more likely to achieve better scores than boys in computation-level arithmetic, whole numbers, estimation and approximation and in algebra. Boys tended to do better in geometry, measurement and in proportional thinking. The most marked differences appeared in transformational geometry, proportional thinking and standard units of measurement, all of which favoured boys in the majority of systems. The authors suggested that the last of these could be due to boys' greater familiarity with units of measurement owing to their (traditionally male) hobbies; differences in the first might be due to spatial visualization again related to experience (this is a common argument; see the review in Chapter 2). Girls tended to do better on whole number computation, common fractions and algebra; however, no reasons are advanced for this. As in the FIMS, it had been hypothesized that girls would out-perform boys on items with high verbal content, but this was not the case. No discussion was put forward for this and, to put these differences in perspective, we should point out that the mean score for both boys and girls in high scoring countries is higher than for boys and girls in low scoring countries. Since in some countries girls can score higher than boys in other countries, the conclusion must be that mathematics ability is not genetically determined. The biological hypotheses for differential performance are therefore not supported; the alternative is that there are factors in the curriculum, the teaching or the status and perception of the subject which affect performance.

At the higher age level, the gender differences were more consistently in favour of boys; in only one system, British Columbia, did girls significantly out-perform boys and then only in two sub-tests. The authors here discuss the selectivity of pre-university samples and point out that at this stage the population is highly selective and predominantly male. Even in those countries in which a high proportion of the population is still in school at this stage, the proportion of the age cohort taking maths is less than 20 per cent, except in Hungary and British Columbia. Furthermore, the selectivity for boys is commonly different from that for girls. Only in Thailand are the numbers of boys and girls similar in this population. In Hungary girls outnumbered boys, while in all other countries boys outnumbered girls significantly. While one can assume that this population as a whole is academically able, one cannot make the assumption that boys and girls in this group are equally able. The authors suggest that whereas there is a strong tendency for more able boys to take maths, the tendency may be for able girls not to choose maths. However, given the perceived difficulty and 'male-ness' of mathematics, it seems more likely that in general girls who study it at this level are in fact more able.

The largest overall group differences occur in Belgium (French), Hungary, Hong Kong, Israel and Japan. The sub-test which provided the greatest and most regular differences in favour of boys was probability and statistics, while algebra (computation) and analytical geometry produced results in which group differences were smaller or favoured girls in a number of systems.

Although this study investigated pupils' attitudes, as did FIMS, these were not analysed by gender in the same way, so we cannot look at the interaction between gender, attitude towards and achievement in maths. The study did, however, unlike FIMS, include some attitude statements in relation to gender stereotypes. Thus students were asked whether they agreed or disagreed with the following:

1 Men make better scientists and engineers than women.
2 Boys have more natural ability in maths than girls.
3 Boys need to know more maths than girls.
4 A woman needs a career just as much as a man does.

[One must question the inclusion of item 4 in this section – it is hardly to do with maths and in fact it performs differently from the others (p. 198); in addition, they are all 'positive male' statements which can themselves be seen as biased.]

On the whole, students tended not to endorse these items. The authors conclude that the low levels of gender stereotyping and the fact that these items were included at all, are evidence of the changing nature of the relationships between the genders and the types of schooling each demands and deserves.

An interesting area is that of pupils' beliefs about their parents. Apparently, pupils believe that their fathers are better at mathematics and enjoy it more than their mothers, while mothers are perceived as thinking that mathematics is more important. At age 13, 38 per cent of the sample thought their mothers could do their maths and 53 per cent their fathers; at pre-university level, the corresponding figures were 6 and 20 per cent. The authors conclude that as in almost all systems boys are exposed to more and more complex maths and that students are reflecting what they have seen operating at both home and school, mothers and daughters have less experience with maths and are expected to participate less in maths.

The authors conclude that we need to find ways of eliminating gender-based barriers to more girls taking maths and succeeding in the subject. One cause for optimism, however, was that the boy/girl enrolment pattern had changed from FIMS to SIMS for the pre-university maths specialist sample, with an improvement in gender equity occurring in most of the countries across the two decades; only in Japan was there a decline in the relative level of female participation in advanced maths.

A detailed analysis of the SIMS data for England and Wales (Cresswell and Gubb 1987) showed no significant gender differences except that boys were ahead at 13+ on measures. The authors find this surprising in the light of the results of the APU secondary surveys and other work in which significant sex differences have been reported. However, it is consistent with the FIMS finding of smaller differences in co-ed schools: the population for this study in England and Wales in 1981 was predominantly co-educational. As for the small sex differences in the older group, the authors support the suggestion made to explain this aspect of the data in the FIMS: the heavier degree of selection for girls has eliminated most of those who would not have compared favourably with the boys.

The authors of the FIMS and SIMS Reports clearly expect boys to out-perform girls in all areas of maths except those with a verbal content. Where this is not the case, they tend to look for within-school factors to explain the unexpected or suggest that there is something unusual in the sample. In their fairly detailed discussions of reasons for (expected) differential performance, they focus on environmental factors, single-sex/co-ed schooling, male/female teachers, attitude to and interest in the subject, as well as access issues. Nowhere is there a discussion of whether the test format is responsible for any differences. Similarly, the test developers' construct of the subject being assessed is not critiqued; although in cross-national studies consideration is made of the topics studied at various ages in different countries so that content validity is an issue, it is not brought up in reviewing performance.

IAEP maths survey 1

The original IEA surveys are so detailed and complex that a long period of time elapses between designing the items and writing up the analysis so the data is almost out of date by the time it is available. In 1988, a new international study was carried out: the International Assessment of Mathematics and Science (IAEP). This survey assessed only 13-year-olds in these two subjects, the aim being to use items already developed by the American National Assessment of Educational Progress (NAEP; see Chapter 6) and to report on performance within a year of the surveys. Five countries (Spain, Korea, USA, UK and Ireland) and four Canadian provinces took part in the survey which was reported by 1989 (Lapointe *et al.* 1989). The analysis of gender differences is much less detailed than in the other studies and this is no doubt due to the shorter time-scale for analysis and reporting. On maths, the report says that although many research studies have found performance differences between teenage boys and girls in maths, this survey suggests a different picture with boys and girls performing at the same level in 10 of the 12 populations assessed (Lapointe *et al.* 1989: 18). Only in Korea and Spain do boys at this age achieve significantly higher in maths than girls. The items were all originally developed for the NAEP and were simply translated for use in other countries, with names, units of measurement, etc., changed where necessary. It is not clear what proportion of items were multiple-choice, but there were no practical tasks.

A more detailed analysis of the UK findings (Keys and Foxman 1989) shows that girls actually scored higher than boys overall but this difference was not statistically significant. The authors say that this result is surprising in the light of APU results which consistently show boys ahead of girls in most areas of maths at 11 and at 15. Their interpretation of this is that possibly girls gain on boys between the ages of 11 and 13 before the boys begin to move ahead again. This might be due to an initial emphasis on number in the early years of secondary schooling, a topic in which girls do well relative to boys. There is, however, no discussion of the appropriateness of test content or items and whether these differed from the APU surveys, or indeed the appropriateness of using American items across a range of countries.

IAEP maths survey 2

The IAEP carried out a second maths survey in 1990, this time covering 20 countries, including 9-year-olds as well as 13-year-olds, and using items submitted by all participating countries (Foxman 1992). At age 9, gender differences were few: only in two countries did boys significantly out-perform girls; at 12, this figure rose to seven countries (Lapointe *et al.* 1992). For England there were no significant differences on the subject overall at either age. When broken down by topics, however, girls' performance is higher than boys' on five of the six topics at age 9, and boys' higher than girls' on four out of six at age 13.

In the one paragraph that comments on these figures, the author's emphasis is on boys catching up with girls and overtaking them. A more positive picture in relation to girls' achievement could have been drawn by looking at actual differences at 9 and 13 as Table 4.1 shows. Indeed, making inferences about progress is invalid, since these are cross-sectional rather than longitudinal studies.

Table 4.1 Differences between the average percentages correct of boys and girls in mathematics topic area (boys % correct − girls % correct) (from Foxman 1992, quoted with permission)

	Age 9	Age 13
Number: conceptual understanding	+0.2	+0.2
Number: procedural knowledge	−3.6	−1.1
Measurement	−0.5	+3.1
Geometry	−0.7	+0.2
Data analysis, etc.	−3.5	−1.9
Algebra	−0.7	+1.3

[Table 4.1] shows the differences in the IAEP boys' and girls' average percentage correct in six topic areas. There is a similar pattern at both ages, with boys' best areas relative to girls being Measurement and Number concepts, while girls' best areas relative to boys are Number (procedural knowledge) and Data analysis. Between ages 9 and 13 boys tend to gain relative to girls across the topic areas, albeit by a small amount (1 to 3 points), but sufficient to keep the profile of performance across topic areas comparatively similar at the two ages. This pattern accords very well with that consistently found by the APU for 11- and 15-year-old pupils, both in terms of the profile of performance and the extent of the gain of boys over girls between the two APU ages. It indicates that a similar profile of gender differences in mathematics performance in several of the main topic areas exists from ages 9 through to 15. Throughout this period, boys appear to gain over girls in each of these topic areas.

(Foxman 1992: 26)

In fact, a footnote to this quotation does point out that some APU data at 11 and 15, as well as GCSE coursework and extended investigations at 14 in pilot national assessments, put girls ahead of boys.

Science

First international science survey

Twenty countries participated in the first IEA international science survey (FISS). There were four populations: $10+$, $14+$, the last year of full-time secondary school, and students from this group who were specializing in the subject tested. The testing and analysis took place during 1970–73 (Comber and Keeves 1973). Items were multiple-choice together with some written 'practical' tests.

In science at age $10+$, the pattern was for boys to perform at about 0.25 of a standard deviation above girls. The exceptions included India and Iran, while boys' superiority was particularly marked in West Germany, Finland and the Netherlands. At age $14+$, the pattern was the same but the difference was larger: boys performed 0.5 of a standard deviation higher than girls. Only for England was the difference relatively low.

At the pre-university level, the differences in performance are even greater (with the exception of Chile, India and Thailand) and they are particularly strong in Finland and Scotland. In these latter two countries the boy:girl ratio at school at this level is quite different with more boys in Scotland and more girls in Finland. Since one of the complicating factors in these surveys is the progressive selectivity in the systems (girls becoming less well represented in the samples as the age goes up and no clear information on the ability level of those who stay on and/or choose science) these results for Scotland and Finland are interesting but also difficult to explain.

Looking at performance in different aspects of science, as with maths more differences appear: it seems that the gender differences are more pronounced in the physical sciences than in the biological sciences, a pattern similar to that found in the APU and NAEP surveys. In biology at age 10 +, the girls in England, India, Sweden and Thailand 'actually perform better than the boys' (Comber and Keeves 1973: 148). Furthermore, this superiority is also found in England, Thailand and New Zealand at 14 + and in India at pre-university level.

In chemistry, the differences fluctuate from country to country. Girls out-perform boys at both 14 + and pre-university level in Flemish-speaking Belgium: 'Perhaps this results from a bias in the sample drawn, but it may well reflect an emphasis given to chemistry in this school system, where the low scores suggest that little chemistry is taught at either level' (p. 148.) It is also surprising to the authors that there is little if any difference between the sexes in England at the 14 + level; again, the reason given is that it may be due to the relatively small amount of chemistry teaching in secondary modern and comprehensive schools at this level.

In physics, there were strong differences between the sexes with few exceptions. The authors put forward, on the basis of performance on items which test understanding, that the key to these gender differences lies in the boys' better understanding of scientific concepts. (This is in line with the arguments evaluated in Chapter 2, that boys are better at understanding difficult conceptual issues.) The authors do not offer any explanation for this: since boys' superiority here fits with their view of the world no explanation is needed, while in the instances where girls do well, some reason (indeed excuse) for this is usually offered, either bias in the sample or limited teaching.

As far as the effect of single-sex versus co-educational schools is concerned, the sex differences were, in line with maths performance, smaller in co-ed schools at 10+ for all countries in the analysis, and at 14+ for all countries except Australia, West Germany, England and Italy. At pre-university level, however, the opposite holds with the exception of Belgium and Italy. However, the authors point out that these differences are not large compared with overall sex differences, and that the reasons for pupils attending single-sex or co-ed schools are complex and differ from one country to another, so that drawing conclusions on the basis of this analysis is difficult. A general point needs to be made here in relation to the comparisons of co-ed and single-sex schooling: not only are there likely to be population differences between the two types of system, but also within systems there can be quite major differences. In the UK, for example, an all-girls grammar school is likely to be different in a number of respects from an all-girls comprehensive school.

Second international science survey

The second IEA international science survey (SISS) took place in 1983–86. Twenty-four education systems were involved; of these, 10 had also taken part in the 1970 study. The samples or populations were the same: 10+, 14+, and science students in the final year of secondary school.

The preliminary analyses (IEA 1988) showed that in all countries boys scored higher than girls at all levels (as in the previous survey). However, the overall difference between the sexes was lower than in 1970 and the authors put forward this explanation:

> . . . the 1970–71 test contained one quarter of the total number of items that assessed performance on practical work through a paper and pencil practical test [*sic*]. This type of item, which has a strong bias in favour of male students, was not included in the 1983–84 tests and could well account for the reduction in the standard score sex differences.
>
> (IEA 1988: 64)

Again, the authors feel the need to explain the better performance of girls, though significantly, this is the first time that bias in relation to type of item has come into the discussion.

At the pre-university stage, boys showed greatest superiority in score in physics and least in biology; in both Hong Kong and Sweden, girls out-performed the boys in biology. A comparison with the previous survey at this level was not possible owing to sample differences.

A study of the results for England (Keys 1987) showed that boys scored significantly higher than girls at 10 and 14, the difference being twice as large at 14. For the older, specialist sample, boys scored significantly better than girls in the groups doing biology and chemistry A Level but there were no gender differences in the group doing physics. This report devotes a whole chapter to sex-related differences and the author investigated the 'male-ness' of the subjects, differences in handling 'scientific' toys or equipment, sex of the teacher and attitudes to science. She concludes that: girls were much less likely to have access to a computer at home; the proportion of students taught science by a woman decreased with the age of the students, and only 14 per cent of the A Level physics students were taught science by a woman teacher; the girls taking physics A Level are a very small group and the hypothesis is that these girls are highly motivated and very able. At age 14, where the biggest differences occurred, boys regarded science as easier than girls did, had more favourable attitudes towards the social implications of science and were more interested in careers in science – these patterns were not as marked at either age 10 or 18, thus there appears to be a grouping of attitude, interest and achievement at age 14. Keys makes the point, however, that the data indicate that differences in physics performance already existed at age 10 and the items on which boys out-performed girls by the greatest amount at 14 were those concerned with content areas which reflected boys', rather than girls', out-of-school interests. This latter finding supports Johnson and Murphy's (1986) suggestion that boys' superior performance in physics (pre-A Level) may be partly explained by the fact that the content is closer to their out-of-school interests and experiences.

IAEP science survey 1

The 1988 IAEP survey found far greater discrepancies between boys' and girls' performance in science than in mathematics with boys out-performing girls (at 13) significantly in all populations except those of the UK and the USA. The greatest difference found was in Korea (Lapointe *et al.* 1989). These non-significant UK differences do not support the results of the second IEA study, where statistically significant gender differences in favour of boys were found at 14, although in the first survey the differences at 14 were relatively low. The authors of the UK report (Keys and Foxman 1989) point out that the second IAEP survey would use a wider selection of items and imply that the findings might be different.

IAEP science survey 2

The second IAEP study in 1990 covered 14 countries at age 9 and 19 countries at age 13. Boys tended to do better than girls in nearly all the countries participating, more so at age 13 than at age 9 and particularly in physical and earth and space sciences. The differences were less in life sciences and, in a number of countries, girls were ahead of boys in questions on the 'nature of science' (Foxman 1992). The survey again found that there were no statistically significant gender differences for the English sample at 9 or 13, although the boys' scores were higher. Looking at performance by topic, boys scored higher than girls on every topic except for 'nature of science' at age 13. Overall, boys' superiority though not great, was more marked at 13 than at 9. The only background issue discussed is the pupils' response to the statement: 'Science is for boys and girls about equally'. A high proportion of English students at both ages agreed with this statement (86 per cent at 9, 97 per cent at 13).

Thus the second IAEP findings confirm the first IAEP study rather than the IEA study, viz. non-significant gender differences in science performance in England. The high agreement with the attitude statement above, which was common to all countries except Korea, might give some indication of why gender differences in science are declining.

The analyses by gender for the IAEP 2 studies in maths and science are fairly limited. However, a section of the English report (Foxman 1992) does look at reasons for differential performance across and within countries. Home variables including number of books in the home and amount of TV watched were found to be significant (i.e. correlated with level of achievement). School factors included homework, use of practical apparatus, ability grouping and time spent on the subject. Overall correlations can, however, be misleading: the two most successful countries, Switzerland and Korea, have very different class sizes; the limitation with this type of survey is that it cannot probe deep enough to explain such differences. One issue which is not addressed is the lack of overlap between test format and teaching methods: English pupils did more practical work in science than other pupils and yet the tests had no practical element. Three-quarters were multiple-choice items and the others were free response short answer items. This obviously raises questions of the fairness of the test to English pupils. It also begs questions of the view of science held by the test developers – the construct which they are trying to measure – as reviewed in Chapter 2.

For our purposes, the most interesting report is the one written by Alison Kelly, *Girls and Science* (1978). This was based on a study which examined in detail the sex differences in the 14-year-old population of developed countries in the FISS study. It is relevant to note that Kelly only included developed countries, presumably on the grounds that cultural differences between developed and developing countries are so great that comparisons among them are invalid. Unfortunately, her study excluded Thailand, which consistently shows unusual patterns of performance by gender. In all the countries considered, boys achieved better than girls in science. The gap between girls' and boys' achievement was similar in all countries but these differences were consistently larger in physics and smaller in biology, with chemistry intermediate. Thus, Kelly states, sex differences are more characteristic of a branch of science than of a country. As we pointed out earlier where girls in some countries achieve higher mean scores than boys in other countries, biological hypotheses cannot be used to account for differential performance. Hungarian girls did better than boys in all other countries in biology; Hungarian and Japanese girls achieved higher scores than boys in all other countries in chemistry; Japanese girls achieved a mean score in physics which was comparable to that of boys in other countries. This last result shows that 'with a suitable mixture of background, attitude, motivation and teaching', girls can score higher than boys even in physics.

Kelly explored three hypotheses to explain these gender differences – culture, school and attitude – all of which fall into our environmental hypothesis involving psycho-social factors. The cultural hypothesis is that girls do not do as well in science as boys because society does not expect them to. If this were the case, then one would expect differences across countries in line with different cultural expectations; since these were not evident, Kelly says that this explanation cannot be accepted. However, since not enough was known about the expectations and encouragement for girls in different countries, it could not be rejected either. The results for Thailand (which was not included in Kelly's study) suggest that cultural effects could indeed be significant.

The school hypothesis suggests that schools present science in a way that is more suited to boys than girls. If the two sexes enter school with different past experiences and knowledge, different interests, attitudes and expectations, then Kelly argues, the same treatment will not necessarily have the same effect on them. Treating boys and girls identically in school may serve to accentuate rather than diminish the existing differences. This is analagous to the equal opportunities argument that equal treatment of different groups will not produce equal outcomes. On the basis of the data, however, this hypothesis could not be supported. Girls' achievement was not related to the number of women science teachers (however, this is a per school figure rather than an analysis of teacher per girl, i.e. the correlation was between the proportion of women science teachers in a school and the achievement of pupils in that school). In fact in England and the USA, girls achieve better scores in science with more men teachers. Girls did not achieve better in single-sex schools once selection factors were allowed for; they did not have different attitudes to science in single-sex schools. Kelly concluded that it was difficult to sustain the idea that the school organization favoured boys, nor did method of teaching have an effect, although the teaching method variables were not well described or measured, being rather gross. There was some tentative evidence that differences are reduced where girls have taken as many physics and chemistry courses as boys.

The attitude hypothesis is that girls will do less well in science than boys because they have less favourable attitudes to science. Kelly found that the girls did have less favourable attitudes to science than boys, and that pupils with more favourable attitudes achieved better than pupils with less favourable attitudes. However, boys with positive attitudes to science achieved much better than girls with similar attitudes in the same country, so attitude alone is not a sufficient explanation.

Kelly concludes that none of her three hypotheses are satisfactory for explaining differential group performance. She identifies a factor which may contribute to differences: the impact of out-of-school learning, a point which Murphy (1990) also makes. Opportunity to learn (i.e. instruction) was important in chemistry for both genders but less so in physics for boys, thus suggesting an impact from out-of-school learning for boys in physics. Kelly points out that there are parallels between the situation of blacks and girls: blacks are not primarily disadvantaged by material factors, but by the psychological consequences of society's response to blackness, which affects all social groups and produces a uniform depression in achievement scores. This argument can be applied equally well to females. She advances an alternative hypothesis based on a cognitive-developmental theory of the acquisition of sex-role stereotypes. In this theory, science is seen as a masculine activity: girls, who are striving to attain a feminine identity, therefore reject things scientific, while boys try to adopt scientific ways in their play activities and hobbies. Boys thus gain an initial lead over girls in science achievement. The onset of adolescence accentuates the development of sex-role stereotypes and feedback loops operate to increase this lead between the ages of 10 and 14.

Despite Kelly's careful analysis of the environmental issues, there is no discussion of the nature of the assessment materials or the taught curriculum.

Writing

The second IEA study included a survey of the teaching and learning of written composition. As yet there is no analysis of the findings by gender in the different countries. The sample in England and Wales was made up only of 15-year-olds in their fourth year of secondary schooling (Gubb *et al.* 1987). The report describing this study and the findings offers only one short comment on gender differences. The order of difficulty of the writing tasks is shown (using mean overall impression score) with the results presented separately for boys and girls (Gubb *et al.* 1987: 15). For every one of the 15 tasks (they ranged from letter writing to fictional narrative via description), the girls' mean score is higher than that of the boys. There is no discussion of this in the text. The section on the Welsh-speaking sample gives a similar table with the following comment: 'Sex differences in written composition are well documented. The results in this study confirm the trend observed by other researchers that on the whole girls consistently perform better than boys' (p. 134).

The fact that girls out-performed boys on every task seems to be accepted as unremarkable in writing, while less clear differences in maths and science are investigated in depth, is perhaps not surprising after all. What comes across in the writing up of these studies is that the authors are writing from a standpoint of assumed male superiority in maths and science, and female superiority in verbal and written skills. Any variation from this (e.g. girls' better performance in science) either needs explaining away (Comber and Keeves 1973) or is glossed over by focusing on boys' performance (Foxman 1992).

Discussion

What these surveys appear to show is that in maths the pervasive better performance of boys in 1970 is much less marked by 1990. In 1980, the 13+ girls were scoring higher than boys in a handful of countries; at 17 the boys did better. In England and Wales, the girls were performing as well as the boys at 13 and 17. In 1988, 13+ girls and boys were performing at the same level in all but two countries (where boys were significantly ahead); in the UK, girls performed better than boys although not significantly so. By 1990, girls were performing as well as boys at age 9 in all but two countries involved and at age 13 in two-thirds of the countries;

in England, there were no differences between boys and girls in the subject as a whole, at both ages.

In science the picture is less variable. In 1970, boys scored higher than girls in all countries (only in England at 14 was the difference relatively small); by 1980, although the pattern of performance was the same, the gap between the boys and girls was smaller. In 1988, 13 + boys scored significantly better than girls in all countries except the UK and USA; by 1990, boys tended to do better than girls in nearly all countries, more so at age 13 than at age 9. In England, however, there were no significant differences between boys' and girls' performance in the subject as a whole at either age. There are continued gender differences in physics, chemistry and biology.

Can we draw the conclusion, then, that gender differences exist in maths and science, which alter with age, and in the UK seem to be reducing over the years? It is clear that there are measured differences in performance on these tests but the extent to which they reflect actual differences in achievement is more problematic. Commenting about changes over the years is also problematic, since the IEA studies are quite different from the IAEP studies, and the second IAEP survey is different from the first. If, however, we see the same general trend across a range of surveys (e.g. including those of the APU and NAEP), we can have more confidence that the trend is real.

A major limitation with these international surveys is the type of item used and the information offered about them. The early IEA studies tended not to release items because of security reasons, i.e. they wished to make sure that items were not 'taught to' in subsequent surveys. The IAEP studies do release some illustrative examples of items used in maths and science. As Goldstein (1991) points out, however, since we know that even apparently innocuous changes to the wording of a test item, its layout or position in relation to other items, can change the response pattern markedly, it is important to know what the items used in these surveys were in order to interpret and understand the responses. The content and context of the item or task are particularly important in relation to the performance of different cultural and gender groups, as our discussion of 'bias' made clear.

In general, the majority of items used in these surveys are of the multiple-choice response type (with the exception of the writing composition task). This, of course, is because of the ease and speed of marking which such items offer. However, there are questions over the validity of such items and we know that they tend to advantage boys. In the later IAEP surveys, some short-answer items were included but all the items are essentially paper and pencil rather than performance tasks. (The second IAEP study included some practical tasks, although only some of the English sample took these and the results were not available for the 1992 report.) Clearly, tests that include only multiple-choice type or short responses to printed stimulus materials are very limited in what they can assess and may distort the performance of groups by the nature of their content and style. Although the surveys (except IAEP study 1) did make careful attempts to map taught curriculum across countries, the extent to which a particular aspect of the subject was tested in the surveys did not (and could not) reflect for each country the extent to which it was taught. This, of course, will have an effect on performance across countries, but should not have an effect within countries between genders. In addition, the first IAEP study did not provide any item statistics (Wolfe 1989), thus we cannot examine the performance of different groups on individual items. Yet item statistics to study differential item functioning (DIF) are crucially important if we wish to make a fair comparison of the performance of different groups. IAEP 2 used the DIF statistic to eliminate items which did not perform in a sufficiently similar way, but this analysis was carried out within countries rather than across countries (Lapointe *et al.* 1992).

Another major limitation of these surveys is that although considerable amounts of background data are collected, they are not sufficiently detailed to allow in-depth investigation of any observed differences. Thus, even if we have confidence in the reality of the observed differences in performance, we are usually unable to explain them. Thus, for example, what the studies appear to show is that the gender gap in maths has narrowed, even reversed, but what we do not know is whether this is due to the nature of the sample, the type of test items, or to genuine changes in attainment in the girls or boys. And while no information on items is available, or detailed background data at an individual level, we can take the discussion no further.

What the surveys are able to do, however, is to show that there is no genetic determinant of performance: if girls in one country can score higher in maths or physics than boys in another, the cause of differential performance must be environmental rather than biological.

The position taken by the authors of these reports is generally that there are differences between the sexes which are real, observable and can be measured, with the result that they do not question the construct as they define it for assessment. This is similar to the position in relation to IQ testing and indeed is a characteristic of the psychometric model. Neither, until perhaps IAEP 2, do they question the type of item and the contribution this might have to causing differential performance. Their model of equal opportunities seems to be the disadvantage model (cf. Yates 1985, quoted in Chapter 1): that there is something lacking in girls who are then encouraged to behave more like boys. The implication is that girls can overcome disadvantage through the acquisition of what is lacking, i.e. skills at which boys are 'traditionally' better.

What is not addressed at all, and will be picked up in the next two chapters, is the status of different subjects (e.g. physics compared with biology), and the impact that this, combined with perceived male-ness or female-ness of subjects, has on pupils' attitude to and interest in the subject.

5

NATIONAL ASSESSMENT PROGRAMMES 1: THE ASSESSMENT OF PERFORMANCE UNIT IN THE UK

National surveys, in contrast to the international surveys discussed in the previous chapter, do not provide comparative data about sub-group performance. They do, however, provide a breadth of information both within and across subjects that is usually lacking in international surveys. Where national surveys have been established over time, as is the case with the UK Assessment of Performance Unit (APU) and the US National Assessment of Educational Progress (NAEP), there is the additional benefit of being able to look at patterns of performance for a population over time. Furthermore, national survey systems have the potential to explore initial tentative findings of educational significance and relate these to factors to do with the population and/or the assessment instruments themselves. We consider national surveys in the next two chapters to establish what they have to say about sub-group differences and similarities and to consider possible explanations for these.

The Assessment of Performance Unit was set up in the Department of Education and Science in 1974. The objectives of the APU were given in a Government White Paper (DES 1974). They were 'to promote the development of methods of assessing and monitoring the achievement of children at school and seek to identify the incidence of under-achievement'. The APU is important for our purposes because it not only provides cross-sectional data on performance by gender, but also carried out in-depth studies of performance in relation to task context and content, and pupil attitudes and expectations, etc. The instruments used also involved a wide range of modes of action and response unlike those typically used in international surveys.

The survey activity took place between 1975 and 1989. The mathematics programme commenced annual surveys from 1978 to 1982 (phase 1) and surveyed again in 1987 (phase 2). The language (English) surveys followed from 1979 to 1983 and recommenced in 1988. The science teams were established in 1978 and surveys were carried out from 1980 to 1984; a programme of in-depth research was then initiated and no further surveys carried out. The foreign language programme began in 1983 at three ages and finished in 1986. A single design and technology survey, at age 15 only, was carried out in 1988–89. The survey activity stopped when the APU was closed in 1991. The closure of the unit followed the introduction of compulsory national curriculum assessment of all school children at ages 7, 11, 14 and 16 in England, Wales and Northern Ireland.

The responsibility for generating the various APU subject surveys was devolved to different institutions. A consequence of this was that different approaches to test construction and analysis were adopted and different emphases placed on the need to research assessment methods and practice. To an extent, this latter difference reflected the state of the art in the various subjects. For example, there existed in the UK a substantial history of assessment of language achievement, whereas there was virtually no previous research and practice of assessment in science, particularly at the younger survey ages of 11 and 13. We will describe briefly the different approaches in order to contextualize the various survey findings. These perspectives influence the scale of the subject survey, the constructs emphasized and the survey purposes prioritized. Having said this, it should be borne in mind that the way in which the surveys are defined not only reflect the assessors' predilections, but also curriculum debate at the time. For example, at the beginning of the mathematics survey programme, practical investigative mathematics did not feature as a substantive element in the educational debate or in teachers' practice, whereas in science the controversy surrounding process science was very much in evidence, although only exerting a minor influence on teachers' practice.

In reporting sub-group findings, we focus on the mathematics, language and science assessments and make reference to the design and technology findings where they reinforce other survey findings or provide additional insights. We discuss the findings from the first phase surveys (i.e. the initial five annual surveys for each subject), and the second phase mathematics and language results. Our aim is to document any significant changes in approach to the issue of equity in assessment. We also identify findings, or interpretations of these, which support or challenge the hypotheses referred to in Chapter 2. In so doing, we consider the general approach to assessment adopted; the characteristics of the instruments used both with regard to the specific items and their administration; and background variables of the population monitored including curriculum experience.

The only sub-groups reported on in the APU findings are males and females. No ethnic or racial sub-groups were identified. The APU findings are therefore limited. Nevertheless, they enable us to paint a broader picture of the potential sources of dimensionality in assessment – sources which need to be explored if equity in assessment processes is to be realized. By dimensionality we refer to the factors or constructs assumed to be being measured by a particular instrument for the population or sub-group for whom the test scores are to be interpreted. Here we are not using dimensionality in its technical sense, but as a means for describing the outcomes, real or assumed, when individuals interact with assessments. In attempting to make sense of any measured sub-group differences or similarities, it is important to consider both the individuals comprising the group *and* the technical assumptions that determine their level of performance and how it is defined. We would distinguish dimensionality within an assessment from factors such as say cultural stereotypes which may alter the accuracy of the measurement but not necessarily its nature. From our viewpoint, dimensionality is not a characteristic of an item in isolation, but rather an outcome of the interaction of the individual, sub-group or population with the item.

Mathematics and language survey design

The mathematics and language teams were based in the National Foundation for Educational Research. They had two ages to survey: 11-year-olds towards the end of the primary phase of education and 15-year-olds at the end of the secondary phase (2 per cent sample). The mathematics framework is described as having 'dimensions of content, outcome, context and assessment mode' (Foxman *et al.* 1991: 24). Initially, the bulk of the assessments were based on written short response items for testing concepts and skills. Each test involved approximately 50 items. Thematic tests (i.e. linked items to look at concept and skill achievement) were not introduced until the final survey in 1987. Problem-solving tests, including structured questions about a problem or a pattern, were introduced in the fourth survey in 1981. Usually, five or six problem situations made up a test booklet. This aspect of the monitoring was expanded considerably in 1987. Attitude measures featured in each of the surveys. In the first two surveys, the one-to-one test situations focused on topic testing, mainly of estimating and measuring skills and concepts such as symmetry and probability. From 1980, problem-solving topics on mathematical and 'everyday' contexts were included. It was not until the second phase of surveys that small group assessments looking at cooperative learning on relatively open-ended test situations were used. At the same time, a probe looking at the use of microcomputers was introduced. These changes in the content and design of the surveys reflected changes in the curriculum, but were also initiated in response to criticisms about the range of the mathematics surveys and to pursue initial findings.

The language assessment included the dimensions of reading, writing, speaking and listening (oracy). The reading assessments emphasized pupils' ability to put reading materials to practical use. The materials included works of reference, literature and everyday materials. In each survey, a series of 10 different writing booklets was designed. Each booklet comprised four parts: a short writing task common to each; one of 10 longer writing tasks; a text-based exercise such as editing or note-making; and short questions probing pupils' writing preferences and experience in writing. The tasks varied in having the subject matter and form of writing fixed or open to the pupil to define. To accompany these tests, samples of pupils' written work produced under normal class conditions were selected by teachers with guidance from the survey team. The teachers had also to complete a questionnaire to contextualize the selected samples to enable the team to interpret them. Attitude measures were included in each survey initially with regard to reading and writing, and later across the modes of language. Oracy was assessed in the last two surveys of phase 1 and again in 1988, the second phase monitoring. The majority of oracy tasks involved both the interpretation and production of sustained talk.

The initial mathematics and language surveys were analysed using the Rasch model to attribute latent variable scores to individual pupils in each sub-category level. The 'latent variable' is the construct or trait that the item or test is assumed to measure. (Examples of such variables would be the abilities defined by the scales in the various IQ tests or in the case of the maths APU assessment, the topic identified in the sub-category – number, algebra, measures, etc.)

The Rasch model makes several statistical assumptions. A central assumption is that the difficulty of an item does not vary. If question A is twice as difficult as question B at one point in time, then it remains twice as difficult at any other time. A second assumption is that the items are unidimensional, i.e. measure a single construct or, equivalently, the items represent a constant combination of two or more abilities for the whole population tested and sub-populations within it. (This assumption is made by all standard item analysis techniques.) Where items have been identified statistically as warranting withdrawal or modification either because of poor discrimination, bad fit levels or low reliability, this tended not to happen unless there were accompanying 'educational grounds' for so doing. The report amplifies this point by reference to error responses:

> If too many pupils of middle or higher attainment give a particular error response instead of the correct response, the expected relationship between the attainment level of the pupil and the likelihood of the pupil answering correctly will be upset. Where such patterns are due to faults in the item (presentation, choice of numbers, layout or wording are possible faults), then remedial action is clearly indicated. Where

this is not the case, then what is revealed is information about pupils' performance.

(Foxman *et al.* 1985: 775)

In making these decisions, the authors were attempting to strike a balance in their words 'between educational grounds for item inclusion and statistical grounds for item exclusion'.

What remains problematic is how the error response patterns for these aberrant items are interpreted. If they are said to reveal information about pupil performance, is this in terms of the construct that the item is assumed to be measuring? Is it valid to infer that incorrect responses reflect a lack of attainment of the construct being assessed? Consider, for example, the error noted in problem-solving situations where 'pupils . . . give responses based on social considerations related to their experiences rather than the mathematics of the problem' (Foxman *et al.* 1985: 434). In these circumstances, the items have not measured the pupils' ability to solve a mathematical problem, as the pupils' responses do not indicate a lack of the abilities assumed to be being measured but rather an alternative perception of what constitutes a solution. (In other words, the assumption of undimensionality does not hold.) Another item testing the same mathematical ability but set in a different context may well enable the same pupils to demonstrate the achievements being assessed.

Bejar (quoted by Goldstein and Wood 1989) considers dimensionality to be 'situation-specific'. This corresponds with the point made above, namely that dimensionality, rather than being a characteristic of the item, is a property of the students' responses to the item under certain conditions. Exploring the way sub-groups interact with items or groups of items is essential when attempting to interpret differential performance.

When assessors set items, it is assumed that the purpose and hence the task itself is self-evident. However, the experiences, motivations and prior knowledge of the students may well lead them to emphasize aspects of items that assessors consider to be trivial and irrelevant to the specific demand made. It is therefore important to consider some of the psycho-social variables identified in Chapter 2 when trying to interpret assessment outcomes, be they successful or unsuccessful ones in the assessor's terms, as both can represent a lack of validity in the assessment.

The choice of the Rasch model, and indeed all other standard psychometric item analysis procedures, indicates the view that the teams held about the nature of their subjects and learners' responses to them; and the purposes to be addressed by the survey data. In this latter case, the teams prioritized the need to monitor trends in performance over time. The Rasch model appeared to offer a way of calibrating each test item so that allowance could be made for its difficulty. In assuming the invariance of relative question difficulty, the teams were suggesting that individual factors (for example, between boys and girls) had little influence on performance; similarly, that teaching and curriculum influences were negligible. Similar points were made in the critique of the psychometric approach to assessment in Chapter 3. Yet as Wood argues, such an assumption 'cannot be reconciled with focused instruction which deliberately seeks to shift, perhaps radically, those relative difficulties' (Wood 1991: 113), and indeed goes against common sense.

Mathematics survey findings: Phase 1, 1978–82; Phase 2, 1987

The approach to the reporting of the mathematics results is described in the review report in the following way: 'Wherever possible, the method used is to compare items and their response patterns in order to appraise the effects of item features, age differences and attainment levels, on performance' (Foxman *et al.* 1985: 33). An individual pupil was allocated to one of five attainment bands by his or her performance on the APU test: (1) top 20 per cent on APU test score, (2) upper middle 20 per cent, (3) middle 20 per cent, (4) lower middle 20 per cent, (5) bottom 20 per cent. It is worth noting that this approach means that an item's behaviour is judged in relation to the ability scale that it also contributes to.

The review of the five mathematics surveys considered sex differences at the sub-category level. The performance profile for boys and girls showed that boys out-perform girls in the applied and practical areas of mathematics, i.e. both 'measures' and 'rate and ratio'. Girls perform at a higher level than boys in 'computation' (whole number and decimals) and 'algebra' (both sub-categories).

At age 11, the only significant differences found consistently for each survey were in 'application of number' and 'rate and ratio'. At age 15, however, boys' scores were significantly higher than those of girls in tests of 'measures', i.e. rates and ratio, units and mensuration, number concepts, general algebra and descriptive geometry. These findings are similar to other survey results already commented on and those of NAEP which we consider in the next chapter.

The APU mathematics team also looked at sub-group performance by ability and found that nearly all the differences in performance between boys and girls at both ages were accounted for by the top 10–20 per cent of attainers. A greater proportion of boys than girls are found in the top 10 and 20 per cent bands of attainers; this is also the case for the bottom 10 per cent. At age 11, there were more boys than girls in the bottom 10 per cent in two-thirds of the sub-categories tested. The performance of the top 20 per cent of 11-year-olds was found to be equivalent to the performance of the middle or upper middle attainers at age 15. Hence it is plausible that a pupil in the top band at age 11 (mainly boys) is likely to be in the top band at age 15. In this respect, the APU results are seen to differ from those of other surveys conducted in the UK (see, e.g. ILEA 1983; Cresswell and Gubb 1987). This difference, the authors suggest, relates to the balance of items used from the different topic areas. For example, it is possible to construct tests using a preponderance of items in topics where girls typically out-perform boys. A similar point was made by Halpern in her attempt to explain some of the apparent trend differences in SAT scores (see Chapter 2).

The attitude measures showed that boys were more confident about their success than girls when tackling questions about 'measures' and measurement tasks in practical situations. Thus the authors note there are parallels between pupils' performance on certain topics and pupils' attitudes. The APU maths findings correspond to those of other researchers, which reveal that boys and girls have different attitudes to mathematics. Boys are more confident than girls and expect to do well. Evidence of this difference is apparent at age 11 and increases at age 15. How different attitudes might contribute to differences in achievement is not speculated upon. The report concludes that 'the pattern of differences between boys and girls both in their attitudes to mathematics and

in performance is established before they leave primary school'
(Foxman *et al.* 1985). The report authors speculate on the possible
link between the sex stereotyping of activities within school as
masculine or feminine and the sex difference in performance on the
'measures' sub-categories (unit, rate and ratio and mensuration).
The authors emphasize the link between pupils' affective and cognitive responses to tasks, but it is unclear whether these are seen to
'cause' differences in performance for pupils with the same achievements or to explain differences in real achievement.

In the discussion of the mathematics findings, there are some
references to the performance of boys and girls on certain items,
although the item data are not presented broken down by sex.
These references are few and far between and it is unclear what
guidelines are used in deciding whether to comment on differential
item performance. The difference in performance at age 15 on
items asking pupils to measure 'lines' is reported for example and
explained by girls' failure to use appropriate scales and units of
measure. The tendency of girls as a group to use less efficient and
accurate problem-solving strategies is also noted in the report of
the sex differences in performance on 'methods used to solve problems'. The example quoted to exemplify this performance difference describes how more girls than boys fail to use a balance,
relying instead on themselves to judge weight. No attempt is made
to explore these differences by reference to other items and pupils'
performance on them. For example, there is no measured difference quoted in the performance of girls and boys on reading scales
where a pre-set length has to be read off a rule. Does this mean
that the problem for girls in measuring lines is to do with *recognizing* which is the appropriate instrument to use? The report authors
also note that pupils in general tend not to use apparatus without
seeking permission first. Could the apparent difference in both
measuring skills and problem-solving methods be due to girls'
greater diffidence in the use of apparatus – a diffidence noted in
many studies of boy/girl behaviour in practical science situations
(Whyte 1988)?

It is interesting to note that there are no reported differences in
the performance of girls and boys on items said to measure spatial
awareness and visualization. This finding is not commented on
despite the well-documented sex differences in performance on

measures of this kind that we discussed in Chapter 2. The authors themselves comment on the limited discussion of sub-group performance in the reports: 'further work on identifying patterns of performance for such sub-samples [girls and boys] will form an important part of the next phase of the APU work in mathematics' (Foxman *et al.* 1985: 777).

A separate publication on attitudes and gender differences (Joffe and Foxman 1988) followed the publication of the review report. A major gender difference reported in this was the change in girls' attitudes from age 11 to 15. Girls at age 15, for example, rate mathematics as less useful than boys, indicate that they enjoy the subject less and find it more difficult. Boys also tend to overrate the easiness of an item in relation to their success, whereas girls over-rate the difficulty. (In responding to attitude rating scales, boys generally use the extreme positive ends more than girls. Girls, as a group, choose the more moderate ratings and express far more uncertainty.) The difference in the sub-categories 'measures' in favour of boys and 'computation' in favour of girls is also considered further. The authors note that the differentiation in performance between 'measures' and 'computation' is even more pronounced at age 11 than age 15 for the items illustrated. Furthermore, the difference between the 'measures' and 'computation' scores is much larger than the 'actual gains made by boys at age 15 compared with those at age 11'. They go on to conclude that the 'average scores of boys and girls in tests will depend on the balance of boy and girl biased items in them. Thus it is possible to make up tests which will favour either gender according to this balance' (Joffe and Foxman 1988: 25). This repeats the point made in the earlier review report.

In this publication, it is also reported that 'some of the largest differences in favour of boys at age 15 were found in the results of items involving visualising 3-dimensional figures' (Joffe and Foxman 1988: 28). At the end of the report on gender differences and attitudes, the authors pose a series of questions, one of which asks 'are the methods of assessment used more favourable to one group than another?' (ibid.: 33). This concern is clearly evident in the reporting of the later surveys to which we now turn.

Second phase: Mathematics

We mentioned earlier the possible invalidity in quoting group comparisons for items that have not been calibrated for each sub-group population. Both the mathematics and the language review reports refer to possible content and context effects on pupils' performance. If such pupil–task interactions exist, then the applicability of the Rasch and similar models to the survey data is called into question. Furthermore if, as the mathematics data suggest, items over time become more or less difficult for one sub-group or another, then curriculum and teaching effects cannot be assumed to be negligible. Findings such as these served to fuel the ongoing debate in the research community regarding the validity of the Rasch model in such applications. Consequently, the Rasch model was rejected for the analysis of the data from the later surveys of mathematics and language performance as 'the constant–relative difficulty assumptions of the model are not tenable in an educational context' (Foxman *et al.* 1991: 148). Consequently, a multilevel model was adopted to an extent to allow some school and pupil level variances to be investigated.

Previously, it had been reported that boys made gains over girls in all areas of mathematics between 11 and 15 years. The written tests of problem-solving strategies used in the 1981 and 1982 surveys revealed interesting shifts in this trend, with girls ahead of boys at both ages (Foxman *et al.* 1991). The report authors comment on the educational significance of these results given the move towards process-mathematics in the UK curriculum. They suggest that girls may no longer be viewed as 'underachievers' in a mathematics curriculum with this emphasis.

At age 15, girls were also found to be 'considerably ahead of boys in situations requiring questions or problems to be devised'. For data representations, although 11-year-old girls performed at a lower level than boys, by age 15 girls' and boys' performance was equal. Performance on the 'computation' sub-category in this report was broken down into whole numbers, decimals and fractions. At age 11, girls were further ahead in whole number skills than in decimals. In all three areas, boys gain relative to girls at age 15, compared with age 11, particularly on computations involving whole numbers. At age 15, girls achieve lower scores than boys in the number skills category, but they remain ahead in whole number and decimal computations. Some of the largest gender differences were found in responses to items which involved three-dimensional diagrams.

In the report of the final surveys at ages 11 and 15, gender differences were the first focus of the reported results in marked contrast to previous reports. It was also clear that sub-demands within tasks were being considered to help interpret differential performance. In this survey, one-to-one practical assessment contexts were used to explore how pupils apply their mathematical knowledge. On items testing mental skills, boys out-performed girls, and assessors noted that boys were significantly more assured and fluent than girls on these tasks. No significant sex differences in performance were found in the assessment of calculator skills and 'estimating and measuring'. In the measurement items, the pupils were *asked* to use particular measuring instruments rather than being allowed to choose, which may account for the similarity in the performance of girls and boys in contrast to earlier findings.

Another issue the mathematics team explored in this survey was the effect of context on performance. In a summary report of the survey findings, it was stated that 'mathematics set in a context is usually harder for girls than for boys, even at age 11' (Foxman *et al*. 1990: 17). However, the everyday contexts used were rarely of the social or domestic type referred to in other surveys and research studies, nor were they concerned with human dilemmas.

English survey findings: Phase 1, 1979–83; Phase 2, 1988

In the language review of performance of 11- and 15-year-olds (Gorman *et al*. 1988), an overview of findings for each dimension surveyed is presented first. This is then followed by detailed discussion of items. The overview refers to differences in the performance of boys and girls if these are significant and consistent. The item data are presented on every occasion broken down for boy and girl sub-groups.

In the review of reading performance, no reference is made to differences between girls' and boys' performance. This is despite a tendency for girls to out-perform boys. The significance of the performance gap is questionable but that in itself is noteworthy.

The review of writing performance (general impression scores) revealed a significant difference between the distribution of scores for boys and girls for each task, with girls out-performing their male peers. The discussion of the results based on a 10 per cent sub-sample of scripts, which were both impression marked and analytically marked (where the marks indicate the difficulties posed by specific components of different tasks), did not include reference to this performance gap, which leads one to assume that girls' superiority in this language mode extends across all aspects of task demands. The overall performance of boys and girls at both survey ages on speaking and listening was reported to be very similar.

In the detailed item analyses for each language mode, reference is made to the performance of high and low attaining groups (i.e. top and bottom 20 per cent). A few references are made to boy/girl differences in reading performance within these groups at age 15, but no patterns in performance for the sub-groups are noted or speculations about influential factors included. This is not the case with the reporting of the oracy item results, although no overall differences in the performance of girls and boys were found for this language mode. This inconsistency in reporting of the data presumably reflects the different chapter authors' interests. To fulfil their brief, the APU monitoring teams were not obliged to provide any particular sub-group breakdowns. The extent to which this was done in the reports indicates both the level of interest within the teams and externally in the educational community.

To contextualize the discussion of the oracy results, comment is provided about boys' and girls' performance in the other categories, i.e. that in each survey at ages 11 and 15 girls achieve higher mean scores than boys in writing on all tasks. This finding is echoed in the second IEA study discussed in Chapter 4. A similar trend in overall results was found for reading, though this only reached significance in some surveys. The picture for oracy performance was according to the authors 'quite different'. There were no overall differences in performance, but boys out-performed girls on particular tasks.

The authors noted that the tasks where boys consistently achieved higher scores had what they termed a 'technological content'. One required pupils to describe a series of bridges, another a set of ships. The authors were unable to offer any explanation for other measured differences in task performance. For example, one task with a scientific content (ball-bearings on a track) showed boys ahead of girls. However, as other tasks with a science content (beetles and gulls) did not, the authors felt there were no grounds to indicate a content effect on sub-group performance. However, this result is not surprising if you consider the well-documented differences in girls' and boys' attitudes to the science content areas. Girls as a group respond more confidently to tasks with a biological content than with a physics content (Johnson and Murphy 1986). Indeed, girls' alienation from typical physics content is a cross-cultural phenomenon (Kelly 1981). As the authors could not detect a 'discernibly consistent pattern' in the performance of girls and boys, they concluded that 'the oracy surveys are largely free of sex bias'.

We noted earlier that the overall results for the analysis of pupils' writing performance did not include any comment on the differential performance of boys and girls. Later in the report where individual items are discussed, it is noted that 11- and 15-year-old boys' relative weakness to girls is across all dimensions of the task discussed (i.e. writing in response to a picture).

On tasks which asked pupils to provide a comparative description, girls at ages 11 and 15 achieved higher mean scores than boys. Boys experienced difficulties on all aspects of the task used to illustrate this category of performance, whereas girls' difficulties were restricted to content and organizational issues. In analysing the performance of pupils on tasks demanding argumentative and persuasive modes of writing, it was found that the small number of boys who were highly rated were responding well across the dimensions of content, organization and style. In general, only a few 15-year-old boys produced writing of a high standard when responding to persuasive writing tasks. The pupils' choice of subject matter in these tasks showed that boys who achieved high scores opted for political topics. Girls' choices of subject matter reflected their reading habits, which show a general orientation towards reading material dealing with home and family concerns. The authors noted that when impression marks and analytical marks were compared for these tasks, it seemed to be the case that markers were impressed by the boys' choice of controversial, overtly political subject matter, it being seen as an indicator of 'originality'. This reference to assessors' expectations and values is interesting and particularly pertinent in assessments using items that do not have a multiple-choice response format.

The discussion of the samples of written work produced under normal classroom conditions included no reference to sub-groups. The discussion focused on such issues as the 'typical length' of pupils' written products and their perceptions of 'best work', issues which one might expect to illuminate possible sources of differential performance between girls and boys.

As with the maths APU surveys, there was an understanding that pupils' attitudes to language were important influences on their performance. The survey of pupils' attitudes to reading and writing revealed that 11-year-old boys and girls preferred to read and write imaginative fiction. By age 15, boys' preferences change and their interests lie in the more factual modes of language. With respect to reading at age 11, more boys than girls enjoyed reading works related to hobbies or which involved finding out how things work. They also were more likely to choose comic books and annuals at home in preference to stories.

Over half the boys at age 15 compared to a third of the girls said they preferred reading books which gave accurate facts, whereas twice as many girls than boys liked to read 'to help understand their own and other people's personal problems'. Fifteen-year-old girls were also more positive than boys about school activities related to reading. More girls than boys indicated that they enjoy reading, whereas boys were more likely to express a reluctance to read.

In the survey of attitudes to writing, pupils were asked to specify the type of writing they most enjoyed doing at school and at home. Eleven-year-old boys tended to prefer factual writing arising out of project work, whereas girls were more inclined to favour letter writing and writing poetry. Eleven-year-old boys were also more likely than girls to express a reluctance to write or a lack of confidence in writing. At 15 years of age, boys and girls also differed in the type of writing they preferred. Girls tended to enjoy writing about their families and writing from personal experience (60 per cent girls, 40 per cent boys). Fifteen-year-old boys' choice of enjoyable writing experiences revealed a preference for explanatory/expository types of writing. Girls, as a group, preferred imaginative writing tasks.

The focus of girls' interests in writing is similar to their reading preferences. This was also found to be the case for boys. A higher proportion of boys than girls, for example, enjoyed writing about their hobbies, sports or recreational interests. The authors make some comment about possible links between interest and performance. For example, with respect to imaginative writing performance, the authors offer two opposing explanations. They suggest that boys' lack of interest might be a consequence of their lack of achievement, i.e. you do not show interest in an area where you 'do not shine'. Alternatively, a lack of interest in imaginative fiction means that boys are less aware of the forms and models used in this genre, hence may lack the 'incentive to *use* their language for exploratory, reflective purposes'.

In a separate publication (Gorman 1987), there is further discussion provided about the imbalance in girls' and boys' exposure to different types of reading material and how this may affect their preferences and skills in writing. The form and presentation of girls' and boys' preferred reading material is quite different with regard to the use of diagrams, style of address, etc. Unlike the discussion in the maths review report, the emphasis here is clearly on the link between learning (both out-of-school and in-school) and measured achievement. Where boys and girls showed a corresponding interest in a particular kind of reading material, there were notable content differences in their choices. For example, at age 15, nine out of ten boys compared with three out of ten girls, expressed a liking for factual magazines. Those concerned with pop music were the most popular with both groups (23 per cent boys, 12 per cent girls). The only other factual magazines recommended by girls were either concerned with domestic issues such as furnishings, gardening and cookery, or about horses. Ten per cent of the boys recommended car or motorbike magazines and 5 per cent football publications; other choices covered a diverse range of boys' hobbies and interests of which fishing was the most popular (Gorman 1987: 17). These differences in style and content of pupils' preferred reading may well influence performance in other subject areas, particularly science.

White, deputy director of language monitoring, comments in a separate publication for teachers:

From data gathered in the surveys of reading attitudes we see that the reading habits of both sexes at age 15 coincide with their preferences in writing. Here too we note that much of what boys read for pleasure (a wide range of hobbies manuals and illustrated technical journals) is unlikely to come under scrutiny in the course of schoolwork. By contrast, girls who choose to read fiction and 'human interest' literature will be accustomed to ways of reading made familiar by English lessons, and constantly reminded of the traditional links between reading and writing.

(White 1988: 33)

She goes on to relate the performance differences emerging at age 11 to the process in secondary school by which boys and girls are channelled into certain subjects and points to the way this can lead to the underachievement of boys in areas of language:

Over the course of secondary schooling a disturbing picture emerges: one in which the majority of the more able group of writers (mainly girls) concentrate their energies on the writing of fiction and other "literature" based prose, while less proficient writers (mainly boys) move, by dint of option choices, further away from the subject teachers who might best be able to help them improve their writing performance.

(1988: 33)

White's concerns are not only for the boys, however. Addressing the coordinators of the National Writing Project, she asks what happens to the good girl writer. The anomaly she raises is that in an educational system which affords so much weight to written assessment, why do the group of pupils (namely girls) who do best at writing at school do so much less well outside it? She argues that the hit-and-miss assessment practice common to schools needs to be reconsidered alongside girls' declining confidence in their writing to begin to understand this anomaly. She also points to the way reading and writing attainments are quite wrongly assigned to one area of the school curriculum (i.e. English) – a situation which has not been helped by the introduction of a subject-differentiated national curriculum for England and Wales. That this area of the curriculum is accorded low status, White also considers significant. This is a point we will return to when looking at assessment outcomes beyond school in higher education institutions. Another point White makes relates to the language modes themselves and the shifting emphasis in teaching, assessment and in life outside of school in favour of oracy skills as opposed to writing skills. You will recall that boys out-perform girls on several of the APU oracy tasks. It is also a finding of many studies of classroom interactions that boys as a group dominate talk. Where this has been found not to be the case, girls' talk appears to be concerned with seeking help and reassurance (see, e.g. Randall 1987).

Second phase: Language

The second phase of the language monitoring involved a mixture of repeated tasks and new tasks. The results were again presented for boys and girls separately, but there was little emphasis on gender differences in the analysis of pupils' performance (Gorman *et al.* 1991). Girls were again found to obtain higher mean scores than boys on reading tasks, the difference being highly significant at the primary age. Similarly in writing, boys continued to do less well than girls. In oracy, as in previous surveys, there were no overall differences in performance between girls and boys; however, there were marked differences in performance on different types of task and types of talk. At the primary level, boys did better than girls on many of the tasks, yet by age 15 girls were out-performing boys on some of these.

The survey of attitudes was repeated and extended to include attitudes to oracy. Fifteen-year-old boys were found to be more confident than girls about their abilities as talkers. In the primary survey, over 47 per cent of the boys and over 34 per cent of the girls preferred to watch TV than to read books. In each case, they obtained significantly lower scores in reading and writing than did pupils who took a different view. This indicates a further link between pupils' out-of-school experiences and their ultimate achievements in school. At the secondary level, an even higher proportion of boys and girls expressed a preference for watching TV (67 per cent boys, 50 per cent girls). In this report, reference is made to the performance of second-language speakers. The survey showed that at ages 11 and 15, second-language speakers achieved significantly lower scores in reading and writing than native speakers of English.

Science survey design

The science surveys were conducted at three ages: 11, 13 and 15 years. The science teams were based at King's College London and Leeds University. In deciding what approach to adopt to the assessment, the science teams reviewed survey experience within the UK and internationally. In summarizing the findings of this review, Johnson (1989: 21) states:

> It was known that different population subgroups interact in different ways with certain kinds of test, and, more importantly, with different questions within any test.
>
> Applications of latent trait and analysis of variance models to achievement data confirm the presence of such interaction effects, in curriculum areas other than and including science . . . In other words, some pupils or pupil groups were finding certain questions relatively more or less difficult than would be predicted from the response behaviour of the entire pupil sample.

Differences in performance between pupil groups would not be important provided they were uniform across all questions within the attainment area defined. This, however, was rarely found to be the case. The science teams, unlike the mathematics and language teams, had, in addition, to cater for widely differing curriculum provision. Science subjects in UK schools at the time were optional at age 15 and rarely taught in primary schools. Invariance of relative question difficulty clearly could not be assumed for science, within or over time, given the known variation in pupils' science learning experiences. Consequently, the science teams opted for a domain-sampling approach. In this approach, a large pool of test questions is generated for a particular 'ability' or 'skill'. This pool is assumed to act like a universe of all such possible questions that might have been developed, although strictly it cannot do so. Any random sample of questions from the pool will be representative of the pool as a whole, and hence the entire ability/skill domain.

In the domain-sampling approach, interaction effects are allowed in principle. The only constraints are that the domains have educational meaning and relevance, and that all the questions allocated to a particular domain are agreed to fit the definition of the domain. The problem with this approach is defining an agreed and implementable domain; a requirement difficult in practice to meet satisfactorily (for a discussion, see Johnson 1989).

The complex model adopted by the science team assumes that a pupil score on a question is a combination of an overall population score for the entire population of pupils on the population of questions, plus an effect associated with the particular pupils, an effect associated with the particular question, class, school and interactions between these. Using analysis of variance procedures, the team attempted to identify sources of performance variation so that their influences can be catered for in the estimation process. The effects on performance have to be identifiable and systematic in their actions, however. Knowledge of systematic performance influences was limited at the beginning of the science monitoring programme. Progress, if anything, was marked by an increasing awareness of just how little was known with regard to interaction effects in an educational assessment context (Johnson 1989). The assumption of the presence of interaction effects and the significance accorded to these had implications for the focus of the science teams' analyses and their interpretation of performance outcomes.

For example, the science assessment framework analysed scientific performance into five broad categories of achievement: use of graphical and symbolic representation; use of apparatus and measuring instruments; observation; interpretation and application (the latter broken down into physics, biology and chemistry at ages 13 and 15); and planning of investigations. The categories were not hierarchical constructs; nevertheless, it was accepted that certain of the skills defined in one category were preconditions for others. Consequently, the categories of performance were not unique and mutually exclusive and were recognized as such when interpreting pupils' performance. It was also understood that within any category or sub-category there were other dimensions to be considered; of these, the science teams highlighted the *content* (i.e. the information, object, event or data in the question) and the *context* (i.e. the overt question setting). A further category, 'performing investigations', was also identified. Tasks in this category represented a synthesis of the component activities in the other categories – a synthesis which the teams judged would provide further and quite different insights into pupils' science achievement.

This category was not defined as a domain. Pairs of practical tasks or individual tasks were administered in a one-to-one test situation.

A wide range of question styles was used in the surveys. In the *written* response mode, pupils were required to: *generate* both short and extended responses; to select correct responses; and to *assess* and *criticize* other pupils' responses. In the *practical* response mode, pupils might be asked: to deliver a variety of measured or estimated physical quantities; to set up apparatus; to follow instructions to carry out standard scientific techniques or an everyday exercise such as wiring a plug; and finally to devise a strategy and carry out a practical investigation. Up to 30 different test packages were administered in a single survey at one age. In total, over 600 different questions were administered at least once in the series of five annual surveys of 11-year-olds and approximately 800 different questions were administered in at least one of the five corresponding surveys at each of the other ages.

Science survey findings: 1980–84

The science teams' publication *Girls and Physics* (Johnson and Murphy 1986) provides a review of gender differences in performance at the sub-category level. In Table 5.1, a difference is included if it occurred across the five surveys and was judged to be both educationally and statistically significant. The suffix indicates the age at which the gender difference occurs. Where there is no suffix, the difference occurred at the three ages tested.

The APU science results provide a similar pattern of differences to that found by other national and international surveys of science content. In addition, they provide information about a wider range of science achievement than had hitherto been available.

Table 5.1 shows that gender differences in favour of boys appear to increase as pupils go through school. However, when pupils with the same curriculum backgrounds are compared, all performance gaps at age 15, except those for applying physics concepts and the practical test-making and interpreting observations, disappear. In the APU science surveys, the gap in physics achievement between girls and boys increases with age.

Table 5.1 A review of APU findings on gender

APU tests	Results	Type of test
Use of graphs, tables and charts	$B_{15} > G_{15}$	Written
Use of apparatus and measuring instruments	$B_{15} > G_{15}$	Practical
Observation	$G > B$	Practical
Interpretation	$B_{13,15} > G_{13,15}$	Written
Application of biology concepts	$B = G$	Written
Physics concepts	$B > G$	Written
Chemistry concepts	$B_{15} > G_{15}$	Written
Planning investigations	$B = G$	Written
Performing investigations	$B = G$	Individual practical

Boys produced higher average scores than girls on *more than 90 per cent* of the physics questions at each age, and for *half* the questions the discrepancies reached statistical significance. Boys' superiority proved to be consistent across all the physical science concept areas included in the assessment (force, pressure, speed, energy, etc.), although the discrepancy was particularly marked in the case of electricity at all three ages.

The *extreme* discrepancy in the performance of girls and boys on questions featuring electricity appears to be a particularly firmly established phenomenon. Girls' weakness in this area was evident across the framework, and was not confined to questions demanding conceptual understanding. Whenever a circuit diagram or an actual circuit was featured in a question, girls performed at significantly lower levels than boys; this applied whether they were asked merely to take instrument readings or whether they had to name specific components in a circuit diagram or to follow such a diagram actually to wire up a circuit. Boys also showed superior competence when using ammeters and voltmeters, and were more familiar with the appropriate units of measurement.

In Table 5.1, a sub-category difference was noted for the use of apparatus and measuring instruments. A review of pupils' performances on the use of individual measuring instruments, however, showed very clearly that there was no *general* weakness on the part of the girls in this area. Girls and boys perform equally well at all three ages when asked to use thermometers, measuring cylinders and weighing scales. There were no differences either in their performances at age 11 with rulers and metre rules (not tested at 13 and 15 years).

There were differences, though, in the ability of boys and girls to use hand lenses and stop clocks at all ages, and microscopes, forcemeters, ammeters and voltmeters at ages 13 and 15 (not tested at age 11); all these differences were in favour of the boys. On *written* questions assessing pupils' familiarity with conventional *units* of measurement (tested only at 13 and 15), boys and girls showed similar degrees of familiarity with units of temperature, time, volume, mass or weight, but as indicated earlier, boys showed a *significantly* superior knowledge of units associated with electrical measurement.

In the sub-category 'making and interpreting observations', girls achieved higher mean scores than boys in at least three-quarters of the questions used. A review of the individual question results suggested that boys and girls actually have different relative strengths in this area. There was a definite tendency for girls to show the better performances on those questions in which they were required to compare and contrast a number of objects or features, and to record their observations or to use them to classify the objects or to identify and use a relationship between two variables. These kinds of question were in the majority (hence the girls' overall test advantage), and they tended to feature biological or earth science resources – leaf specimens, rock specimens, photographs of cloud formations, seeds, and so on. Boys, on the other hand, tended to show the better average performances on the handful of questions in which scientific explanations were demanded for the observations made.

Girls appeared to have a slight edge over boys in terms of using graphs, tables and charts at age 11; by the age of 13, the sub-category difference was inconsistent in direction; by the age of 15, there were consistent performance discrepancies in favour of boys. Girls at each age produced higher scores than boys on two-thirds of the questions featuring tables, bar charts, pie charts, flow charts and Venn diagrams. In contrast, boys at every age achieved higher scores on questions dealing with coordinate graphs. These questions were much more in evidence in the item banks at age

15. The report authors speculated on the mathematical demands made by the different data forms and considered gender differences across mathematics and science. It seemed possible that it was a combination of demands which affected girls' and boys' scores. It would depend on the direction of each effect whether score differences occurred. For example, it would be possible to imagine a coordinate graph task focusing on a physics content, involving units girls are less familiar with and demanding a mathematical operation they are reported to be less well able to achieve. Such a task might show a large difference between boys and girls; however, if any one of the features mentioned was to change, the scores could be altered.

There were a number of performance discrepancies across the framework which could be attributed to spatial ability differences between boys and girls. This was a general weakness reflected in performances on a number of different questions featuring objects in motion. Another example of a general performance weakness which might indicate less well-developed spatial skills was noted in questions which required pupils to produce two-dimensional reproductions of three-dimensional illustrations – a possible overlap with the findings quoted in the maths review report. However, these questions also demanded the production of conventional scientific diagrams to represent sets of apparatus or electrical circuits shown in drawings. It is plausible, therefore, to attribute *this* weakness to other effects. Again, the potential for combined effects, i.e. the content and the type of task demand, was more apparent when questions showing differences were scrutinized.

This review of items revealed a series of potential sub-demands which could exert differential effects on some girls' and boys' performance. The report went on to consider if these achievement effects could be related to other differences between boys and girls. (A similar type of exploration to that conducted by the language team into pupils' out-of-school reading habits and preferences.) This decision indicates something about the authors' views about the nature of gender differences. If such achievement differences were assumed to be innate, there would be no recall to seek explanations for them.

If, on the other hand, they are the outcome of differential learning experiences, etc., then ameliorating strategies could be developed. The science team collected background information about pupils' interests and experiences within school and outside of school in relation to science. The evidence collected led the report authors to comment:

> It would generally be agreed that boys' activities afford greater opportunities than do those of girls for acquiring relevant experience with which to consolidate their later conceptual learning in physics. In particular, boys would have a much greater opportunity of accumulating a working knowledge of mechanics, of developing spatial ability and of gaining an early familiarity with electricity (again, all aspects of performance in which girls are generally weaker than boys). Moreover, this wider range of experiences of boys with activities related to science can be expected to have an effect both in terms of the confidence of pupils in later laboratory work and their ability to perceive the relevance of some of the scientific tasks set in secondary science courses. The different kinds of activities in which boys and girls engage would also afford practice in the use of *different* kinds of measuring instruments.
>
> (Johnson and Murphy 1986: 21)

Indeed, with regard to measuring instruments, it was precisely those instruments which girls as a group did less well on that boys and not girls claimed to have experience of outside of school. Boys' preferred reading habits also provide another form of science-related experience. In contrast, most girls, although avid readers, do not compensate for their lack of physical science experience through their choice of reading matter.

In scanning questions which showed a difference in score between boys and girls, it was clear that it was not just electrical content which inhibited some girls. Questions set in contexts girls saw as overtly 'masculine' (e.g. questions about tyre damage, aircraft, submarines, heavy industry, car spare parts, etc.) were responded to by fewer girls than boys and the scores achieved by the girls were also lower. However, on questions concerning health, nutrition and reproduction, and on many questions set in a clearly 'domestic' context, girls tended to perform at higher levels than boys at all ages. On these questions, fewer boys than girls responded. It also appeared immaterial whether or not such questions demanded pre-existing knowledge or understanding.

In conclusion, it was noted that boys' and girls' different out-of-school experiences would alter both their confidence in science and their actual achievements. Boys' experiences outside school could provide scientific learning opportunities on a range of different aspects of science attainment. To develop strategies to facilitate girls' learning in science, it would be necessary to better understand the source of their different interests as well as their consequences.

The final science surveys at each age included instruments specifically designed to explore some of the tentative hypotheses identified in the earlier publication. These included a range of questionnaires to probe pupils' interests, experiences and reactions to school and assessment activities. At age 11, the questionnaires established again the polarization in boys' and girls' out-of-school interests. The activities that girls claimed to take part in 'quite often' at home or otherwise out of school were: looking after pets (57 per cent), weighing out ingredients for cooking (60 per cent), and knitting or sewing (46 per cent). For the boys they were: looking after pets (57 per cent), making models (50 per cent) and playing pool or snooker (59 per cent). The greatest differences in 'activity rates' for girls and boys occurred for the 'tinkering activities', e.g. making models from Lego, etc. (50 per cent boys, 23 per cent girls) and playing with electrical toys (45 per cent boys, 16 per cent girls). There was, in addition, an overwhelming preference expressed by both girls and boys to do more of the things they already engaged with. The report authors concluded that 'some definition of appropriateness of interest has taken place by this age' (DES 1988a). The questionnaire data also revealed the large differences in girls' and boys' use of equipment and instruments outside of school (not inside school), with girls making less use than boys of every item except for weighing scales.

The review of sub-category performance confirmed the presence of content–pupil interactions which differentially affected girls' and boys' responses to tasks. Contents to do with animals, botany and domestic and social issues were seen to advantage girls, whereas tasks about physical objects and events were more likely to advantage boys. The type of data included in an item also appeared to affect pupils' performance. Boys appeared to achieve higher scores when handling spatial data; girls, on the other hand, tended to outperform boys on items involving non-coordinate forms of data. The authors summarize these findings in the following way:

> Where data are presented in discontinuous form, with cate-
> gorical variables and consequently an increased likelihood of
> a verbal medium, girls tend to perform better than boys.
> Numerical or graphical data and spatial–dynamic patterns
> tend to result in higher performance on the part of boys.
>
> (DES 1988a: 111)

The language demands of items were also identified as a possible
influence. For example, the high level of language demand in items
used in the practical test of 'observation' were quoted as the possible reason for girls' superior performance. Girls' greater achievements might therefore be due not to their science skills, but their
linguistic skills. The report authors also challenge boys' superiority
in tests of the application of science concepts, noting that items here
tend to require multiple-choice response or short written answers
– modes of response seen to favour boys and which we discuss in
more detail in Chapter 8.

At age 13 (DES 1989), findings revealed that out-of-school
activities that were identified as relevant to science in school corresponded largely to those in which boys engaged and girls did
not. It was also the case that girls expressed little interest in these
activities. The authors concluded that 'given that scientific activity
reflects the values and interests of those most commonly engaged
in it, it is quite possible that in identifying 'science relevant' activities one might in fact be imposing a stereotypical view of the
subject'. This source of potential bias clearly has implications for
assessment as well as curriculum and echoes Kelly's view of the
'masculine' image of science.

Another questionnaire looked at pupils' interests in science topics
and their applications. The results showed that girls only expressed
an interest in topics or applications related to people or other
animals, their function and the relationships between them and
other living things. The boys showed an interest in more topics
than girls, particularly those with an orientation towards physical
science. Boys, unlike girls, were interested in knowing more about
both the concepts and their applications. The authors pointed out
that 'expressing an interest in a topic suggests an understanding
of what is entailed and its relevance to oneself. It is possible, therefore, that different pupil interests reflect different understandings
of relevance.' They go on to ask if it is the 'processes by which

pupils perceive relevance to themselves and therefore interests in particular topics and subjects' which need to be explored. Again this point links with the image of the subject and how this resonates or not with gender-stereotyped expectations in society and school.

Boys and girls at age 13 were found to share very similar perceptions about the sex appropriateness of particular jobs. These shared views conformed for the most part with conventional patterns of employment in society. When asked to consider the importance of science for jobs, the findings showed that for boys perceiving a high science content in a job made it more popular with them, whereas for girls in general it tended to produce another barrier between them and certain careers.

In the review of sub-category performance, a very detailed analysis of sub-skills at the item level was carried out. The team found no evidence of girls' weakness with coordinate data forms, nor did boys seem to be disadvantaged by extended written response demands. This adds further weight to the point made earlier that it is a *combination of demands* which affects girls' and boys' scores rather than a single attribute of a task such as data form or response mode. In looking at the type of data included in items, there was evidence that sex-related differences in performance were associated with spatial patterns. A special set of items targeting this type of data handling was therefore included in the age 13 survey. The results did not reveal a general weakness of girls for the manipulation of spatial data, but showed that on questions concerned with the equal angle law of reflection at a plane surface, girls tended to perform at a lower level than boys, irrespective of the context and content of the item. One of these items was based on snooker and it may be recalled that this is one of the out-of-school activities that 59 per cent of 11-year-old and 64 per cent of 13-year-old boys claimed to 'quite often' or very often engage with (i.e. playing pool, snooker or billiards), hence experiential differences may also be affecting performance here.

Content effects were observed in pupils' responses to certain of the practical investigations, with girls rejecting an investigation involving an electrical circuit and some boys rejecting an investigation of which floor covering was the most suitable for a kitchen. The investigations were administered face-to-face so pupils were asked about their reactions. The girls were found to reject the problem from an expressed belief that they do not have the knowledge necessary to solve the problem, irrespective of whether it is demanded. The boys rejected the problem from a belief that the knowledge they do have, labelled as 'science', cannot be applied in these 'non-scientific' circumstances. There is possibly some indication of the effects of differences in confidence here related to pupils' self-images.

In another problem situation, pupils investigated which material would keep them warmest when stranded on a mountainside. They were expected to compare how well the material kept cans of hot water warm. Many girls were observed to be doing things apparently off-task. For example, they cut out prototype coats, dipped the materials in water and blew cold air through them. These girls, when talked to, revealed that they took seriously the human dilemma presented in the task. It therefore mattered how porous the material was to wind, how waterproof and whether, indeed, it was suitable for making a coat. Conversely, the boys tended to consider the issues in isolation and judged the content and context of tasks to be irrelevant. It should be noted that the girls' performance was often very adequate in scientific terms in that they competently investigated several variable effects or combinations of them (Murphy 1990); however, as the task did not correspond to the one set by the assessor, their responses typically were judged to be inadequate.

The review of item performance at age 15 (DES 1988b) revealed a similar pattern to that found at age 11, but not age 13, i.e. that boys are on the whole more successful than girls when handling coordinate graphs, while girls are better at dealing with other representational forms. Girls' superior performance on the majority of observation tasks could not, however, be explained by their greater facility with language, which was posited in the age 11 review report. The questionnaires about careers surveyed at age 15 repeated the findings at age 13. The only 'female' occupation for which at least half of the pupils considered biology or physics to be of some value was nursing. Physics was considered by the majority of pupils to be of some importance to all the most 'male-appropriate' occupations. Physics and chemistry were perceived to be the science subjects with the highest 'job value', following behind English and mathematics. Proportionally more girls than boys claimed to find physics, chemistry and mathematics difficult, echoing the maths survey findings. In response to the questionnaire on awareness of and interest in various scientific applications, boys were better informed about a wider range of applications than girls. Girls, as a group, were more interested than boys in the medical applications and boys were more interested than girls in the physical science applications. These findings overlap with those at age 13.

The later research of the APU Science Project paid little heed to similarities and differences in the performance of sub-groups. This reflected, to some extent, a general decline in interest in the topic of equity at policy level.

Design and technology survey findings: 1988–89

The design and technology project team, like the science team, was based in a university department. The first survey was conducted in 1988–89 for the population of 15-year-olds and provided some interesting and related findings in support of the earlier science results (Kimbell *et al.* 1991). For example, it was found that 15-year-old girls appeared to be better at identifying tasks, investigating and appraising ideas than boys, while boys seem to be better than girls at generalizing and developing ideas. Boys also out-performed girls in modelling, whereas girls dramatically out-performed boys on evaluating products. The difference in performance on evaluating products is such that low-ability girls (by exam entrance) nearly out-performed high-ability boys.

The results also showed a marked effect on performance due to context. Girls out-performed boys in contexts concerned with people, whereas boys did better in industrial contexts. This corresponds to the science team's findings but differs from that reported in the final maths survey. The context effects were less marked for pupils of higher ability.

The design and technology team found, as did the science team, that sub-effects within tests influenced performance. Hence, in one test, the structure, context and openness all favoured the girls and consequently they did very much better than the boys. In another test, the reverse effects obtained and boys did very much better than girls. As the authors comment:

Wherever the effects that we have described overlap and operate to the advantage of the same group then we must expect that group significantly to outperform other groups. Only occasionally, of course, do the effects all operate in the same direction. More often, if one effect operates in favour of one group this is balanced by a different effect favouring other groups . . . The total effect is to reduce the gender bias in the results.

(Kimbell *et al.* 1991: 208)

The survey data included information about curriculum background, which is very diverse in the design and technology area. To explore curriculum effects by gender, the team attempted to control for ability. They did this by identifying a middle ability group (by exam entrance). There remained a problem of cell size, but the team felt that where findings were significant it was worth reporting them. However, the tentative nature of the findings should be borne in mind. The reduction in gender effects once curriculum and ability were taken into account was particularly noticeable in the Craft Design and Technology (CDT) area. The report authors comment:

The strengths (dominantly reflective) that girls typically bring, when linked to a CDT course that typically (from the data) enhances active procedural capability, creates a combination of strengths that allows them to achieve high levels of performance – which show up particularly well in our modelling tests.

(Kimbell *et al.* 1991: 213)

The findings also showed overlap with the science team's results about the different attention boys and girls pay to aspects of phenomena in investigations. Analysis of pupils' performance on the evaluation component, for example, revealed that 'the gender groups prioritise different aspects of evaluation – the boys always referring to manufacture, the girls only when it is obviously required – but that once the aspects are identified the girls are very much better at it' (ibid.: 214). Boys were found to be more able to 'get to grips' with reflective aspects of capability when they were practically engaged with developing a solution. Girls, on the other hand, were better able to empathize with users and identify the critical issues without 'the benefit of practical engagement'. We referred earlier to girls' superior performance on the 'planning' sub-category in science, which again was about practice but assessed in the written non-active mode.

The design and technology tasks were also analysed with regard to the conceptual demands made and it was found that boys were more familiar than girls with concept areas related to structures and appropriate use of materials. Boys' 'complete dominance' in the concept area related to 'energy systems' was also remarked upon. Girls typically focused on aesthetic variables in problem-solving activities in contrast to boys. These findings again correspond well with the science APU results in terms of the variables focused on in the observation tasks and the practical investigations.

Across the APU surveys, there had been brief comment about the influence of assessors' expectations on performance. These expectations were seen to favour either group depending on what was being assessed and by whom. The design and technology surveys found further evidence of these effects. The team comment: 'there is some evidence that women mark girls' work higher and men mark boys' work higher. For example, 95% of all female markers mark girls' work higher than their male marking partner' (Kimbell *et al.* 1991: 134).

In the pilot survey, the team had found that markers were influenced by their view of a 'typical' boy's response, or a 'typical CDT' response. In the main survey, consequently, marking was carried out blind. The team speculate that these results do not therefore arise because of different assessor expectations of girls and boys as groups. They do, however, suggest that the curriculum background of the assessors (female markers were predominantly home economics teachers, whereas male markers were largely from the craft, design and technology discipline) was influential. They comment: 'we believe they (the female assessors) were simply more in tune with the typical value positions and approaches associated with girls' work. Exactly the same comment applies to male markers and boys' work' (Kimbell *et al.* 1991: 154).

Discussion

The evidence from the APU surveys reveals a relatively stable pattern of performance within subjects (see Johnson 1989, for example). Where performance trends alter, this tends to arise because the definition of the subject has been altered by extending the range of achievements monitored and the ways in which these were elicited. The overall findings do show greater variation within groups than between groups, thus lending little support to biological explanations for performance differences. Indeed, perhaps one of the most valuable aspects of the surveys has been to demonstrate how differences across subjects are reduced when curriculum background is controlled or when out-of-school experience is taken into account, indicating that differences in achievement are related to differences in opportunity to learn to a large extent. This effect has been demonstrated across the subjects monitored and for a variety of different achievements including spatial abilities.

The differential learning opportunities afforded to boys and girls are evidenced in various ways. For example, a group may be advantaged or disadvantaged relative to another because they have different experience of the *context* of the task (i.e. the setting), the *content* (i.e. what the task is about), the *task demand* (e.g. write a letter to a friend) or the *mode* and *style of response* favoured in the particular subject, to name but a few. Where these effects occur, differences in performance can represent differences in achievement but not necessarily potential. However, differences in performance may underestimate real achievement because the pupils' perception of the task is at odds with the assessors.

The surveys also provide additional powerful evidence about the influence of attitudes on achievement. The correlation between attitudes and performance has been noted here and in other international surveys discussed in Chapter 4. The different attitudes of girls and boys as groups to subjects or aspects of subjects reflect pupils' learnt behaviours about their own capabilities and what constitutes appropriate behaviour for them. These different attitudes alter pupils' level of confidence, which in turn influences their performance. Attitudes can also influence what pupils see as significant in tasks, which, depending on their gender and the image of the subject, can focus them onto the task at hand or lead them to perceive an alternative task or no task at all. The effect of different attitudes can therefore enhance or depress performance on a task irrespective of achievement.

Another major contribution of the surveys to the general equity debate is the technical evidence about variance in item response over time and between different population sub-groups. The surveys provide no solutions but do highlight the need for methods to explore 'unknown' sources of performance variation. In any assessment situation, most pupils and pupil groups produce inconsistent performance from one question to another within a test. The factors that lead to this variation are difficult to identify and even more difficult to quantify and counter. It is the dynamic interaction between pupils and questions which determines the apparent homogeneity or heterogeneity in tests or question pools; these properties are not innate to the question alone, neither are they necessarily stable qualities. Empirical evidence can be used to improve homogeneity within a group of questions but such homogeneity does not necessarily provide evidence of a single ability or skill. It can be said that pupils perform in similar ways when confronted with the questions in the group. They might nevertheless be deploying quite different abilities and skills to achieve the results.

In a similar way, performance patterns produced by an entire pupil sample are not necessarily replicated by all the identifiable pupil groups in that sample. Neither is the performance of one group necessarily an even performance across a domain or sub-domain. Nevertheless, comparisons of the performance of identifiable pupil groups is helpful and necessary to assist the interpretation of test scores. Such action brings into question the validity of comparing the performance of sub-groups with quite different background experiences. In this regard, Johnson in her technical review of the APU scientific surveys, challenges the assumption that underachievement can only be synonymous with relatively low achievement. In her view, it is 'only where we are prepared to make the assumption that relatively low performance signals underachieved potential that a search for explanations which might inform responsive action becomes meaningful' (Johnson 1989: 106). We return to the issues raised here in Chapter 8.

The APU surveys have demonstrated that consistent differences between the performance of boys and girls are due to sub-effects related to the items and/or their administration. The overall difference depends on the combination of effects within the item and the test instrument overall. Thus it would be possible to engineer group differences or remove them by changing the assessment items. In maths, for example, changes in the topics assessed, an increased emphasis on process, and the use of abstract as opposed to 'real' contexts would, it is suggested, favour girls. In English, a greater emphasis on oracy, a change in the 'typical' style of response valued and the inclusion of technological and political content in tasks would, on the other hand, be to the advantage of boys. In science, girls' performance relative to boys would be improved by broadening the view of relevance, allowing more open-tasks and modes of response and using contexts involving social and human concerns. This is a gross oversimplification but hopefully it serves to illustrate the point. Altering the characteristics of items can affect group differences by advantaging one group but in so doing another group would be disadvantaged. This follows because up to a point what is being measured are learnt gendered behaviours and/or expectations rather than achievements. The findings, therefore, support the hypotheses concerning the influence of psycho-social variables on performance both in terms of how boys and girls come to view themselves and become viewed by others and how subjects become constructed and achievement within them defined.

Murphy (1990) reviewed the science survey findings with regard to gender and set them in a wider context of more general assessment implications. Consequently, it is worth reiterating some of the points made to help clarify the issues. For example, concerning the finding that differences in students' performance are related to their different experiences, both in school and out, she suggests:

> The different experiences of students does not just affect the skills they develop but also their understanding of the situations and problems where their skills can be used appropriately. To interpret assessment results and to plan effective classroom strategies it is necessary to focus on both the nature of the differential experiences as well as their consequences . . .
>
> A lack of experience leads some students to define areas of the curriculum where they expect to be successful or

conversely unsuccessful. Any tasks set in these areas are subsequently avoided by many girls and boys. This has the effect of lowering their performance in assessment and also ensuring that in class they miss vital learning opportunities. The effects of alienation must be distinguished from differences in ability in order to correctly interpret achievement for formative purposes.

(Murphy 1990: 4–5)

She comments on the findings of the probes into pupils' perceptions of, and approaches to, problems:

The different purposes that girls and boys have learnt to attend to outside of school alter their perception of what is relevant and noteworthy, given the same circumstances. This is a crucial point for assessment. Typically purpose is either missing in assessment tasks or assumed to be implicit and unproblematic with the result that students have to import their own in order to make sense of tasks. The purpose defines what knowledge students consider appropriate to draw on and ultimately what task they tackle. The APU results indicate that girls' purposes are more often at odds with those of science assessors than boys and their performance more frequently misinterpreted as a consequence.

(Murphy 1990: 4–5)

One can also anticipate similar effects arising through cultural and class differences, for example. Where a subject has a more 'feminine' image – home economics, aspects of language, for example – one can imagine the reverse situation occurring with boys rather than girls being disadvantaged as a group.

The differential effect of task content on pupils was noted across the surveys, yet assessors assume that the content of a task is largely irrelevant. These content performance effects arise from the combination of avoidance by some students, and the heightened confidence of others. These findings occur across the full ability range. The dilemma for assessors is that such questions are sources of assessment invalidity, which need to be eradicated for the summative purposes of reporting and evaluating. On the other hand, they provide the teacher with invaluable formative insights to aid curriculum planning. Hence how we view and treat performance differences will depend on our purposes as assessors.

The APU findings for science and design and technology revealed that the problems that girls and boys perceive and the solutions they judge to be appropriate are often different given the same set of circumstances. Children enter school with learning styles already developed, some of which are not only different to that advocated in various subjects, but incompatible with them (Cohen 1986). Furthermore, how pupils express their understandings will reflect their different experiences and these differences in style. Murphy comments:

> Typically girls tend to value the circumstances that activities are presented in and consider that they give meaning to the task. They do not abstract issues from their context. Boys as a group conversely do consider the issues in isolation and judge the content and context to be irrelevant. This latter approach is generally assumed in assessment practice. Research (Murphy, 1982; Harding, 1979) that shows that boys do better than girls on multiple-choice items relates to these differences. Girls, in taking account of features of items that the assessor regards as "noise" or padding, see ambiguity in the responses offered and commonly either do not respond as no one answer "fits" or give more than one response.
>
> (Murphy 1990: 6)

In looking across the APU findings, Murphy identifies the different styles that girls and boys use to express themselves – styles which reflect their reading habits. However, style can affect an assessor's response to a specific piece of writing. The study of Goddard-Spear (1983) showed that the same piece of science writing, when attributed to girls, received lower marks from teachers than when they were attributed to boys. Nor is blind marking always the answer. The design and technology team used blind marking yet some markers commented on how easy they thought it was to identify girls' and boys' responses.

A move away from reporting achievement by scores to the use of written records, students' self-assessments and student-selected pieces of work will not have the beneficial effects hoped for if assessors do not disentangle features of style from the criteria that they are attempting to assess. Being able to evaluate whether the judgements about performance are valid with regard to the construct being assessed is perhaps the biggest problem that faces teacher-assessors.

The APU reporting of findings related to gender reveal an interesting trend. There was a growing interest in the issue of group differences and equity through the early to mid-1980s. This is evident in the science and language review reports and the second phase reporting of the maths surveys. We then see an apparent decline in interest in the reporting of the final language survey and in the absence of comment on gender in publications of the science team through the late 1980s and into the early 1990s (SEAC 1990a, b, 1991a, b, c, d). This lack of attention to equity issues towards the end of the 1980s reflects in part the removal of the topic from the political agenda. In principle in the UK, teachers and assessors should provide equality of opportunities, but the problem of how actually to develop and put into practice fair forms of assessment does not seem to be a political concern. However, we now know a good deal about such issues and effecting change remains firmly in the jurisdiction of the education community. We will return to this when we consider national assessment policy in the UK in Chapter 7.

6

NATIONAL ASSESSMENT PROGRAMMES 2: THE NATIONAL ASSESSMENT OF EDUCATIONAL PROGRESS IN THE USA

The 1966 Equality of Educational Opportunity Survey (EEOS) conducted by Coleman in the USA revealed that differences in existing school inputs made relatively small differences in school output. The survey involved a large sample of schools, teachers and children and established that minority children entered school with a serious educational disadvantage (as measured by standardized tests) and that this disadvantage increased as they continued through school (Coleman *et al.* 1966). This research (referred to in Chapter 1) has been the subject of widespread criticism, nevertheless the results had a significant impact on the educational establishment. One outcome was an increased demand from the public and federal government for accountability from the school systems. Three years after the Coleman Report was published in 1969, the National Assessment of Educational Progress (NAEP) project – now known as the Nation's Report Card – was established 'to obtain comprehensive and dependable data on the educational achievement of American students' (Mullis *et al.* 1990).

Initially, NAEP was administered by the Education Commission of the States. At the present time, it is the Commissioner of Educational Statistics who is responsible by law for carrying out the NAEP project. In 1988, Congress established the National Assessment Governing Board (NAGB). It is this Board which develops NAEP policy, selects which subject areas are to be assessed, determines the assessment objectives and develops and designs the assessment instruments, their administration and analysis. The Board is also responsible for ensuring that 'all items selected for use in the National Assessment are free from racial, cultural, gender or regional bias' (Mullis *et al.* 1990: 3). NAEP is funded by the Office for Educational Research and Improvement, US Department of Education, under a grant to the Education Testing Service, Princeton, New Jersey.

Since 1969, NAEP has assessed national samples of 9-year-olds, 13-year-olds and 17-year-olds and from 1983 began sampling students by grade as well as age. In addition, samples of young adults between the ages of 26 through 35 have periodically been assessed. The subject areas tested include reading, writing, mathematics, science and social studies, as well as literature, art, music, citizenship, computer literacy, history and geography. Several of these subjects have been assessed many times. Areas of high public interest such as reading, mathematics, science and writing are assessed every 4–5 years, other areas every 6–8 years. The American surveys are particularly interesting because they look at ethnic group differences and collect a range of background variables related to schools though not necessarily related to the sub-groups under discussion.

Assessment design

NAEP assessments are developed through a process of consensus. This is to ensure that it reflects 'the thinking of a wide variety of individuals – state and district curriculum specialists, teachers, school administrators, researchers, parents, concerned citizens, officials and business people' (Educational Testing Service 1987: 5). Panels of experts develop the objectives for the subject assessment and writers develop the questions to fit these specifications. The items are then reviewed by subject matter specialists, measurement experts and sensitivity reviewers. This latter group have the task of eliminating items potentially biased or insensitive to certain sub-groups. In this regard, the items for a subject do not represent any particular curriculum as was the case with the APU items.

In all of the NAEP assessments prior to 1983–84, the battery of subject items was divided among mutually exclusive booklets and each booklet administered to a nationally representative sample of students. After 1983–84, this procedure was changed. The items were divided into 15 minute blocks and each student received a booklet containing three blocks of items. The blocks are distributed in such a way so that each block appears in the same number of booklets and each pair of blocks appears in at least one. This change in procedure was to allow data to be analysed within and between booklets, thus increasing the potential of the data.

NAEP summarized student performance in reading, mathematics, science, US history and civics on a 0–500 proficiency scale designed to describe overall student achievement in each curriculum area. To provide meaning to the results, performance is characterized at four or five 'levels' on the proficiency scales. The results are reported in terms of the percentages of students achieving each level. NAEP uses item response modelling (IRM) to estimate average proficiency for the nation and the various sub-groups of interest. Item response modelling as we mentioned in the last chapter assumes that only a single latent variable is measured by items. Levels are defined by describing the types of items that most students attaining that level would be able to perform successfully. The items are grouped by each of the levels and subject experts are then asked to interpret the items and describe what students at the level knew and could do compared to students at the next lower level.

Individuals' overall performance on a test is used to assign them to a level. The items that individuals at a level succeed on (65 per cent probability of success) are then used to describe the construct that that level 'measures'. The only basis for classifying an item at a proficiency level is the estimated probability of success of students at different proficiency levels. The content and the demand of the item or the weightings of the different types of items included in the test do not feature directly in this classification. Yet the numerical values for the NAEP scales are intended to be interpreted from a criterion-referenced perspective, i.e. to identify what students know and can do. Any item answered correctly more frequently by individuals at a lower level than a higher level would be rejected as having poor discrimination. As such the system only works if items are unidimensional. This is a similar perspective on aberrant items to that adopted by the maths and language APU surveys, which used the Rasch model for analysis (another example of IRM). Again it is worth noting that any such aberrant items also contribute to the level achieved by the individual. The writing assessments were not summarized on a continuum of proficiency with criterion-referenced levels. The writing levels were to do with adequacy of task accomplishment, i.e. unsatisfactory, minimal, adequate and elaborated.

The results for NAEP like the APU are not reported for individuals, schools or school districts, and not until recently were state-level results available (i.e. from the 1990 testing).

We will review findings from the reading, writing, mathematics and science surveys up until the late 1980s and make brief reference to the civics and history assessments. The intention is first to present the NAEP description of sub-group performance and then to consider how such performance is explained. In so doing it is important to bear the above caveats in mind concerning the basis of NAEP scores. We then consider what the descriptions suggest about the views of equity and achievement underpinning the surveys and their reporting, and review any relationships between the hypotheses set up in Chapter 2 and explored through Chapters 3 and 4.

A review of reading performance

A review of the survey findings for 1970–71 and 1974–75 (Tierney and Lapp 1979) showed that at age 9 girls out-performed boys and black children performed at a level 13 percentage points below white children in overall reading performance. At age 13, girls were ahead of boys by five percentage points, while black students' level of achievement was seven percentage points below that of their white peer group. At age 17, a similar gap between females and males was noted, while the gap in achievement between black and white students increased to 19 percentage points. The authors were critical of the measures used by NAEP. In their view, they were inadequate as they did not represent a comprehensive examination of reading, nor were the measures used designed to be appropriate for students who were learning English as a second language. Four areas of potential bias in the measures were identified: the range of vocabulary used; the syntactic formations deployed; the use of idiomatic expression; and the cultural knowledge assumed in the items. No associated concerns about possible gender bias in the assessments were referred to in the report. Criticisms such as these challenge the educational validity of the NAEP measures and the assumption of 'unidimensionality'. The possibility of biasing factors may mean that ethnic and racial sub-groups within the test population are responding to the same set of items along different dimensions. Hence to interpret their performance on an IRM scale is to misrepresent their actual and potential achievements. The comparative data offered is therefore to be viewed with caution.

The Reading Report Card (NAEP 1985) looked at trends in reading across four assessments from 1971 to 1984, the two already discussed and two later ones. In this report, IRM was used to generate a 'common scale that for the first time allows a direct comparison across ages'. The scale is said to allow performance to be compared across groups and sub-groups whether tested at the same time or a number of years apart. The NAEP reading scale measures proficiencies from 0 to 500. Five levels are used to define the scale: level 150, rudimentary skills and strategies; level 200, basic skills and strategies; level 250, intermediate skills and strategies; level 300, adept skills and strategies; and level 350, advanced skills and strategies.

Critics of the NAEP reading scale (for example McLean and Goldstein 1988) challenge both the technical and educational grounds for it. Central to these criticisms is the view that language and language learning is not unidimensional and that reading performance depends on both the task and the context. The NAEP perspective is considered naive and to yield measures unrelated to the processes of teaching and learning. Consequently the basis of the scores are considered suspect as is the use of the same items to measure trends in performance over time. (Similar criticisms concerning the assumption of invariance of relative question difficulty were described in the discussion of the APU Maths and Language assessments in Chapter 5.)

The statistical techniques used by NAEP to study dimensionality in the reading items were also judged to be inappropriate and the evidence provided about the items 'fit' inadequate to justify the claim of unidimensionality. Criticisms of this kind apply equally to the range of NAEP subject surveys. The descriptions of sub-group performance need therefore to be set in the context of the view of the subject underpinning the assessment and the nature of the scale used to determine scores.

Results in the report are presented for black, white and Hispanic students based on *observed* racial/ethnic identification, which is made by the assessment administrators according to the following categories: White, Black, Hispanic, Asian or Pacific Islander, American Indian or Alaskan Native and Other. Sample sizes did not allow reliable estimates for all sub-groups but all students were included in determining the national estimates of average reading performance.

The overall trends reported by NAEP showed a marked improvement in the achievement of minority and disadvantaged urban students between 1971 and 1984, which had reduced the gap between their performance and that of other students. Nevertheless, the reading proficiency of these students remained low, the average reading proficiency of black and Hispanic 17-year-olds being only slightly higher than that of white 13-year-olds. The report noted that males' reading proficiency trailed that of females in all four reading assessments with the gap only narrowing slightly between 1971 and 1984. The influence of home environment as judged by the availability of reading material in the home and the level of parental education was shown to affect performance at ages 9, 13 and 17. The more reading material available and the higher the level of parental education, the better the students' reading proficiency.

In looking in more detail at the findings for black students, it was noted that improvements had occurred across the range of reading skills. Nevertheless, only 16 per cent of black 17-year-olds were judged to demonstrate adept reading skills and strategies compared to 45 per cent of white students of this age. This trend was mirrored in the performance of Hispanic students. It is those students with adept reading strategies who were found to do well in their overall school performance and to have the greatest likelihood of going on to further academic study and to achieve success in the workplace. In addition to this finding, the report noted that four times as many black children as white children had reading skills below the rudimentary level, which placed them at greater risk of experiencing overall failure at school in the future.

The Reading Report Card 1971–1988 (Mullis and Jenkins 1990) looked across the last five national assessments of reading using IRM to trace student achievement. We will consider some of the problems that have arisen in the trend analyses for reading as they provide a background to the specific findings discussed here and inform issues which apply generally to all of the NAEP trend data.

Briefly the items used to establish the NAEP scales are assumed to be unidimensional, moreover any change in the proportion of correct responses to an item over time is assumed to reflect changes in the population's achievement rather than in the difficulty of the item. Established NAEP scales can be extended to include new items (as long as those items are assumed to exhibit the same 'trait') by comparing students' responses on new items with students' responses on the established scale in order to assign a difficulty value.

As we mentioned in Chapter 5 the assumption that a change in the facility of an item indicates a change in the population's achievement suggests that teaching and curriculum influences are negligible. The comparison of the 1984 and 1986 NAEP reading results on the basis of a set of common (bridge) items revealed a dramatic decline in the performance of 9- and 17-year-olds. NAEP considered this size of decline to be unlikely and treated the 1986 results as anomalous and did not report them. The extensive investigation conducted by NAEP into these anomalous results suggested that student performance was affected by changes in the administration of the common items, i.e. the order of the items, the format of the test booklets. To overcome these effects and to enable links to be made between the 1988 and 1984 survey results NAEP used a 'bridge' sample as well as a main sample in the 1988 survey. The 'bridge' sample were the same age as students assessed in 1984, were administered a sub-set of the same reading items at the same time of the year using the same method. The main sample differed in each of these respects. These controls were seen by NAEP to safeguard the stability of the 'measure' and so allow comparisons to be made.

Critics of the NAEP strategy remain sceptical, however, on at least two counts. Firstly NAEP's solution seeks to control the assessment context rather than to understand how it influences students' performance. This is of particular concern given that the effects on students were not consistent across sub-groups defined by gender and race. Secondly a change in the proportion of correct responses to an item can be described as a change in achievement but whether this is due to changes in the population or in the item or an interaction of both of these factors cannot be established. Such concerns about the meaning of the NAEP reported trends, particularly for sub-groups, would apply across the subjects surveyed and should be kept in mind when considering NAEP findings.

Students were assigned to racial and ethnic sub-groups in the 1988 survey on the basis of their response to the following questions:

> Are you: A, American Indian or Alaska Native; B, Asian or Pacific Islander; C, Black; D, White; E, Other (What?) Are you Hispanic? A, No; B, Yes; Mexican, Mexican American or Chicano? C, Yes; Puerto Rican? D, Yes; Cuban? E, Yes; Other Spanish/Hispanic (What?)

The NAEP convention employed in both the 1984 and 1988 assessments is to identify trend differences as significant only if they are at least twice as large as standard errors. The results quoted in this report vary slightly to those quoted in the 1985 report due to refinements in the weighting procedures applied. In all subject reports of assessments from 1984 onwards, these reporting procedures apply.

The findings of the assessments showed little change for white students at ages 9, 13 and 17. Black students, on the other hand, are reported to have made 'striking gains' from 1971 to 1988. Across the 9-year period from 1971 to 1980, the difference in average performance between black and white 9-year-olds decreased from 44 to 32 scale points. However, in 1988, the difference between their average reading proficiency scores remained almost 30 points. Black 13-year-olds' reading proficiency steadily increased across the assessment. The difference between black and white populations of students in 1984 was 27 scale points, and in

1988 it was 18 scale points. A similar decrease in achievement difference was noted in the 1988 assessment of 17-year-olds. This was despite the increasing population of black students remaining at school. The difference in average reading performance between black 17-year-olds and their white peers showed a systematic reduction from 53 scale points in 1971 to 41 points in 1984. By 1988, the achievement difference was reduced to 20 scale points, which nevertheless remains a substantial difference in the average reading proficiency of 17-year-olds. In 1975, Hispanic students tended to out-perform black students. In 1988, this was no longer the case: black students across the ages assessed performed as well, if not better, than Hispanic students.

This improvement in sub-group performance is discussed in the report. It is suggested that students who are 'disproportionately likely to be disadvantaged, have [perhaps] benefited from compensatory programs in the initial school years and from recent reforms at the high school level, resulting in substantially improved achievement' (Mullis and Jenkins 1990: 15). This view contradicts the findings of the Coleman Report with regard to school effectiveness. However, it must be remembered that very different measures of achievement were used.

Across the variety of subject areas assessed by NAEP, the results for males and females support numerous research studies including the APU surveys, that show females out-performing males in reading and writing, while males are ahead in mathematics and science. The assessments indicate that the reading proficiency of females had remained fairly constant from 1971 to 1988. In contrast, 17-year-old males tended gradually to improve across the assessments. At ages 9 and 13, improvements noted in the 1970s were followed by declines in the 1980s. The improvements at age 13 were slight and offset by the declines, whereas at age 9 the improvements were greater, hence overall there was a slight reduction in the gender difference in reading achievement between 1971 and 1988 for males both at ages 9 and 17. These results were discussed in the context of the changing trends in Scholastic Aptitude Test (SAT) results that we referred to in Chapter 2. Mullis and Jenkins accept that some of the relative decline in female verbal SAT scores can be attributed to changes in the test-taking population, but not in terms of the ability of the male test population as Halpern (1992) does, but rather in terms of female disadvantage with regard to schooling and home support. Nor do the authors consider the possibility of item effects or overall test content bias. They conclude in opposition to Halpern that '*real changes* may be taking place in the relative verbal achievement of females and males' (Mullis and Jenkins 1990: 20, our emphasis). Whatever our view of this claim, it does suggest support for environmental explanations for performance differences.

In *Learning to Read in our Nation's Schools* (Langer *et al.* 1990), the results for the 1988 reading assessment were related to the level and quality of instructions and support students receive from their teachers. In this report, the range of performance for different sub-groups was the initial focus. The authors comment:

> By grade 12 the average performance of Black and Hispanic students only reaches the level of eighth grade White students nevertheless, at any given grade some White students were among the least proficient readers and some Black and Hispanic students were among the most proficient.
>
> (Langer *et al.* 1990: 17)

The differences in average performance of black and Hispanic students and their white counterparts was attributed largely to differences in socio-economic status rather than to any variables related to the assessments themselves. However, this conclusion is only based on a comparison of average reading proficiency for students attending schools in advantaged urban, disadvantaged urban and extreme rural communities. The early advantage of attending either kindergarten, pre-school nursery or day-care was noted for black and Hispanic students as well as white students: 52 per cent of Hispanic students, 59 per cent of black students and 61 per cent of white students were reported as attending pre-school, nursery or day-care. However, no information is provided in the report about the quality of education available at this point for the various sub-groups. A higher proportion of Hispanic students (50 per cent) pursue general as opposed to academic programmes of study in high school, compared with 34.5 per cent of black students and 31.5 per cent of white students. This may indicate differences in expectations and self-image both of the students, teachers and society.

The reading proficiency of females is described as significantly higher than that of males across the grades with 'no reduction in

Table 6.1   Reading habits in grades 8 and 12 (percentages)

	Grade 8		Grade 12	
	Males	*Females*	*Males*	*Females*
Fiction	29.0	46.0	25.0	39.0
Non-fiction	21.0	11.2	32.0	17.0

the gap at the upper grade levels'. The report looked at the reading habits of males and females and noted a similar trend to that measured by the UK national assessment of performance (Gorman *et al.* 1988). Males read less fiction and more non-fiction than females (see Table 6.1). Overall, more males report rarely reading or never reading than females (26 per cent males, 11 per cent females at grade 8; 22 per cent males, 15 per cent females at grade 12). As in the APU surveys, there was a decline in interest in reading for the population as a whole as they get older.

The report includes a very informative breakdown of instructional variables such as time spent on reading, reading skills emphasized, etc., but none of these were related to gender, race or ethnic sub-group performance, only to ability groups or to cohorts of students following different programmes of study at high school. Hence the potential for looking at possible differences in learning opportunities and access is limited in the report. Within the general pattern of instruction, students in 'low'-ability classes (by reading) were more likely to be asked to do 'daily workbook assignments and somewhat less likely to engage in daily discussion or read books they choose themselves' (Langer *et al.* 1990: 50). This may indicate different within-school experiences for those sub-groups doing less well at reading overall. It was noted that in disadvantaged urban communities, i.e. those with higher proportions of black and Hispanic students, teachers of half the students reported receiving only some or none of the instructional materials they required.

The section on teacher characteristics did report by race and ethnicity. For example, Hispanic students and those students attending schools in rural areas were more likely to be taught by inexperienced teachers. In reviewing the teaching force for grade 4 students, it was noted that males and minority groups are under-represented with only 12 per cent of fourth graders having male reading teachers and only about 22 per cent taught by black or Hispanic teachers. The overwhelming majority of students are taught by female teachers (88 per cent).

The second part of the report focuses on how well students read by reference to the 1988 NAEP reading assessment. The reading tasks and evaluation methods differ from those reported in *The Reading Report Card 1971–1988* (Mullis and Jenkins 1990). The majority of the reading tasks involved multiple-choice response formats but there were in addition some open-ended tasks. The reading text of the tasks was either 'informative' or 'literary' and performance was assessed in terms of how well students could construct meaning and examine and extend their understanding of a passage. The average results for students show that on the construction of meaning from information passages, white students out-performed black and Hispanic students across the grades by about 10 percentage points, and females just out-performed males. Black and Hispanic students performed similarly. This was also the case with literary passages. The differences between males and females on constructing meaning from literary passages as opposed to informational passages increases with females ahead of males across the grades. The scores for examining meaning were low for all students. Interestingly, the proportion of literacy to informational tasks alters across the grade assessments. At grade 4, there were 11 literary passages and 13 informational ones; at grade 8, there were 6 and 21, respectively, whereas at grade 12 there were 4 literary compared to 22 informational. There were also very obvious content differences in the passages: some were scientific; others overtly 'masculine' such as 'soccer'; and yet others, which may have seemed more oriented towards females such as High Tech Pizza, were set in an industrial context and contained a great number of technical and scientific terms. No comment is made about potential content effects on sub-group performance.

A review of writing performance

A review of writing trends based on three assessments of writing achievement conducted from 1974 to 1984 is reported by Applebee *et al.* (1986). The writing tasks used in the assessment were selected to reflect the differing purposes for which people write at home, at school and in the community. The purposes identified were labelled as informative, persuasive and imaginative. The discussion of trends is restricted to those writing exercises administered using identical procedures in at least two of the three assessments, i.e. a rather small data set of three to five writing tasks at each age tested.

The assessment results showed the writing performance of 9-year-olds was relatively stable from 1974 to 1979. Performance then decreased on the persuasive task from 1979 to 1984, while informative writing skills remained about the same. There was some improvement on imaginative writing performance during that same period. Thirteen-year-olds' performance showed increases on some tasks but decreases on others during the period between 1974 and 1979, with more declines than improvements. However, there was a steady improvement from 1979 to 1984, so that by the early 1980s 13-year-olds' writing performance had recovered to 1974 levels. At age 17, performance decreased from 1974 to 1979 and recovered somewhat from 1979 to 1984.

The results were analysed by sub-groups (identified by assessment administrator) in order to 'help explain trends for the nation as a whole'. The results suggest that trends in performance during the 10-year period from 1974 to 1984 were similar for white, black and Hispanic students. The greatest differences appeared at age 9. Black 9-year-olds showed comparatively more improvement than their white counterparts from 1974 to 1979, but trends in the performance of the two groups were very similar from 1979 to 1984. The performance of Hispanic 9-year-olds improved on all three writing tasks in 1984. For both 13-year-olds and 17-year-olds, the trends for white, black and Hispanic students were parallel. It should be noted, however, that very few black and Hispanic students were sampled on each writing task, so the results need to be interpreted with caution. The report concludes that at all age levels, the majority of students did not write adequate responses to the informative, persuasive or imaginative tasks included in the assessment. The performance of black and Hispanic students at all three ages generally showed lower writing achievement levels than white students, although the trends as described for the three groups were similar.

The report also examined trends in instruction and found similar trends for sub-groups defined by sex, race and ethnicity. The amount of time spent on writing instruction increased over the first half decade and levelled off between 1979 and 1984 for 13-year-olds and 17-year-olds. The report showed an increased amount of time spent on the process of writing for 13- and 17-year-olds, which continued from 1974 through to 1984. Black and Hispanic 17-year-old students reported somewhat more time devoted to writing than did their white peers. The report concluded that little is known about the impact of various writing instruction methods on achievement and it may be that 'simply spending more time discussing writing is not helpful'.

The report focused on trends in performance, and as male and female achievements followed similar patterns over the decade, unlike the trends for reading, no comment is made about the differences in scores, generally in favour of girls, that occurred across the ages tested. It is perhaps noteworthy that there is no comment here concerning females *sustaining* their superiority on this aspect of verbal skills, in contrast with the report of the findings for reading. There were also some notable differences in male and female reports on writing instructions. For example, at age 13 in 1984, more girls (54 per cent) than boys (40 per cent) reported that they usually drafted or rewrote a piece of work before handing it in.

The levels of writing performance for the population were reported as being substantially the same in 1988 as in 1984 (Applebee *et al.* 1990a). Many students continued to perform at minimal levels on the writing assessment tasks and relatively few performed at adequate or higher levels. Six writing tasks were reported on at grade 4, three assessing informative writing, two tasks requiring persuasive writing and one on imaginative writing. At grades 8 and 11, the six tasks were split between informative writing and persuasive writing. Overall, 12 tasks were included in both the 1984 and 1988 assessments of writing. To compare the overall writing performance of sub-groups over time, estimates of how well students in each grade would have done on the 11 tasks assessing informative and persuasive writing were computed and summarized on a common scale of 0–400.

The overall performance of white students closely resembled the national profile with a significant decline at grade 8 between

1984 and 1988 and no significant changes at grades 4 and 11. The average writing proficiency of black and Hispanic students remained stable across all three grades. Consequently, the gap between these students and white students was slightly reduced at grade 8. However, the gap remained large. In 1984 and 1988, Hispanic and black eleventh graders were judged to write less well than their eighth-grade white peers. Hispanic fourth graders tended to write better than their black counterparts, but the performance gap between black and Hispanic students was reduced between grades 4 and grade 11. This improvement in black students' scores relative to Hispanics mirrors that measured in the reading domain but is less dramatic.

Females performed on average better than males across all grades. Between 1984 and 1988, the performance of fourth-grade girls increased significantly, while the performance of boys remained the same. At grade 8, females' performance remained stable, while that of males decreased. At grade 11, performance by both groups was stable with females ahead of males by over 20 scale points. These results correspond to other surveys, both national and international.

The assessments also documented trends in attitudes, writing behaviours and instructions. The results showed that there was little change in the writing instruction received by students despite numerous curriculum initiatives over nearly a decade. The best writers tended to be students who valued writing, had positive attitudes towards their writing, used writing extensively for personal and social reasons, and received feedback on their writing from their teachers. Unfortunately, none of these analyses were done by sub-group, so there are no indications of potential relationships between sub-group performance, attitudes and instruction. It is interesting to note this lack of analysis, particularly as the collection of this background information was intended 'to improve the usefulness of NAEP achievement results and to provide an opportunity to examine policy issues'.

A further report (Applebee *et al.* 1990b) provides two perspectives on students' writing achievement: the relationships between students' overall writing performance and various factors; and students' performance by task for the 1988 assessment. The grades referred to in this report are grades 4, 8 and 12 assessed in 1988.

Again much of the analysis presented in this report does not relate sub-group performance to background variables. We shall discuss the exceptions to this. Teachers were asked to comment on the amount of class time spent each week teaching students how to write and helping with their writing. The most common amount of time was 60 minutes per week. However, teachers reported spending more time with black and Hispanic eighth-grade students: 32 per cent of black students and 35 per cent of Hispanics received more than 60 minutes compared to 26 per cent of white students. There were no reported differences in time spent instructing males and females. Teachers also commented on the time they expected students to spend on writing assignments each week. Again the average time was 60 minutes, with 47 per cent of black students and 52 per cent of Hispanic students being expected to spend over 2 hours on such assignments, compared to 39 per cent of white students.

The assessment items involved students in responding to different writing modes and the overall performance of students was analysed within each mode. Again there was no breakdown of performance by sub-group – a particular loss with regard to gender as differences within mode have been identified in other surveys (Gorman *et al.* 1988). A special study to explore the effects of increased response time on students' performance was carried out as part of the 1988 assessment. This study showed that minority students did not appear to improve their performance when given additional time to respond to informative and persuasive tasks, although some improvement was noted on narrative tasks for black eighth-graders and Hispanic fourth- and eighth-graders. For males and females, the benefits of additional time were also primarily evident on the narrative tasks.

Civics and history assessments

The trends in performance on the civics assessment show some similarities with those already discussed (Anderson *et al.* 1990). From 1976 to 1988, the performance gap between white students and their black and Hispanic peers narrowed across time at both ages. This was the result of significant gains in civic achievement by black and Hispanic 13-year-olds and a decline in the achievement of white 17-year-olds. At age 13 in 1988, the average civic proficiency of whites was 51 per cent compared with 46 per cent for blacks and Hispanics. The performance gap between white and black students, and between white and Hispanic students, remained larger at age 17 than at age 13, despite the decline in white students' performance. The average civic proficiency for white students was 61 per cent compared to 53 per cent for blacks and 54 per cent for Hispanics. The performance of 13-year-old males remained relatively constant across time, while the performance of girls improved significantly from 1982 to 1988. There were no gender differences in performance at age 17.

In 1988, the items used in the assessment of civics were primarily multiple-choice. Four levels of civic proficiency were defined and reported on the 0–500 scale: level 200, recognizes the existence of civic life; level 250, understands the nature of political institutions and the relationship between citizen and government; level 300, understands specific government structures and functions; level 350, understands a variety of political institutions and processes.

There were more male eighth- and twelfth-grade students achieving the highest levels of civic proficiency than females. At grade 4, there were large differences in the performance of white students compared with blacks and Hispanics. Three-quarters of white fourth-graders achieved the lowest level of proficiency compared with approximately 50 per cent of black and Hispanic students. In the twelfth grade, the percentages of black and Hispanic students achieving the higher levels of proficiency were far smaller than the percentage of white students doing so.

A significantly higher percentage of females than males performed at the lower two levels and a significantly higher proportion of males than females performed at the third level. These gender differences in performance at grade 8 echo the differences found by NAEP in other subjects. Males in grade 12 out-performed females at levels 3 and 4, which corresponds to performance disparities found in other subject assessments. The report noted the consistency found across the subjects in the lower performance of black and Hispanic students compared to their white peers. The report indicated grave concern about the lack of knowledge of the 'system' demonstrated by black and Hispanic students and the implications of this for the future. Societal changes were seen to depend on citizen participation, which in turn was linked to knowledge of how the 'system' operates. The 'masculine' image that civics has is clearly apparent in the test items and is further supported by the limited involvement of women and other minority groups in 'overt' political life. What is also evident in the assessment items is that content, like mode of response, is not considered to confound the trait being assessed. There are several instances where items could have been presented with a content that was accessible to a wider range of students, but there is little evidence of an awareness of this as an issue.

The items used in the history assessment (Hammack 1990) were all multiple-choice. Four levels of proficiency were defined and reported on the 0–500 scale: level 200, knows simple historical facts; level 250, knows beginning historical information and has rudimentary interpretative skills; level 300, understands basic historical terms and relationships; level 350, interprets historical information and ideas.

The assessment found that males tended to out-perform females and white students again tended to out-perform black and Hispanic students. (The latter two groups' performance was comparable as in the civics assessment.) There is a statement in this report which refers to the relationship between traditional sex roles and school behaviour and learning patterns. However, no attempt is made to interpret the results from this perspective. What gender differences there are in performance reveal that across the grades more males than females achieve the higher levels of proficiency. For example, at grade 4, 19 per cent of males compared to 13 per cent of females achieve the second level. At grade 8, similar performance was found at levels 1 and 2, but 16 per cent of males and 10 per cent of females attained level 3. At grade 12, 51 per cent of males achieved level 3 compared to 41 per cent of females, and twice as many males as females achieved the highest level of proficiency (7 *vs* 3 per cent, respectively).

At each grade, the average proficiency of white students was 24–28 scale points higher than that of minority students. Eighty-five per cent of white fourth-graders performed at or above the lowest proficiency level, compared with about 50 per cent of black and Hispanic students. This pattern was repeated at grades 8 and 12.

A review of the sample of test items included in the report revealed definite attempts to make the items accessible to minority groups and females. However, there is clear cultural bias in whose history is being assessed. This bias and the attempts to address it reveal some interesting insights. For example, on tasks which referred specifically to female characters (feminists, etc.), a cursory look at the test results indicates girls performing at a higher level than boys. For example, in grade 8: on women and voting (males 65 per cent, females 75 per cent); Eleanor Roosevelt (males 50 per cent, females 55 per cent); Harriet Tubman (males 71 per cent, females 76 per cent/blacks 78 per cent, whites 74 per cent). These content effects appear across the levels defined and at other grades. Similar results (i.e. a reversal in the trend) occur for black students. For example, in grade 8: on Martin Luther King, Jr and non-violence (whites 48 per cent, blacks, 89 per cent); Martin Luther King, Jr (whites 44 per cent, blacks 66 per cent); Booker T. Washington (whites 35 per cent, blacks 45 per cent). These content interactions are not remarked upon in the report.

A review of mathematics performance

The mathematics assessment, like the other assessments, is summarized on a 0–500 proficiency scale. Student performance is characterized by five proficiency levels on the scale: level 150, simple arithmetic; level 200, beginning skills and understanding; level 250, basic operations and beginning problem solving; level 300, moderately complex procedures and reasoning; level 350, multi-step problem-solving and algebra. The 1986 data were also computed for five different mathematics content area sub-scales: (1) knowledge and skill in numbers and operations; (2) higher-level applications in numbers and operations; (3) measurement; (4) geometry; and (5) algebra. The assessment included both open-ended and multiple-choice questions covering a wide range of content and process.

Linn and Dunbar (1990) consider the NAEP trends for mathematics in the context of international rankings. They quote the 1981–82 findings of the Second International Mathematics Study (SIMS) by the IEA (see Chapter 4). Of the 20 countries participating at the eighth-grade level, US students ranked 10th in arithmetic, 12th in algebra, 16th in geometry and 18th in measurement. Of the 16 countries involved in the assessment of senior high school students, the US ranked 14th in algebra, 12th in elementary functions / calculus and 12th in geometry. They concluded that US twelfth-graders' performance compared unfavourably with students in Japan, Hong Kong, Sweden, Israel, Finland, New Zealand and England. The other international comparison Linn and Dunbar provide uses the international assessment conducted in 1988 by the IAEP of 13-year-olds from Ireland, Korea, Spain, the UK, four Canadian provinces (from three of these provinces, separate populations of French- and English-speaking students were tested) and the USA. The 12 populations of students were assessed using maths exercises from the 1988 NAEP mathematics assessment. The US students ranked last or next to last on each of the five types of problems in mathematics. The problems associated with international rankings, including sampling, differences in curricula, language, etc., were discussed in Chapter 4 and we commented there on the limitations of such data. However, descriptions of USA performance in this international context provide a useful background when we consider how the performance of minority groups and females might be being viewed by educationists and assessors in the USA.

For example, the most dramatic changes in the NAEP mathematics findings from 1973 to 1986 were the consistent gains made by black students. Nevertheless, the average performance of black and Hispanic 17-year-olds was more comparable to the performance of white 13-year-olds. Across the four mathematics assessments, the average performance difference between white and black students had narrowed steadily at all three ages tested (9, 13 and 17), a similar trend to that noted for reading. Hispanic students' performance at age 17 and 13, in comparison to their white peers, showed a steady improvement and in this assessment black and Hispanic students' performance was comparable. However, at age 9, the gap between white students and Hispanics remained constant at about 20 scale points (Mullis *et al.* 1990).

The 1986 data were analysed for ethnic groups across the five content sub-scales. The findings showed that for both knowledge and skills as well as higher-level applications, the white and Asian-American grade 3 students out-perform Hispanic students who tended to out-perform black students. At grades 7 and 11, the advantage in overall performance demonstrated by Asian-American students remained across all five content areas. Hispanic students at grades 7 and 11 performed significantly better than black students in higher-level applications, measurement and geometry (Dossey *et al.* 1988).

Trends in average proficiency levels for males and females follow the population trends with some notable differences. For example, although the average performance in 1986 of 9-year-old and 13-year-old boys and girls was similar, these results represent significant gains from 1978 for boys and comparatively consistent performance for girls. At 17 years of age, on the four mathematics assessments, males out-performed females. However, the significant improvement in performance of females and not males in the 1986 assessment does suggest that females may have begun to close the gap. Wilder and Powell (1989) provide a further breakdown of these gender differences in performance. At all three grade levels, there was a consistent advantage for females in the areas of knowledge and skills, and a consistent advantage for males in the area of 'higher-level applications'. Females tended to out-perform males on tasks 'where there is an obvious procedural rule to follow', but males had an advantage when the strategy for solving the problem was less apparent (Dossey *et al.* 1988).

This finding and comment parallels Maccoby and Jacklin's (1974) review of differences in the mathematical ability of males and females. It is also a finding that corresponds with the early UK surveys of mathematical performance carried out by the Assessment of Performance Unit (Foxman *et al.* 1985). However, in the later APU surveys, girls were ahead of boys at ages 11 and 15 on written tests of problem-solving strategies (Foxman *et al.* 1991). Other differences in the 1986 NAEP assessment showed males ahead of females at grades 7 and 11 on the geometry scale, which the report identifies as consistent with the well-documented difference in favour of males on tests of spatial ability (Dossey *et al.* 1988: 54), and on the measurement scale at all three grade levels, although not significant at grade 7. The report authors relate this finding to the differential experience of measuring instruments documented in the science survey data findings, which correspond well with the UK APU surveys.

Wilder and Powell (1989) comment on the attitudes of males and females to mathematics as measured in the NAEP assessments. The attitude questions asked do not allow performance correlations to be addressed. In general, students' interest and confidence in mathematics decreases with age, as is the case in science, but this effect in mathematics is more pronounced for females than males at grades 7 and 11. Fewer girls think they are good at mathematics and at age 13 more females think mathematics is more for boys than girls. Again these findings echo those of the APU surveys discussed in Chapter 5.

In the summary of findings from 20 years of NAEP (Mullis *et al.* 1990), the authors consider such gender differences as 'perplexing', particularly as the students take similar courses. The trend for the gap to increase with age in mathematics is viewed as especially 'perplexing'. Such views merely reinforce the lack of attention being paid by the assessors to the nature and sources of gender and group differences. It is perplexing to us that Mullis *et al.* appear not to have read any of the abundant literature in the area, even that available specifically in the context of assessment research. The work of Mallow (1987) on alienation, for example, would provide simple insights into the mechanisms by which early sub-group differences can become compounded and lead to later low achievement irrespective of ability and courses studied. The same phenomenon was observed and then researched in the APU science assessments (Johnson and Murphy 1986). No such attempts to explain differences characterize the NAEP approach to reporting test scores and differences. There are obvious differences in content of the test items but no reference is made to these. Similarly, there are instances where a context is established but effects on sub-group performance are not considered.

Review of science performance

The science data, as with other subject data, were analysed using item response scaling technology and were summarized on a common proficiency scale of five levels: level 150, knows everyday science facts; level 200, understands simple scientific principles; level 250, applies basic scientific information; level 300, analyses scientific procedures and data; level 350, integrates specialized scientific information. This scale was computed across five content area sub-scales – (1) nature of science; (2) life sciences; (3) chemistry; (4) physics; and (5) earth and space sciences – for the 1986 survey. The items used included both open-ended and multiple-choice items and covered a wide range of content and process areas as well as a variety of contexts (Mullis and Jenkins 1988).

The science assessment, and this report in particular, while sharing the same problematic assumptions about the unidimensionality and difficulty invariance of items nevertheless reveals a different approach to the interpretation of the NAEP survey data. The reference to constructs such as 'process', content and context are not reflected in other reports. Similarly, the breakdown by content areas as in the maths assessment indicates some recognition of the multi dimensionality of scientific achievement. This slightly more probing approach is reflected in the analysis of subgroup behaviour by background variables which we will refer to later.

The overall picture of science performance is somewhat similar to the mathematics picture (Mullis *et al.* 1990). The lack of science in the elementary curriculum was considered in the interpretation of fourth-graders' performance. For example, in this context, it was viewed as encouraging that 70 per cent of 9-year-olds demonstrated an understanding of simple scientific principles. However, the results for 13- and 17-year-olds were considered 'disappointing'. Only half of the 13-year-olds and 80 per cent of the 17-year-olds demonstrated even a basic understanding of scientific information and how it might be applied. Nine per cent of grade 8 students and 41 per cent of grade 12 students were considered to be only 'moderately versed' in science and only 8 per cent of 17-year-olds were judged to have any degree of specialized subject knowledge. The performance of 17-year-olds in 1986 returned to where it had been in 1977, but remained below the level achieved by 17-year-olds in 1969 and 1973. The performance of 9- and 13-year-olds was essentially static between 1970 and 1986.

On ethnic group performance, the differences found were considered erratic. White students scored better than black students but the difference in scores varied. The trend for Hispanic students was similarly erratic. The average proficiency of 13- and 17-year-old black and Hispanic students appears to remain at least 4 years behind that of their white peers (Mullis and Jenkins 1988: 7). Only 15 per cent of black and Hispanic 17-year-olds were judged able to analyse scientific procedures and data compared to nearly 50 per cent of white students in the 1986 survey.

The performance of these groups is discussed in the report of the 1986 science survey in terms of possible causal relationships, although the NAEP data was unable to provide evidence of these relationships because of the multiplicity of the potential variables affecting the data (Mullis and Jenkins 1988). However, the conjectures proffered by the authors make a significant and interesting change from the usual reporting style. The data revealed no clear messages about course uptake and performance. For example, students who took courses in the life sciences and chemistry performed better in these content areas than those who did not (across the sub-groups). White students who took physics had much higher proficiency on the physics sub-scale than those who had not taken the course. However, the proficiency level of black and Hispanic grade 11 students on the physics sub-scale was about the same whether they had taken physics courses or not. White students in grade 3 were found to be consistently more likely to report having used various scientific apparatus than were black and Hispanic students. This was also the case at the seventh grade. This experience gap between white and minority students in some instances increased between grades 7 and 11.

The survey results for males and females showed a consistent trend for males to out-perform females from 1977 to 1986. An analysis of the earlier NAEP assessments up to and including 1982 showed that boys on average performed significantly better than girls across the grades on tests of physical science and, to a lesser extent, earth science, with only small discrepancies in favour of boys for biology. In 1986, a 6-point scale difference was found at age 9 in overall proficiency scores which increased to 9 points and 13 points at ages 13 and 17, respectively. Males' superior performance was notable at the older ages and the higher levels of the proficiency scale. The panel for dissemination of the NAEP results considered these performance gaps in the 1986 science results and judged the 9-year-olds' gap in performance insignificant, but expressed concern at the increased disparity that occurred with age for males and females (Ashworth 1990). In 1986, at age 17, roughly 50 per cent of the males, but only a third of the females, demonstrated the ability to analyse scientific procedures and data. The performance gap in physics between eleventh-grade girls and boys was found to be extremely large, and it could not be explained by differential course-taking patterns. Indeed, in some cases, the proficiency gap increased with course-taking for high school-aged students (Mullis and Jenkins 1988). Chemistry course-taking, for example, seemed to be much more beneficial to males. Course-taking in physics appeared to improve all students' performance, but did not reduce the gap between males and females and may have increased it. A similar concern, indeed 'distress', is expressed by the report authors who suggest that research is needed to 'discern factors – societal, personal, educational or other – that underline gender differences in science proficiency and to guide appropriate intervention' (Mullis and Jenkins 1988: 60). This is a clear statement of a view in support of psycho-social rather than biological factors to explain differences.

The NAEP science surveys also collected information about early experiences and attitudes (see Tables 6.2 and 6.3). For instance, in the 1979 and 1982 national science surveys of 9- and 13-year-olds, the children in the survey samples were asked whether they had ever worked with each topic in a list of ten. The findings are illustrated in Table 6.2 and show differences in experience among the 9-year-olds that also emerged, though to a lesser extent, for 13-year-olds.

Table 6.2 Differences among 9-year-old boys and girls in terms of the percentages claiming to have worked or experimented with particular named topics

Topic	% Pupils		Discrepancy in favour of	
	Boys	Girls	Girls	Boys
Batteries and bulbs	61	47		
Magnets	68	57		
Floating and sinking	58	48		
Dissolving	55	54		
Living animals	65	63		
Mirror	41	43		
Seeds	61	64		
Living plants	63	68		
Shadows	43	48		
Sound	55	67		

From Johnson and Murphy (1986: 19).

Table 6.3 Differences in the percentages of young boys and girls reporting use of particular measuring instruments at home or otherwise out-of-school[a]

Measuring instrument	% 9-year-olds		% 11-year-olds		Discrepancies in favour of	
	Boys	Girls	Boys	Girls	Girls	Boys
Compass	65	52	69	48		
Microscope	54	40	49	34		
Stopwatch/clock	57	45	66	52		
Spring balance	35	25	28	20		
Hand lens	86	81	70	59		
Metre stick	67	62	22	16		
Thermometer	81	83	53	49		
Weighing scales	84	87	75	81		

[a] ▦ American 9-year-olds: ■ British 11-year-olds.
From Johnson and Murphy (1986: 21).

The NAEP enquiries also explored pupils' familiarity with a range of common measuring instruments and simple tools, and the results are very much as one might expect. Table 6.3 illustrates the differences in the proportions of American and British boys and girls who claimed to have used each instrument (at home or otherwise out of school in the case of APU). These results are perhaps particularly remarkable for the striking degree of coincidence of the American and British findings. They also indicate the cross-cultural phenomenon of gendered societal expectations in support of the environmental hypotheses concerning differential learning opportunities.

In 1986, roughly the same percentages of boys and girls at age 9 reported having used basic scientific equipment. However, fewer girls than boys had experience of more advanced apparatus (e.g. a microscope or telescope). This gender difference with regard to microscopes vanishes at grade 7; however, the use of telescopes, barometers and electricity meters remained far more common for boys than for girls in the USA and the UK and were reflected in performance differences on tasks in the APU surveys at ages 13 and 15. White students in grade 3 were more likely to have used various scientific apparatus than were black and Hispanic students whose experience was similar. The greatest discrepancies between whites and blacks and Hispanics was primarily in experience with simple devices, yardsticks, magnifying lenses, etc.

The positive relationship between students' experience using various kinds of scientific equipment and their science proficiency is commented on in the science report (Mullis and Jenkins 1988). The authors, however, are unsure of the causality of the relationship. Is it their greater facility and involvement in science which leads boys to use the equipment more or does their increased experience enhance their proficiency? Either way, it seems clear that the interaction between positive experience and engagement increases achievement.

The probe into students' reported experience in applying their science knowledge showed more males than females at grades 7 and 11 having attempted to fix something electrical or mechanical, whereas females were more likely to have tried to diagnose an unhealthy plant or animal. The 1986 survey of attitudes to science showed males having more positive attitudes to science than females, as was found for mathematics. There is no report for ethnic groups, although the differences were small given the general low response of students.

In the report on *Accelerating Academic Achievement* (Mullis *et al.* 1990), no reference to the attitude measures or differences in experience are considered when reviewing sub-group differences or when making recommendations about how to improve student performance. This may be because there were few consistent relationships between reported attitudes and science proficiency. However, the panel for dissemination, when reviewing the differences between girls' and boys' performance, cited growing evidence of differential within-school treatment and opportunities in science instruction. Teacher expectation and interactions, textbook content, and parent and peer attitudes were also quoted by the panel as agents in deterring the science participation of girls. The panel recommended that science should include 'an abundance of hands-on activities related to concepts in electricity, magnetism and other areas, structured so that girls play an active rather than a passive role'. Teachers were also to be made aware of 'the more subtle behaviours that communicate low expectations to particular students' (Ashworth 1990).

Discussion

The picture of sub-group performance that emerges from the NAEP surveys is summarized in the report *Crossroads in American Education: A Summary of Findings, The Nation's Report Card* (Applebee *et al.* 1989: 11):

> In general, it appears that the performance gaps, as measured by differences in average proficiency, have narrowed across time, particularly for Black students. Decreases in the disparities in reading and mathematics performance are the most consistent among the subject areas across time, with the gap decreasing gradually, while the gaps in science performance are the least stable. For Hispanic and Black students alike, the gap in science achievement relative to White students increased until 1982, before narrowing between 1982 and 1986.

The apparent performance gap between black and Hispanic students and their white counterparts remains uncomfortably large, however, particularly in science. Overall, the performance of 17-year-old black and Hispanic students is close to that of white 13-year-olds in the areas of reading, mathematics and science – as the report comments, a difference of 3–4 years of additional schooling. The performance of Hispanic students in earlier assessments tended to be superior to that of black students, but the picture at present shows more comparable performance between the two groups. This reflects the improvement in black students' performance in certain areas such as reading.

The performance of males and females is summarized in another report, which concludes:

> The average performance results for males and females reinforce the evidence that females have an advantage in reading [and also writing] and that males have an advantage in mathematics and science. The results also reveal performance disparities favouring males in U.S. history, civics and geography.
>
> (Mullis *et al.* 1990: 47)

The role that NAEP plays with regard to equity in education is to help monitor the extent to which it has been achieved. For example, in a NAEP report on *Accelerating Academic Achievement* (Mullis *et al.* 1990), a chapter is devoted to the question 'What is the status of equity in educational achievement?' The chapter starts by quoting the general state-wide objective concerning equity, i.e. that 'the distribution of minority students in each level will more closely reflect the student population as a whole' (Mullis *et al.* 1990: 44). It is in this context that performance by race, ethnicity and gender is then reported and compared. If we consider the chapter's conclusion, the role of NAEP becomes even more apparent:

> The NAEP results offer evidence that our nation has the capacity to raise the achievement levels of minority students. Yet they also highlight the substantial amount of work that remains to be accomplished in this area. If, by the year 2000, the achievement levels of minority students are to more closely reflect the achievement levels of the nation as a whole then progress must accelerate in this decade toward reducing racial/ethnic and gender performance disparities.
>
> (Mullis *et al.* 1990: 56)

In this sense, then, the process of assessment itself stands outside of the educational issue. Where potential causes of sub-group differences are indicated in the NAEP findings, these are reported. There is, however, no evidence in the various reports that the findings themselves, be they of differences or similarities, are considered to be anything but valid and reliable. The process of assessment is assumed to be a neutral technical procedure. To understand this we need to recall the NAEP brief to provide 'dependable data on educational achievement'. To this end, NAEP has invested much effort in evaluating and improving their methodology and analyses, as it is through these means that they consider validity and dependability are achieved and scores acquire meaning. It is therefore unsurprising given this and the fact that there was never any intention for the project to *research* the issue of equity and assessment, that there is an absence of any critical comment on the performance of tests and items in them.

However, a review of sex and ethnic differences in US middle school mathematics and science funded by the Ford Foundation (Lockheed *et al.* 1985) usefully places the NAEP findings in the wider context of other studies. Note that only the 9- and 13-year-old samples are considered in this review. The following performance effects were established across the range of studies including NAEP:

- ethnic but not sex differences in performance in mathematics (Asian and white students out-performing black and Hispanic students);
- ethnic and sex differences in performance in science (whites out-performing blacks and males out-performing females on some tasks).

The review explored assessment-related factors to see to what extent they could account for ethnic and sex differences in performance. The authors concluded that the discontinuity between the child's language and the language of assessment had a detrimental effect on performance, as did cultural bias in the tasks used and the responses valued. Familiarity or lack of familiarity with test format was similarly found to enhance or depress students' performance and differentially affected certain ethnic groups. Finally, the authors comment on the test domain in science:

> We were interested to note the relative absence of research interest in the relationship between the context of science assessment and science performance; it seems that much more attention has been paid to exploring deficits in cognitive ability than to determining whether assessments relying upon tasks and apparati associated with upper-middle class White males could possibly explain the observed differences.
>
> (Lockheed *et al.* 1985: 35)

Wilder and Powell (1989), in their survey of sex differences in test performance, do consider the characteristics of the tests. They quote Hudson's (1986) analysis of the items used in the NAEP mathematics assessment of 17-year-olds in 1977–78 and 1981–82. Hudson's results for a large sample of students demonstrated that in both years the tests were more difficult for girls with equivalent mathematics backgrounds. She found some evidence of bias in items at times in favour of females and at other times in favour of males, which could not account for the performance gap. Hudson did find, however, large sex differences in students' choice of distractors. Females were much more likely to use the 'I don't know' distractor than males, a point which echoes some of the discussion in Chapter 5. Marshall (1983) also found that distractor-type differentially affected the performance of males and females.

Hudson continued her research by asking an additional sample of high school students to articulate their approaches to the items. She concluded that males and females thought about the problems in quite different ways. Females responded in ways consistent with the notion of 'learned helplessness' to items they found difficult. They were less willing to guess, used the 'don't know' option more and gave up more easily than males.

In the later reports for mathematics and science, there is a noticeable change in approach to the NAEP data in that potential links between sub-group performance and other variables are suggested. It is, however, clearly stated in the reports that no *causal* relationships can be substantiated by the NAEP evidence.

The NAEP findings provide little support for biological explanations for performance differences. The gaps in performance between different racial and ethnic groups appear to be narrowing and there is clearly a view that ameliorating strategies can improve the position of black and Hispanic students in relation to their white peers. We should also recall that some black and Hispanic students perform at the highest levels of proficiency and similarly some white students' performance corresponds to the lowest levels of proficiency. Factors that have been identified as influencing students' level of performance include socio-economic background. Economically disadvantaged pupils are said to enter school '*appearing* to be behind their peers and are therefore placed in remedial classes'. Consequently, they are 'poorly prepared to pursue higher-level science and mathematics course work in high school' (Oakes 1985, quoted in Mullis and Jenkins 1988: 8). The availability of educational resources in the home environment and parental level of education were also found to affect performance.

Differences in out-of-school experiences have been identified for ethnic sub-groups and links with performance established. There is also evidence of different within-school experiences between sub-groups related to resources, teaching staff and the forms of instruction received, which may exert a detrimental effect on black and Hispanic students' performance. These factors all affect the opportunities students have to learn, an hypothesis we discussed at the end of Chapter 5 and which is further supported by the evidence here.

Attitudes were also found to vary as were expectations with regard to academic achievement for black and Hispanic students in relation to white students. No consistent relationship between attitudes and performance were established in the NAEP surveys, but other research points to the significance of these in terms of the way students perceive tasks in relation to themselves. Hudson's work is of interest here. She established that there were differences in approach to problems for males and females and related students' typical responses to their attitudes to the subject and to themselves. Female attitudes had a detrimental effect on their performance (Hudson 1986). Wilder and Powell (1989) identify psychosocial variables such as these as important ones that warrant further research attention.

Another factor raised for consideration concerns the language of assessment (Lockheed *et al.* 1985). We mentioned in Chapter 5 that assessors assume that the purpose of an assessment item is self-evident. Language plays a critical role in communicating meaning in many subtle ways. It is easy to imagine how sub-groups may be differentially affected by the language used in tasks. The biases in the range of vocabulary used, the syntactic formation deployed and the use of idiomatic expressions were noted in the NAEP reading assessments (Tierney and Lapp 1979). One of the overwhelming findings of the APU science surveys was that students failed to achieve on items not because of errors but because of answering alternative tasks. Finally, with regard to racial and ethnic group performance, we cannot ignore the influence of the content and context of items.

The definition of a test domain represented in an assessment instrument can have a critical effect on the ultimate performance of ethnic groups. It is possible to alter the content of a test to advantage or disadvantage certain groups while maintaining the construct that the test is said to be assessing. We identified examples of this in the civics and history assessments. The evidence already referred to in the book makes it clear that aggregation of items to provide meaningful sub-scores depends on educational criteria not considered in the NAEP global aggregation procedure.

The content and context of items can also affect what students consider to be relevant in a task. We noted in Chapter 5 Cohen's

(1986) point about differences in learning styles with regard to gender.

Cohen makes a similar point about students from different ethnic and racial backgrounds whose learning styles (developed out of school) are at odds with those advocated in various curriculum subjects. These differences in style, if not taken into account by assessors, can have various detrimental effects on performance. For example, students may fail to respond to assessment items and so be unable to demonstrate their achievement; alternatively, they may pursue different tasks to those assumed by the assessor; or provide alternative, albeit equally adequate, solutions; or merely express their responses in ways which are devalued in certain domains and which are consequently attributed lower scores by assessors. Issues such as these bring into question the possibility of unidimensional measures and indeed the desirability of using such measures to inform curriculum policy.

Gender differences in performance are different in kind to ethnic group differences; however, there are useful parallels that can be drawn between the sources of these differences. One of the potential gender influences identified in NAEP work was students' differential out-of-school experiences (see, for example, the explanation for the difference between male and female performance on the mathematical measurement scale and the lower achievement of females in science: Dossey *et al.* 1988; Mullis and Jenkins 1988). In other cases, differences in sub-group performance are linked to possible sex differences in ability; for example, the documented difference in male and female spatial ability is raised to account for the performance gap between male and female students on the mathematics geometry scale (Dossey *et al.* 1988). In the science report, reference is also made to the differential treatment and opportunities afforded to male and female students, particular mention being made to teachers' higher expectations of boys than girls and the way they challenge boys and not girls during questioning sessions. The stereotypes in textbooks and the overtly masculine image of science are also raised to account for performance differences between male and female students. How these variables influence performance is not generally speculated upon, however.

The NAEP report authors, in attempting to interpret test differences, do not question the appropriateness of the items used or the model of analysis employed. The representation of the various curriculum subjects by the constructs defined on the proficiency scale and associated sub-scales are also reported uncritically. Indeed, test outcomes are used as a basis to challenge existing curriculum provision and pedagogy in schools.

To a large extent, though not entirely, these omissions are consistent within the theoretical perspective on achievement embodied in the model of analysis adopted by NAEP. If the assumptions in the model obtain then measured sub-group differences reflect differences in achievement on the defined construct. It follows from this that in any interpretations of performance differences, the measured differences are accepted as unproblematic. What is at issue, for NAEP is to *account* for the differences rather than to explore their validity. The issue of bias does not obtain, that is, that the test score has different meanings or implications for sub-groups of test-takers. However, all of the evidence presented so far would suggest that the assumptions in the NAEP model are untenable. Indeed, what is perhaps more difficult to explain is the adherence of NAEP to an IRM scale in the light of educational research findings and the insights provided by technical critiques of the use of such scales (Goldstein 1993b). The tenacity of people's beliefs about the nature of achievement in the face of conflicting evidence should not be underestimated in the field of assessment. The discussion in Chapter 7 of the national assessment system in the UK makes interesting reading against the backcloth of APU research reported in Chapter 5 for example.

In recent years, when NAEP results have been used to target problems with the school curriculum, concern has been expressed about the validity of the meaning attributed to NAEP scores. The fact that items, for example, demand an interaction of subject dimensions, i.e. processes, content, procedural and conceptual understandings and draw on knowledge of other subjects and within-school and out-of-school experiences has been cited as part of this concern. Items of varying complexity may appear at all levels of proficiency, hence what is actually being measured at a level on a NAEP scale may be masked. Research (e.g. Witt *et al.* 1990) suggests that analysis by item might reveal quite different trends in NAEP results, therefore we must be cautious when interpreting and comparing sub-group performance.

7

NATIONAL CURRICULUM ASSESSMENT

Introduction

The largest detailed assessment programme of recent years in the UK has been that related to the national curriculum. The national curriculum prescribes what shall be taught in the compulsory school years of 5–16. Subjects within the curriculum are divided up into sections or attainment targets, and these attainment targets (ATs) are described as a series of ten hierarchical levels by statements of attainment (SoAs) which act as assessment criteria.

National curriculum assessment involves continuous assessment by teachers throughout the key stages (5–7, 7–11, 11–14 and 14–16 years) against the attainment targets of the national curriculum, and assessment by external tests at the end of the key stages. Information from the assessment is for publication and reporting purposes at ages 7, 11, 14 and 16. The GCSE will be used to assess the national curriculum at 16. The blueprint for national assessment, the TGAT Report (DES 1988c), proposed that for the external assessment at 7, 11 and 14, standard assessment tasks or SATs be used; these were to be performance-type assessments with a range of response modes and style with practical, oral and written activities in a range of contexts so that the tasks would have face and content validity (i.e. match normal classroom tasks) and would not have undesired washback effects on the curriculum. These tasks have been used in 1990 and 1991 but presented serious problems of manageability and concerns about reliability (see Gipps 1992b; Torrance 1991). This original SAT model is being watered-down at Key Stage One and abandoned at Key Stage Three in favour of timed written exams. From late 1992, the name SAT was dropped – because of concerns from Educational Testing Services in the USA over confusion with their well-established Scholastic Aptitude Test, also known as the SAT (see Chapter 8) – and the assessments are now called standard tasks at age 7 and standard tests at 11 and 14 (STs). We shall refer to the tests as SATs since that is what they were, and were called, at the time.

At the time of writing, only age 7 (end of Key Stage One) and age 14 (end of Key Stage Three) were included in the testing programme, with ages 11 and 16 due to come on stream in 1994. In this chapter, we shall review the development of the assessment programme thus far to evaluate the test development agencies' approach, and that of the supervising body the Schools Examination and Assessment Council (SEAC), to equity issues and thereby explicate the hypotheses for differential group performance on which their model of assessment is built. This chapter is necessarily less detailed than other chapters, since the national curriculum assessment programme was in its infancy at the time of writing.

Key Stage One: Pilot testing 1990

The development programme began with a pilot survey in 1990 on a sample of pupils at the end of Key Stage One, i.e. year 2 (ages 6 and 7). The first national testing of all year 2 pupils followed in 1991. The pilot study involved three separate development agencies which developed different models of SATs, although within the framework of the SEAC requirements. At Key Stage One, certainly, the development teams took seriously the issue of assessing young bilingual children.

The Consortium for Assessment and Testing in Schools (CATS, based at the University of London) tried delivering assessment activities to bilingual children in a mixture of English and their first languages (CATS 1991a). This decision was based on teachers' expressed concern about very young bilingual children's disadvantage relative to their monolingual peers. However, the trialling process persuaded the CATS team not to translate materials for bilingual children, since most of the materials were in the form of directions to teachers with the SAT delivery being through teacher presentation. Thus instructions to teachers made it clear that they could administer the tasks in a mixture of English and the children's first language where this was appropriate. Other adults who were bilingual speakers were encouraged to assist the teacher, although only teachers were to administer the SATs. These arrangements were not without problems. Some children were not used to having their home language used in schools at all and found its sudden use disconcerting. Some schools had no access to adult speakers of the children's first languages and, of course, there are difficulties in translation: some words and concepts do not have direct equivalents in other languages. (None of these arrangements were permitted in the English SATs.)

As far as the assessment material was concerned, attempts were made to remove potential gender and cultural biases by the use of sensitivity review procedures. Assessment material was reviewed with the help of teachers and others in the LEAs where piloting was taking place. Where doubt persisted, 'advisers' views were canvassed and in the case of potential gender biases a small-scale trial was organized. The report of this team indicates that they felt this approach had been successful in removing inappropriate test content.

Analyses of the performance of a sample of bilingual children were carried out. Bilingual children were defined as all children with first languages other than English (apart from Welsh speakers; Welsh-speaking children were part of a separate development exercise.) This group of bilingual children therefore contained a broad mixture of children from very different language, cultural and social backgrounds. However, it was possible to identify one subgroup of Bengali-speaking children ($n = 353$). Overall, the bilingual children tended to perform better on the SATs than their Teacher Assessment (TA) had indicated.

This was particularly evident in the case of speaking and listening, while in maths the difference between TA and SAT was less clear. The development team therefore felt that the SATs did provide an opportunity for bilingual children to show their true performance. Although the children performed relatively better on SATs than TA, the bilingual children overall performed less well than other groups on the SATs. This, of course, would be expected, since these children are still in the early stages of becoming fluent English speakers and this would limit their learning in a range of areas. The feeling of the development team was that these children's good performance on the SATs allowed teachers to reconsider their opinions of the children's attainments and that this had been a worthwhile exercise.

As for gender differences, both the development team and some of the teachers were concerned about the suitability of some sections of the assessment materials for both boys and girls; specifically that some material was clearly male-oriented while other material was clearly female-oriented. The analysis showed that while there were many statements of attainment (the assessment criteria) which had proved easier for one sex than the other, there was no clear evidence that the SAT as a whole contained overall gender biases. 'The consortium therefore maintains its view that the prevention of potential gender biases is best tackled through the achievement of overall balance rather than by the removal of each assessment which fails to produce similar statistics for boys and for girls' (CATS 1991a: 103). This group was, therefore, explicit in not trying to aim for equal outcomes.

The National Foundation for Educational Research/Bishop Grosseteste College Consortium state that their assessment materials were produced with the aim of making as fair an assessment as possible of bilingual pupils (NFER/BGC 1991a). Their approach was to encourage the administration of SATs in a mixture of English and first languages and to raise teacher awareness of the problems that might be faced by bilingual pupils. Teachers were advised that all the activities could be introduced in the first language of pupils if possible. In maths and science, assessment might also be in the first language where this had been used for teaching purposes. English assessment was to be carried out in English only, although non-standard English dialects were acceptable in response. In the same way as the CATS consortium, they did not consider it necessary to produce SAT material in different languages, since the materials were mainly aimed at the teacher.

Where no bilingual support was available, teachers were encouraged to use mime, sign language, repetition or rewording, drawing and other methods including children's mutual help to explain the tasks. As with the CATS consortium, advice was that bilingual children were to be put into groups together so that they could work in their own language and feel more confident in engaging in the task. It was recognized that this would not help the small group of bilingual children who had no access to speakers of their first language. In respect of 'bias' in relation to gender, culture and ethnic group, the assessment materials were regularly reviewed by experts in the equal opportunities area. This team also felt it important to raise teacher awareness of bias issues in general and in particular of the different ways in which their 'delivery of SAT materials might encourage a biased response' (NFER/BGC 1991a: 28). It is not clear what was meant by this.

The NFER consortium analysed not only the SAT results by different group but also the teacher assessment results. They found that in maths, teacher assessment placed more boys at the extremes of achievement, i.e. at W (working towards level one) and level three, whereas more girls were in the middle range of achievement, at level two. (It was assumed that the majority of pupils would be at level 2 in attainment at Key Stage One, with a smaller proportion at levels 1 and 3.) In science, however, there were differences across the different attainment targets, with girls tending to be more highly rated by their teachers in the biological areas and boys more highly rated in the physical sciences; this as we have seen is a commonly observed pattern of reported gender difference. In English, on the other hand, the boys overall were judged to be at a lower level with the girls more likely to be at levels two and three. Teachers in the pilot study supplied information on the ethnic origins of the children and these were then grouped as white (89 per cent), black (3 per cent), Asian (6 per cent) and other (2 per cent). Children in white and other groups were more likely to be placed at level two on teacher assessment than the black and Asian groups. This pattern was particularly prevalent for English. Similarly, teachers provided information on the language used in the home and these were grouped into English (93 per cent), Indian (5.6 per cent), East Asian (0.4 per cent), European (0.9 per cent), Middle Eastern/African (0.4 per cent) and miscellaneous (0.2 per cent). (There are, of course, methodological problems in asking teachers to identify home language, since in many cases their information will not be exact. Also, to put together 'Indian', when there are many languages in the Indian subcontinent, adds to the crudeness of the measures. However, given the limitations on time and money under which the team was working, one may take the view that this was better than nothing.) The average ratings by the teachers of the smaller groups were lower than the ratings of Indian and English first-language children, and in turn the ratings of the Indian first-language children were lower than those of the English first-language children. As might be expected, on the English attainment targets overall, children whose first language was English were most likely to be judged at level two, while for those whose first language was not English equal numbers were judged to be at level one and level two, with more working towards level one and fewer at level three than English speakers.

The SAT assessment confirmed the pattern which had been produced in the teacher assessment data: the performance of bilingual pupils was lower in general than for other pupils by up to one level. The bilingual children seemed more insecure initially when presented with new work as in the SATs; when this was the case, the peer group became a very important source of support for the child beginning to learn English. In an assessment situation, however, this posed difficulties for the teacher in deciding whether the intervention of another pupil had clarified the child's understanding of the question or supplied the correct answer. The misunderstanding of instructions was a serious problem for bilingual pupils: they appeared to relax and respond better when questions were rephrased in the mother tongue; they became more motivated and handled tasks more confidently. When activities were lengthy and complex, there was a particular burden on bilingual children and examples of misunderstanding did not always come to light. Teachers felt that the bilingual children found it particularly difficult to show their true ability in maths and science. This was largely due to the difficulty of assessing oral responses in science interviews and the difficulties these children experienced in the group discussion element of science and maths investigations. In English, too, there was often the feeling that assessment did not show the real, hard-won achievements of bilingual children in their language development, as they often fell into the large band of achievement between level one and level two. Teachers were, however, keen to offer the full range of assessment to bilingual pupils so as not to restrict their opportunities.

Teachers in the 193 NFER pilot schools were asked to report whether they felt that SAT activities disadvantaged one gender rather than another. The authors of the report say that there was a noticeable absence of complaint in this respect. Where children worked in groups which were mixed, some teachers found that the boys were more dominant and the girls took a passive role, a commonly observed pattern of gendered performance. One teacher suggested science assessments in particular should be administered in single-sex groups. There was comment on bias in the illustrations provided in the pupil worksheets; for example, on the toys and games worksheet there were only males in the pictures showing different types of boats, which served to highlight the problem the authors found in achieving an overall balance of materials. The choice of reading books, however, met with widespread approval for featuring girls, boys, women and men in various active ways and presenting good role models. There was, on the other hand, concern that the booklist did not contain enough 'multicultural', particularly Asian, books. The only other comment on possible ethnic bias in the material concerned the specifying of an electric kettle and an electric cooker in one SAT activity. Some teachers commented that in Asian homes gas cookers are normally used and this was felt to leave some children at a disadvantage, though it must be noted that gas cookers are widely used and children other than those of Asian origin could have been disadvantaged. The report concludes: 'In other respects our materials prompted little comment on bias and we take this silence to be evidence that they were satisfactory in this respect' (NFER/BGC 1991a: 77–8).

The results for the SATs showed clear evidence of differential performance between boys and girls. In maths and science, as in the TA data, girls performed mostly in the middle ranges of achievement (levels 1 and 2), while there was a tendency for more boys to achieve at the extremes (working towards level 1 and at level 3): there was a higher incidence of level 3 scores for boys in both maths and science (except for the processes of science attainment target). In most cases, the differences between the distributions were highly significant. In English, scores were higher for girls overall except in listening and speaking where boys' and girls' achievements were balanced. In the other attainment targets (ATs), girls performed most frequently at levels 2 and 3, whereas boys were more often assessed as at working towards level 1 and at level 1. Significantly higher scores for girls were evident in reading. It was not felt by the test developers that any of the differences in scores were attributed to bias or unfairness in the tests but rather to actual differences in performance between boys and girls, and these differences did match the TA results.

As for the analysis by ethnic group, throughout the SAT data black, Asian and other groups performed in general less well than white groups, and Asian groups less well than black groups [this latter finding is not in line with other research on black and Asian performance with older pupils in the UK (see next chapter) and, the authors report, may be due to a particular aspect of the sampling or to the fact that the Asian children were beginning bilingual learners]. In English, the statements of attainment (SoAs) which involved pupils participating in extended discussion in a group or with a teacher appeared to discriminate particularly against black, Asian and other minority groups: where pupils had to describe what had happened in a story and predict what may happen next, demonstrate inference and deduction, etc., there were many more problems for the minority groups.

The third consortium, the Manchester University based Standard Testing and Assessment Implementation Research (STAIR) group, actually developed SAT material in English and Punjabi, the latter being written in Urdu script and an English transliteration of the Punjabi (STAIR 1991). Their aim was to address the three main difficulties in assessing the achievement of bilingual learners: the child's understanding of exactly what is required; the assessor's understanding of the child's response and the comfort and ease of the child in the assessment context; sources of invalidity in assessment which we discussed in Chapter 1.

The researchers found that girls had higher teacher assessments than boys, particularly in English, and that this was confirmed by their performance on the SAT. Through statistical analysis (not the DIF technique), they concluded that there was no bias in the task and that these results reflected real differences in performance. The researchers did not have enough confidence in the statistics they used, however, to conclude that there was no 'ethnic bias' in the assessment of maths and science. Whatever was happening, there was less of a difference between these groups in maths and science than there was in English. The authors conclude that 'the SAT has reduced the most marked differences in favour of girls in teacher assessment and that elsewhere there is little obvious sex bias in either direction' (STAIR 1991: 156). This report otherwise makes little comment about bilingual pupils or bias in regard to ethnic group.

The report from SEAC, which draws together the findings from the three consortia in relation to the pilot study, discusses various issues under the heading 'Differential Performance and Bias'. It points out that one needs to draw a distinction between the finding that different groups of children had different results and the conclusion that these differences are evidence of bias: some categories of children will show higher average performance than others, but it is important to check as far as possible from the evidence that those differences are reflections of real differences of attainment and are not due to something else. The examples they give are: a question may be less meaningful to one group of children; the assessor may interpret a criterion in different ways for different pupils; decisions may be taken to enter one group of children for some of the assessment but not others; the teacher's lack of familiarity with the area (e.g. science), which results in global assessments of children's performance which might involve over- or under-estimating (SEAC 1991e).

It is clear that at this stage of the development of national assessment materials, both the test development teams and the Council overseeing their work were thinking in terms of conceptual issues in the design of the assessments, rather than simply carrying out item analyses on the results. Thus there were sensitivity reviews of the material (looking for stereotypes or facial bias) and thought was given to how different groups of children understood the tasks; recognition was also given to sources of invalidity in the scoring and to teacher expectation effects. In our terms, then, at this stage of the Key Stage One development, environmental and psychosocial factors were being considered, as well as the content and administration of the tests, as contributing to differential group performance. It is important to recognize this because as we move into the later stages of development and production, and pressures of time increased for the teams, these concerns are less evident. The focus moves to the results and there is a commentary on measured group differences but no serious discussion of how these might be caused.

What is not clear is the extent to which, if any, the pilot experience was built upon in the next phase: the contract to develop the 1991 SAT material for Key Stage One was won by the NFER/BGC consortium, but the framework was modified with fewer attainment targets tested in more depth.

Key Stage One: Summer 1991 testing

Reports on the Key Stage One 1991 national assessment programme come from three different sources: first, from a sample of LEAs and schools studied by the NFER; second, from a report published by the Department of Education and Science, which contains all the national assessment results forwarded to the department by LEAs; and, third, from an evaluation funded by SEAC and carried out by the University of Leeds. We shall look at each of these in turn.

The NFER carried out a number of pieces of research into the results of the Summer 1991 Key Stage One assessment. For teacher assessment (TA), they analysed questionnaire responses from 240 schools containing Year 2 children and 11 special schools drawn from a nationally representative sample (SEAC 1991f). This was supported by 'case studies' in 38 schools chosen in consultation with LEA advisers to represent specific issues. In the event, schools with large numbers of ethnic minority pupils and those with special needs were under-represented. This is perhaps why there were few comments reported by case-study schools about difficulties in assessing children (via TA) who were not fully fluent in English, except that some teachers found it difficult to assess fairly 'know that' and 'understand' in science for these children. For the SATs, the sample of teachers filled out lengthy questionnaires, which included three questions about the suitability of the SAT materials for children who are not fluent in English or whether any activities disadvantaged any particular group, 'e.g. girls, boys, ethnic minorities?' (NFER/BGC 1991b). About 60 teachers in the sample taught children not fully fluent in English; only one-third of these teachers considered the SATs which assessed the maths and science processes as satisfactory. No details are given of why the teachers viewed them so, but presumably because they are highly language-dependent (as reported in the pilot, above). Twenty-two per cent of teachers felt that the SATs disadvantaged one group or other, but again no further details are given, nor is this finding further discussed. That over one-fifth of teachers thought the SATs biased is, one might think, highly significant, although the NFER and SEAC do not seem to recognize this as an issue. Over 90 per cent of the headteachers in the sample said that they thought the materials were free from gender or racial bias – the disparity between the heads' views and those of the year two teachers is probably due to the fact that the teachers were more familiar with the material and actually observed the children performing on it. Similarly, more heads, 42 per cent, were satisfied with their suitability for children not fluent in English.

A pupil record sheet containing the final results for children assessed was obtained from 260 schools covering 5345 children. The schools were chosen to form a nationally representative sample, but in the event the South-East region was slightly under-represented as were infant schools (SEAC 1992a). Using these final results (i.e. a composite of TA and/or SAT), analyses of differential performance were made. Girls performed significantly better in all areas of English and similarly in maths (although the differences were less marked). At the subject level, in science there were no gender differences, although there was a difference (in favour of girls) in profile component 2 (knowledge and understanding of science). The results were also analysed by ethnic group: ethnicity was reported by teachers and grouped as white, black, Asian and other. The authors report that the total size of the minority sample ($n = 460$) was too small to draw reliable inferences, but nevertheless go on to say that black and Asian children did less well than white children in all three subjects. Similarly, for the 300 children for whom English was not reported to be the home language, performance was significantly lower than for those for whom it was. (Evidence was also obtained that younger children (i.e. summer born) and those who had spent less time in school performed less well.) This evaluation report does not discuss these differential performance issues in any detail but makes the point that 'Fuller research is necessary in order to explore these indications in depth and to suggest reasons for them, and strategies to be applied in response to them' (SEAC 1992a: 87). What is interesting is that the NFER authors do not compare them with some of their findings about the suitability of the materials for the different groups studied, as included in their earlier report mentioned above (NFER/BGC 1991b). Finally, we must note that details of scrutiny for item content bias or analysis of statistical item bias during the development of the Key Stage One SATs for 1991 do not appear to be available.

The DES (1991) report is based on the assessment of approximately 500 000 7-year-olds. This is not the full population of 7-year-olds, since three LEAs did not send forward their results. In addition, LEAs who sent forward their results did not all send the entire set, presumably because they had not received the results from all schools. This sample also includes 10 000 pupils in independent schools and these are included in the national figures (but not where individual LEAs are analysed). This report, unlike the NFER report, does not separate out teacher assessment and SAT result and compare the two. It only includes the final results which were sent to the DES. The results for each profile component of the subject and attainment target are given broken down for gender. The girls show higher attainment than boys in all subjects but the difference is most marked in English. In English overall, 83 per cent of girls were at level 2 or 3 compared to 72 per cent of boys. While approximately equal proportions of boys and girls perform at level 2, the differences are most marked at either ends of the achievement spectrum: 25 per cent of boys score at level one, whereas only 16 per cent of girls do; while 21 per cent of girls score at level 3, with only 14 per cent of boys doing so. This same pattern is repeated for the separate attainment targets of listening and speaking, reading, and writing. The differences in maths between boys and girls are less marked than for English: 67 per cent of girls are at level two compared to 64 per cent of boys, while the same proportions of boys and girls are at level 3. In profile component 1 (i.e. number, algebra and measures) the relative performance of boys and girls closely reflects that in maths as a whole, while in profile component 2 (space, shape and data handling) there was less difference in their performance, although a slightly higher proportion of girls were at level 2. In science, boys and girls performed on average at a very similar level, although within the separate attainment targets there tend to be higher percentages of girls scoring at level two and fewer girls scoring at level one.

The Leeds University Evaluation (SEAC 1992b) looked at a sample of children (10 per school in a representative sample of schools within a total of 17 LEAs). This evaluation looked at the teacher assessment results, the SAT results and made additional detailed assessments of the children's achievement, since part of the evaluation's task was to check on the validity and reliability of the SAT and teacher assessment results. The TA and SAT results were collected from an overall sample of 2500+ children: a smaller group were given the extra assessments. [It is interesting to note that there are generally low levels of agreement between teacher assessment and SAT for the attainment targets which were also tested by SATs. For science, the correspondence is particularly poor. The best levels of agreement were in reading, spelling and maths attainment target 13 (handling data).] The gender differences observed are roughly similar to those described in the overall figures given by the DES: at the subject level, the profile component level and the attainment target level, girls' scores are significantly better than those of boys in English. In maths and science at the subject and profile component level, there were no statistically significant differences between girls and boys. However, a more detailed breakdown at attainment target level showed that girls significantly out-performed boys on some of the attainment targets: maths 2 (number), maths 5 (algebra), science 5 (human influences on the Earth), science 13 (energy) and science 16 (the Earth in space). In maths, only maths 5 was assessed by SAT as well as TA: girls did not perform significantly better on the SAT. In science, only science 5 was also assessed by SAT and girls performed significantly better on this as well as TA. Thus from the NFER and Leeds evaluations, and the DES figures, it is clear that wherever there are gender differences, it is in favour of the girls and these differences are particularly marked in English.

The Leeds evaluation also looked at the performance of children from different ethnic backgrounds. Although schools were asked to record details of ethnic background along the lines of the categories used in the 1991 census, the numbers in some of the groups were very small, so that in the event the only groups used for analysis were black Caribbean, Indian and Pakistani as well as white. Pakistani children tended to attain lower levels in all three subjects than other ethnic groups, while black Caribbean and

Indian children tended to attain lower levels than white children in English and maths but not science. The report offers, by way of explanation: 'A major factor in some of these differences was the fact that the home language of many of the children from different ethnic origins was not English' (SEAC 1992b: 101). This, of course, may explain differences between 'white' (if they were English-speaking) and Indian or Pakistani, but would not explain the difference between the Pakistani and Indian samples. The analysis by 'English home language' and 'non-English home language' showed that at the subject and AT levels, for both TA and SAT, the former group scored significantly higher than the latter in all subjects.

Despite the difficulties, acknowledged by the Leeds team, of obtaining valid and reliable information about the social background of children, analysis was carried out by social class. Information was collected on the children's post code (zip code): this information is widely used in market research to identify social background but is a crude measure. The large number of categories were collapsed into four social background groups to give: high-status affluent housing, higher intermediate status, lower intermediate status and low status. Using what the report describes as 'these fairly broad indicators of social background', the analysis of both teacher assessment and SAT revealed a declining pattern of performance with declining status of residential neighbourhood. However, there is no suggestion in the report that the materials were biased in relation to social class background.

The Leeds evaluation offers no discussion of any reasons for differential group performance other than the 'obvious' one of mother-tongue. The observed social class differences are in the 'expected' direction and this may be why there is no discussion of whether the materials themselves were equally appropriate for/fair to all social class groups (or indeed ethnic group or gender). It may, of course, be that the evaluation team saw their task as looking at outcomes rather than causes. Either way, the level of discussion of differential group performance and its causes is disappointing compared with the pilot reports.

Key Stage Three: Pilot testing 1991

As with Key Stage One, a range of consortia was involved in developing SAT materials. One of these, the CATS consortium, carried out pilot testing on a roughly 2 per cent sample in English, maths, science and design and technology. The reports of these pilots contain information about differential performance by gender and by ethnic group and for some also by language, so we will look at the CATS reports in some detail.

Maths

In maths, for a total of 17 500 pupils, background data were available as well as SAT and TA scores. (CATS 1991b) A cross-tabulation of ethnicity and special educational need indicated that a higher percentage than average of Pakistani, black African and black Afro-Caribbean pupils were categorized by their schools as having special educational needs. For Pakistani pupils this was 20 per cent, black African 18 per cent and black Afro-Caribbean 17 per cent. The cross-tabulation of sex with special educational need indicates that 70 per cent of the pupils identified as having special educational needs are boys; these figures do not include the 2 per cent of children who had a statement of special educational need. In the SATs, girls scored approximately 0.2 levels higher than boys on every attainment target; this was similar to the difference observed in TA scores. The authors conclude that the results indicate that the SAT was unbiased in the assessment of girls and boys in that its results reflect those of TA. As for ethnicity, the results suggested that the SAT was not biased in terms of ethnic group either, but the sample sizes were too small for any firm findings to be stated. Data were collected on the degree of fluency for each pupil whose home language was not English; again sample sizes were small but it appears that fluent pupils performed as well as English first-language pupils in teacher assessment and SAT in mathematics and sometimes better. It was also clear that in teacher assessment, non-fluent pupils attained approximately one level below other pupils.

Feedback from the teacher questionnaire throws some light on the teachers' views about the suitability of the SATs for children who are not fluent in English (although only 50 teachers responded to this part of the questionnaire). What became clear from these responses is that the nature of the SAT rendered it accessible to pupils who were not fluent in English. Aspects which contributed to this included: interaction with the teacher, the practical elements of the tasks, a normal classroom atmosphere, interactions with other pupils, and the variety of presentation and assessment modes. The conclusion made is that for pupils who were not fluent in English, written materials cannot enable the demonstration of attainment without teacher–pupil interaction. Eighty-three per cent of these teachers felt that pupils who were not fluent in English *could* engage in the SAT activity. Thus the style of the activity was appropriate for most of these pupils. However, only a third of teachers thought that the SAT enabled pupils to demonstrate appropriate attainment. This comment no doubt is related to the fact that overall the attainment of non-fluent pupils was below that of others in both the SAT and the TA. However, analysis of the SATs showed that pupils who were *not* fluent were scoring higher on the SAT than in the TA, which suggests that the TA awarded by the teachers may have been an underestimate due to the pupils' perceived language difficulties, and that the SATs facilitated high performance for non-fluent pupils to a greater extent than it did for others. The pilot report of the maths scheme states that: 'if pupils who are not fluent in English are to be entitled to a fair assessment it is essential that the SATs retain the interactive, practical and flexible aspects'.

English

For English, a total of 12 208 pupils had background information, TA and SAT results (CATS 1991c). This sample was made up of 90 per cent white Europeans, 90 per cent of whom had English as their home language; 10 per cent of the pupils were identified as having some special educational need (of whom 1.5 per cent had *statements* of special educational need). The mean achievement of girls in the SAT was half a level higher than that of boys, with more than twice as many girls scoring at the higher levels of 7, 8 and 9 (at Key Stage Three the full range of levels 1–10 are available to pupils) with the boys correspondingly over-represented at the bottom levels 1, 2, 3 and 4; this matches the pattern for English at Key Stage One. The difference between the mean levels of attainment for girls and boys was even wider in teacher assessment, which suggests that the boys had benefited slightly from the SATs, though the authors do not suggest the existence of bias in TA on such a small difference. The slightly higher than expected levels for boys on the SATs may indicate that the sort of test condition present in the SAT favours boys rather than girls, say the authors. However, a detailed analysis of gender differences on specific attainment targets comparing SAT and TA show that the same differences apply between genders within attainment targets. Thus the authors conclude that the differences observed are not ones generated by any particular SAT or attainment target, but reflect real differences in the respective attainments of girls and boys in this population of pupils.

Ten per cent of the sample was classified as belonging to ethnic groups other than white European. The mean levels of attainment in the SAT were considerably below the average of the whole group for both Pakistani and Bangladeshi pupils. Those for Afro-Caribbean, Indian and African pupils were slightly lower, while those for Chinese and 'other black' pupils were higher than the mean. (Since there were only 29 Chinese pupils in the sample and only 35 African pupils, it seems unwise to draw conclusions from these figures but the authors do not seem to make this point.) The same pattern of distribution is observed for teacher assessment. The below-average levels of these groups of pupils is consistent with other national data and the authors feel that the SAT was neutral in that it neither raised nor lowered their attainment levels. The lower levels for Pakistani and Bangladeshi pupils were probably accounted for by linguistic and gender differences: there is evidence in their data that the boys heavily outnumber girls in the samples of pupils from Urdu-, Bengali- and Punjabi-speaking families. (There were few single-sex schools in the sample and it is likely that Muslim girls were in single-sex schools, while boys are more likely to be in mixed schools.) This absence of girls would partly account for the lower performance of the Pakistani and Bangladeshi group. Just under 10 per cent of the sample had a main language other than English at home: the mean levels of attainment in the SAT were noticeably lower for Urdu, Bengali and Punjabi speakers, while for those who were Hindi, Welsh and Gujerati speakers levels were higher than average. The authors conclude that this is unlikely to be the result of bias in the SATs, since the mean levels of teacher assessment showed a very similar pattern. (It is clear throughout these CATS Key Stage Three pilot reports that the authors are using the correspondence between performance in teacher assessment and SAT to indicate lack of bias in the SAT. It is possible, however, that there is some tautology in this argument, since it was the same teachers who were also administering and marking the SAT.)

Science

The science sample involved 16 000 pupils in 137 schools in 37 LEAs. When the mean levels in each attainment target in the SAT were compared, there was a difference in performance in favour of the girls ranging from 0.1 to 0.3 of a level (CATS 1991d). However, when the attainment targets were broken down, in only 5 out of 139 SoAs in the SAT did the performance of boys and girls differ significantly. The authors argue that these findings are echoed by teachers, 97 per cent of whom felt that there was no gender bias in the assessment materials. When the mean assessment levels were compared, girls were similarly awarded TA levels which were higher than boys by 0.1 to 0.2 of a level. The performance of pupils from different ethnic backgrounds was compared despite there being very small numbers in some of the groups (e.g. 48 Bangladeshi pupils compared with 10 067 white pupils). Looking at their differences in performance on the attainment targets for TA and SAT compared with the total sample, the authors conclude that it appears that assessment within the pilot SAT did not disadvantage pupils in any of these ethnic categories. As for analysis of bilingual learners, the numbers of pupils in the sample who spoke anything other than English as their main language at home was very small. This group was made up of Welsh (2.85 per cent), Gujerati (0.97 per cent) and Urdu (0.58 per cent) speakers. As a result, no analyses by level of fluency of English speaking was carried out.

Design and technology

The evidence from the design and technology SAT suggested that there was very little that girls did not do better than boys (CATS 1991e). They had better mean scores at both overall levels and attainment target level. This difference was largely the same as for teacher assessment. The boys appear to be slightly under-predicted in TA, however. The pattern observed in Key Stage One for English that the girls are more highly represented at the higher levels and the boys more highly represented at the lower levels, was again the same in design and technology at Key Stage Three; this pattern was there for teacher assessment and was 'exaggerated' in the SAT scores. This pattern runs right through the attainment targets. In this subject area, there were no analyses made by ethnic group or English-language fluency. The guidance material suggested that teachers employed their usual means of helping bilingual learners gain access to the activities. Some feedback suggested that there was a very demanding level of language required in the activities and that this disadvantaged the bilingual pupils.

Teachers also rated pupils in the design and technology sample for fluency in English. They used four categories in ascending order of amount of help needed. The pattern shown in SAT score matched the categorization of the level of help required, i.e. the higher the fluency the higher the score. However, those least fluent in English scored slightly higher in the SAT than the teacher assessment. The authors conclude either that the SAT benefited these pupils or that they had made some progress with their language since the teacher assessment had been made. We might also surmise that teachers had underrated the less fluent English speakers.

Discussion

The report from SEAC which draws together the Key Stage Three findings in the 1991 pilot (SEAC 1991g) from the various agencies (not just the CATS reports discussed here) concludes that in all subjects girls are attaining higher levels than boys. This it goes on to say is not surprising, except in the case of maths, 'since the evidence at GCSE shows girls doing considerably less well than boys in this subject' (p. 26). They ask the question as to whether this is anything to do with the way the assessment is being made at Key Stage Three. It will be important to consider, it goes on, whether the smaller number of new attainment targets in the new curriculum structure in 1992–93 will militate against girls. This report does not discuss performance by ethnic group (presumably because the sample sizes were small) but points out that for bilingual learners performance was 'relatively high'. This they suspect is because teachers were able to provide the normal classroom support for these pupils during the SATs, that the materials were generally accessible to pupils whose home language is not English, and that the opportunity for these pupils to demonstrate their full potential if the SATs change to timed written tests will be reduced (as will be the case for pupils with special educational needs).

Conclusions

A general picture emerges at ages 7 (in 1990 and 1991) and 14 (in 1991) of girls scoring higher than boys particularly in English and maths; more boys scoring at the extremes; minority ethnic groups scoring lower than 'white' children; those whose home language is not English scoring significantly less well; teacher assessment lower than the SAT score for children from ethnic minorities and/or whose home language is not English.

The very gross analyses of performance by ethnic group, particularly at Key Stage One, and the small size of the samples involved, however, mean that it is difficult to know how much weight to place on these findings. In addition, there is no evidence given of statistical analyses for differential item functioning and no information about sensitivity review procedures in the development of the tasks and materials for 1991. (Indeed, the rather hastily produced reading comprehension test and spelling test for Key Stage One in 1992 appear to be highly culturally specific and unfair to groups other than English-speaking middle-class.) Some attempt was made to ask teachers about 'bias' in the materials, but more information is available about this at the pilot stages than at the later stage; this is unfortunate, since the tasks changed quite considerably from one stage to the next. It could also be argued that it is the test developers' responsibility to *avoid* bias, not merely to ask teachers for their opinion as to whether or not it is present. There were also changes in the SAT model for Key Stage Three from 1991 to 1993: the government insisted on a shift away from performance assessments to short, timed, written tests that can be taken in controlled conditions. This has considerable equity implications for some of the test-taking groups, for, despite the disappointing level of analysis of differential performance and 'bias', an interesting point has emerged. The SAT-type activity with its emphasis on active, multi-mode assessment and detailed interaction between teacher and pupil may, despite the heavy reliance on language, be a better opportunity for minority and special needs children to demonstrate what they know and can do than traditional, formal tests with limited instructions. This point is made quite strongly in the SEAC review of the Key Stage Three pilots:

> The relative success of the 1991 SATS for children with special educational needs and English as a second language will be reduced in 1992, unless procedures are established to allow the 1992 tests to be used flexibly with these pupils . . . [and] . . . The differential performance of boys and girls is likely to be affected by the change to a largely written mode of assessment. It is important that this is monitored.
>
> (SEAC 1991g: 2)

At age 7, there is unlikely to be a complete shift to timed written tests but similar concerns arise as the SAT model is diluted and practical interactive tasks in a normal classroom setting are reduced. In an independent study of national assessment in primary schools, teachers reported strong feelings that the national assessment programme at age 7 was inevitably unjust for bilingual children (Gipps 1992a). Since their English language skills were still in the early stages of development, these children were disadvantaged in any assessment that was carried out for comparative purposes. These teachers felt that formal summative (or accountability) assessment for comparison is, at this age, unfair for such children and thus runs counter to their notion of equity. These teachers had similar views about children from disadvantaged backgrounds, but their feelings about bilingual learners were particularly strong.

The working definition of 'bias' that has been used by the CATS team at Key Stage Three is at first sight perhaps neat, but is in fact deeply flawed. Correspondence between TA and SAT is seen to offer evidence that the SAT is not biased. However, this can be criticized on two grounds. First, it is teachers who are responsible for making the judgements in *both* TA and SAT, so making major distinctions between them seems unwarranted. Second, there are many reasons why TA and SAT need not align. Indeed, the Leeds evaluation at Key Stage One (SEAC 1992b) found rather less of this alignment than was expected. In principle, these were good reasons for expecting that SAT and TA would align, viz. the same children being assessed by the same criteria and by the same people. In fact, however, there was considerable variation in the interpretation of the assessment criteria (the SoAs) and the determination of mastery by the teachers. Mastery decisions could have been different in TA from those required for the SAT: for the SAT, children only had to get all but one of the SoAs correct in order to be credited with that attainment target, while for TA no such rule was in operation and we do not know how the teachers made their mastery decisions for TA. SATs were also carried out later in the term when the teachers might have been clearer about the assessment *and* the children may indeed have progressed in terms of what they were able to achieve.

Thus, expecting TA and SAT to agree is problematic in itself (and the evidence at Key Stage One indicates that in many instances they did not agree), so taking agreement to be evidence of lack of bias is even more worrying. Indeed, the SEAC review of Key Stage Three, which was written later than these other documents, appears to be suggesting that TA and SAT are different. While TA may be less standardized and accurate than SATs, because it covers a much wider range of attainments over a longer period of time, it is more thorough and offers a better description of a child's overall attainment. As SATs become shorter tests covering less of the national curriculum, this difference, between TA and test results, will increase. TA is useful for teachers and parents in providing information on an individual's strengths and weaknesses, but will be less use for comparing performance across schools. 'The two forms of assessment should not therefore be regarded as identical' (SEAC 1991g: 34).

This review also makes the point that the shift to shorter written tests may depress the scores of girls and reinforce the current imbalance of subject take-up beyond GCSE, unless TA has a major role to play in determining national assessment results. At the time of writing, TA seems to be becoming less important within the national assessment programme; we will indeed have to monitor the effect of the changes in the testing programme.

In our terms, the consideration of differential performance and its causes within the national assessment programme have been limited. SEAC, the supervising body, did not articulate a (theoretical) position in relation to equity issues. This is not to suggest that the individuals concerned did not care about such issues, but that they did not appear to articulate a rationale on which test development was to be based, although the consortia did by and large state their position at the pilot stage. Lack of guidance, however, and increasingly, lack of time, led to limited considerations of group differences in performance and insubstantial or even invalid analyses of these.

What is clear is that none of these consortia or SEAC was looking for equal outcomes (as discussed in Chapter 1), so there was no attempt to eliminate items in order to bring group scores into line. Factors within the test material itself were acknowledged to contribute to differential group performance, so each consortium carried out sensitivity reviews of material using panels of teachers and others to eliminate any stereotyped or 'biased' material. Factors within the administration were also considered in relation to the particular qualities of the SAT, and it was acknowledged that some of the SAT's key features rendered the assessment tasks more accessible, and therefore more fair, to SEN pupils and pupils whose second language was English than traditional formal assessments.

By and large, the reports do not question the findings in relation to gender and other differences in performance (except to question girls' superiority in maths at 14), since the pattern accords with much of the evidence we already have in relation to the performance of different groups. There is no explicit discussion of the causes of this pattern; certainly, biological factors are not mentioned and the only environmental factor referred to (in relation to teacher assessment) is teacher expectation related to stereotype. No doubt because the findings fit perceived 'current wisdom', there is felt to be no need to investigate any further. Similarly, presumably because they have to assess the curriculum as given, there is no questioning of the constructs being assessed, although there must have been considerable discussion about the constructs when the SoAs were actually used as assessment criteria. Interestingly, the finding that pupils whose second language is English often scored higher on the SAT than on teacher assessment is presented as an argument for the equitable or benevolent nature of the assessment programme.

To conclude, it is of concern that the national curriculum assessment programme is moving towards a more traditional testing model (secondary schools are buying optical mark readers in the American style) which has implications for equity issues, while at the same time equity issues are slipping down the agenda. The current government has little interest in equity, and the speed of test development is so great, and the curriculum and assessment changes so regular, that the test development agencies have little time to carry out detailed analyses and trialling to ensure that the tests are as fair as possible to all groups.

8

EXAMINATION PERFORMANCE

In this chapter, we shall review the research into differential performance in examinations at 16 +, first in relation to gender and then in relation to ethnic and racial group. We focus next on examination performance at 18 in the UK and college-entry tests in the USA. We follow this with a look at the few studies there have been on gender differences in performance at degree level.

Examinations at 16 +

Differential performance by gender

A recent review of gender bias in examinations (Stobart *et al.* 1992a) argues for social rather than physiological explanations to account for male and female differences in examination performance, i.e. environmental and psychosocial factors as opposed to biological hypotheses. The authors cite the 'relative changes in performances over the past century' which in their view 'are likely to reflect changing social structures and expectations rather than the rapid evolution of the female brain and nervous system' (ibid.: 5).

A not dissimilar point is made by Halpern in her critique of the apparent trends in SAT-V scores (see Chapter 2). While this view of the importance of social explanations corresponds to our perspective, it must be remembered that research into gender differences has tended to follow initiatives in assessment practice. Hence these documented 'relative changes' often correspond to a shift in the values underpinning assessment. For example, in the UK, course-work was introduced into many examinations at 16+ because it provided opportunities to measure valued aspects of students' achievement that traditional measures could not cater for. Recent controversies concerning what should be assessed in particular subjects have also highlighted the different values of various pressure groups in education: the furore over the assessment of empathy in history, and the decision to assess spelling in subjects at GCSE are but two examples of this. These changing values determine how subjects are defined and what constitutes 'success' in them. Therefore, although social factors are clearly influential, we should also consider the possibility that the redefinition of achievement may result in a new emphasis on the 'innate' or learned abilities of one sub-group rather than another.

Mode of response in assessment

Harding's research in the late 1970s was initiated in response to teachers' concerns that girls were experiencing difficulty with the 'Nuffield approach' to learning science in the UK (Harding and Craig 1978). This was at a time when girls' under-representation in the physical sciences at GCE and CSE were already a cause of grave concern. The introduction of Nuffield science courses and corresponding exam syllabuses marked a move away from 'cookbook' exercises to verify theory to a 'guided discovery' approach to learning. Hence students were more involved in the 'process of being a scientist' and were expected to exhibit an understanding of this process in practical and written assessment situations. Harding and Craig's analysis focused on three Nuffield science teaching project examinations in physics, chemistry and biology, and one examination in each of these three sciences from 'more traditional syllabuses' in use at the time. The sample selected was also stratified by school type, i.e. single-sex/mixed, and grammar/comprehensive/direct grant/independent. While no overall differences in performance were found, sub-group differences did emerge. These revealed that: boys from mixed schools were more successful in science examinations than girls from mixed schools; girls from single-sex schools did better than their peers in mixed schools; and boys in comprehensive schools were more successful than girls in comprehensive schools.

The candidates' results were also compared for different *parts* of each examination. Sex differences in performance in favour of boys on three of the four multiple-choice papers were found. The one paper containing essay questions ('conventional' biology) was the only part of any examination in which girls were significantly more successful than boys. Writing later about these findings, Harding (1979) quoted Ferguson's research into the University of London Schools Examinations Board GCE O Level Biology in support of her view that the mode of examination was biased. The London Board changed the exam format in 1976 and introduced a multiple-choice paper. Ferguson (1977) found that boys gained significantly higher mean marks in the multiple-choice paper, while girls gained the higher means in the essay questions. In conclusion, Harding (1979: 284) comments: 'we frequently equate achievement with ability and yet evidence discussed here suggests that achievement may be contextually related, differently so, for boys and girls as separate groups'.

A further study by Hoste (1981) analysed a CSE Biology examination and found significant differences in boys' and girls' choice of question combinations and in their performance on different assessment modes. Hoste (1981: 7) stated:

> . . . there is a divide between the practical and multiple choice section of the examination on the one hand and the structured question section on the other. In the former boys score more highly (after allowing for ability in Biology) on nine out of ten items whilst in the latter girls score more highly on sixteen out of seventeen items.

With regard to the multiple-choice items, Hoste could find nothing in common apart from mode of response on the questions where boys out-performed girls. Hoste explained girls' superiority on structured tasks in terms of their greater verbal skills.

Murphy (1980) undertook a review of GCE O and A Level entry statistics and examination results for the years 1951–77. The review revealed sex differences in entry patterns which had changed over the years. For example, in 1951, the A Level entries for males and females in English and French were similar, but by 1977 almost twice as many females as males were entered for both. The gap between male and female entries overall since 1963 had narrowed for O Level and, to a lesser extent, during the 1970s, for A Level entries.

The statistics showed that females in almost every subject achieved a higher pass rate at O and A Level than males. Murphy identified two popular hypotheses about the sources of gender differences as possible explanations for the findings. The O Level pattern of performance, for example, might reflect the advantage girls gain from their earlier maturation. This was a hypothesis discussed in Chapter 2 for which there was little supporting evidence. The superior performance of girls at A Level could be attributed to their being a 'smaller more select group' (Murphy 1980: 8). Murphy saw some support for this latter explanation in the narrowing of the difference between the A Level pass rates of males and females as their entry statistics came 'more into line'.

Murphy looked in detail at the Geography O Level examination set by the Associated Examining Board (AEB) to explore other possible sources of these sex differentiated trends in the overall statistics. The pass rates for girls and boys had always been similar on this exam until changes were made to the assessment scheme in 1977. A consequence of these changes was that 10 per cent more boys than girls achieved grades A–C. Murphy's explanation for the higher performance of boys was the advantage they gained from the introduction of an objective test, i.e. one with a multiple-choice response format. Boys were found to perform at a higher level on the objective paper than the written paper. Murphy (1980: 11) concluded that: 'the average advantage gained by the male candidates on the objective test paper of between 5 and 7 marks stands out as being clearly the most important factor which contributes to their higher overall pass rate'. An extension of the enquiry to include all AEB examinations which provided both multiple-choice and an alternative mode of assessment showed that the performance of boys is improved relative to girls when objective tests replace written tests (Murphy 1982).

Newbould's work at the Cambridge Test Development and Research Unit has been cited in recent publications as providing further evidence that boys perform better on objective tests relative to girls than on any other test form (Newbould and Scanlon 1981). However, Newbould's comments on the analysis of boys' and girls' performance on A Level Biology, Chemistry and Physics reveals a more complex perspective on the issue (Newbould 1980). He suggests that males outscore females more in certain situations than in others. One such situation is within a multiple-choice test. Furthermore, within such a test, 'there are tendencies, if no more, to suggest that this "sex-bias" is more likely to occur in some subjects rather than others and where the specific demands of the items focus upon higher skills or non-verbal operations (Newbould 1980: 9).'

In Newbould's (and Murphy's) view, the issue is not the form of response itself, but the 'way in which the form is perceived within the context of the subject' (Newbould 1980: 9). Newbould concludes that it is the skill demanded by the item that is the major factor in creating 'sex-bias'. This would suggest that it is the constructs used to define achievement and how mode of response mediates these that needs to be explored in a search for 'fairness' in examinations.

Murphy (1981) used Assessment of Performance Unit (APU) tasks to follow up some of the issues raised by this research into mode of response. In her small-scale study, four schools were used and in each school one second-year and two fourth-year classes were sampled. The study was unusual in that the *same task* was used but with either a multiple-choice response option or a free response option. As multiple-choice answers typically represent quite generalized correct responses, the free response items were dual-marked, first in a way that directly corresponded to the demands represented in the multiple-choice item correct response, and second allowing for a more finely judged response. It was hoped in this way to take careful account of the construct being assessed. Differences in the ability of the sample were allowed for when comparing sub-group performance. Pupils' perceptions of the tasks and feelings about items were collected to help interpret the data.

The findings showed no significant differences on the tests at age 13 but at age 15 boys were out-performing girls across the range of tests used. This was consistent with the APU survey results at age 15 for similar tasks assessing pupils' ability to interpret information. Murphy's interpretation of these findings was that using the same task and ensuring that identical mark schemes were used for both response forms had helped to keep the construct being assessed 'stable' across the different modes of response. The findings at age 15 showed the general superiority gained by boys on this aspect of science irrespective of mode or the skill being assessed. The interview findings revealed the link between pupils' affective and cognitive responses to assessment tasks: all pupils considered the free response items to be more difficult and the results reflected this. Boys at age 15 in particular expressed their anxiety about the free response mode of assessment. Girls, on the other hand, expressed a dislike of multiple-choice items because 'you don't have to think'. Girls rather than boys expressed a concern about their lack of knowledge of the information to be interpreted in the items, although in theory no specific knowledge was required to answer them. This is another instance where girls' lack of self-confidence in their ability is seen to affect their response to assessment items. There is a link here with Hudson's (1986) findings about girls' characteristic ways of responding to items that we discussed in Chapter 6. Murphy suggested that the different modes of response tended to alter the constructs being assessed in the different parts of the examinations. However, unlike Newbould, she considered these altered constructs to reflect gendered learning styles which may be accorded different values depending on the subject being assessed. In this sense, the researchers agree about the subject dependency of the effects.

More recent research has also focused on the influence of method of measurement on scholastic achievement. Bolger and Kellaghan (1990) examined the performance of 15-year-old boys and girls in Irish schools on multiple-choice standardized tests and free response examinations of mathematics, Irish and English achievement. The two forms of tests covered the same content and skills but did differ in the type of demand made and whether choice on items was available. The results revealed that males performed relatively better than females on multiple-choice assessment compared with free response examinations and the converse was true for females. The effect of measurement method was found across the domains. In the authors' view, the generalizability of the effect brought into question the hypothesis that the method–gender relationship is due to the superior verbal ability of girls. As Chapters

2 and 5 show, this was often an argument put forward to explain a female advantage on measures of a range of abilities.

The explanations the authors considered included the differential familiarity of the male and female samples with the test items. Thus Bolger and Kellaghan suggest that females perform less well than males on items in the standardized tests as these were 'novel', whereas items in the examinations corresponded to typical school assessment tasks and were therefore familiar. Another explanation considered to have merit was the influence of assessors' expectations and values on judgements made on the free response assessments. Markers in the study were aware of the gender of the pupils because of the different colours of the examination answer books given to girls and boys. The third explanation offered concerned the differential response of males and females to distractors. (These issues are also commented on in Chapters 2, 5 and 6.) The authors focus on the evidence concerning the greater tendency of males than females to guess the answers to multiple-choice questions (Harris 1971; Hanna 1986). Rather than attempt to guess an answer, girls tend to omit items (i.e. they provide no response or, if the option is available, use the 'don't know' response).

In Chapter 6 we referred to Hudson's findings concerning female use of the 'I don't know' option. Adams' (1986) research into sex differences in scores on the multiple-choice Australian Scholastic Aptitude Test (ASAT) produced findings that are relevant to this discussion. The ASAT test covers the humanities, social science, science and mathematics and the sample of year 12 students corresponds to the age of Hudson's sample of high school students. Although Adams was not concerned with the method of measurement, he was interested in exploring the nature of the sex difference in performance that had been found in ASAT scores. What he did find was a very large effect that the students' scores on the confidence in success attitude scale exerted on their ASAT scores. In Adams' words: 'For some undetermined, perhaps social reason, females had a significantly lower confidence than males' (1986: 274).

When confidence in success was taken into account, 'sex had no significant effect on ASAT score'. Once again there is an apparent link between students' self-image and learnt expectations and their response to assessment tasks. The question remains whether it is the method of measurement which acts as a barrier to the students demonstrating their achievements.

Anderson's (1989) findings are also of interest, although he targeted an undergraduate sample. He looked at the effect of method of measurement on undergraduate mathematical achievement. Anderson found that for different student groups on four different types of objective test, there was a consistency in the relative performance of male and female undergraduates with males out-performing females. These performance differences were accounted for in part by the higher non-response rate of women compared to men. Anderson attributes this result to females being less willing to guess and having less confidence in their ability compared to males. Anderson quotes his findings about the greater non-response rate of women as support for Sherman's (1974) argument that much of the sex difference in science performance reported by NAEP was an artefact of sex differences in test-taking behaviour rather than ability, a similar point to that made by Hudson. According to Sherman, self-confidence leads males to attempt more items, whereas lack of confidence leads females to fail to respond or to opt for the 'I don't know' category. In Sherman's view, opting for 'I don't know' may reflect a fear of risk-taking, a fear of being wrong or even a lack of motivation in the female test population.

Introduction of GCSE

The introduction of GCSE examinations in England and Wales in 1988 heralded yet another shift in views about the nature of achievement. The enhanced role given to course-work (i.e. continuous assessment by teachers) was in response to concerns about the validity of the context of terminal examination assessment; in particular, whether all pupils' achievement could be revealed under pressurized timed test conditions. Another major element of the shift was the move away from norm-referenced to a more criterion-referenced assessment. Criterion-referenced assessment was considered to provide the 'users' of the education system (e.g. pupils, parents, employers, etc.) with a more detailed and informative breakdown of pupils' competencies. A rank ordering provided by norm-referenced assessment only indicates individuals' success in relation to their peers and not in terms of the knowledge, understanding and skills achieved by those individuals. The weighting of the continuous assessment component varied from 100 to 20 per cent, depending on the subject and on the syllabuses offered by the centres responsible for the GCSE exam. The coursework is marked by the teacher of the pupil and moderated by someone external to the school. Pupils are entered for the GCSE on the basis of teacher judgements of their ability, although parental choice may also play a part.

Stobart *et al.* (1992a) provide a useful account of the main differences in examinations at 16+. In 1989, girls accounted for 51 per cent of the total GCSE entries. Very different patterns of entry for girls and boys occurred between subjects. For example, in English the entrants were composed of 90 per cent girls and 83 per cent boys; in maths there were similar proportions, 90 and 80 per cent, respectively. However, girls accounted for only 28 per cent of the entrants in physics, 44.5 per cent in chemistry and 62.8 per cent in biology. Few of the major subjects were found to be producing equal outcomes for girls and boys. For example, girls out-perform boys in English and the position is reversed in mathematics. In physics, girls out-perform boys but this may be because the more able girls opt for physics (see the A Level discussion later). There is perhaps some support for this explanation when we consider that boys achieve more grades A–C in biology than girls (51.5 *vs* 44.2 per cent). In English literature and French, more girls than boys enter for the exam and girls significantly out-perform boys. Overall, then, there are different patterns of entry and outcome by gender in the current 16+ examination, a not dissimilar picture to that painted by Murphy (1980). Tables 8.1 and 8.2 provide a breakdown by gender for entry and outcome for GCSE from 1988 to 1990.

Quinlan (1991) hypothesized that the introduction of coursework would differentially affect the performance of girls relative to boys depending on the weighting and type of course-work required. His analysis of entries and grades achieved from 1984 to 1990 showed that where GCSE has 'led to an increase in written coursework, of which part is done outside class time, the performance of females will have shown greater improvement than that of males. This is not the case in subjects where coursework takes the form of continuous assessment within lesson time (e.g. science subjects)' (Quinlan 1991: 1).

Table 8.1 All GCSE groups percentage grades A–C, 1988–90

Subject	Male (M) % A–C			Female (F) % A–C			Difference (F – M) %			Mean difference
	1988	1989	1990	1988	1989	1990	1988	1989	1990	1988–90
Biology	48.7	51.8	53.9	41.0	44.4	47.0	−7.7	−7.4	−6.9	−7.3
Chemistry	50.9	53.3	55.2	47.1	49.7	52.7	−3.8	−3.6	−2.5	−3.3
Economics	47.8	53.5	53.9	45.3	54.5	52.0	−2.5	1.0	−1.9	−1.1
English	36.8	41.6	46.0	50.5	55.2	58.0	13.7	13.6	12.0	13.1
English literature	44.8	41.9	50.7	56.5	55.4	63.1	11.7	13.5	12.4	12.5
French	46.9	49.9	45.6	52.1	55.3	51.9	5.2	5.4	6.3	5.6
Geography	39.0	43.6	44.0	45.1	49.0	51.0	6.1	5.4	7.0	6.2
History	41.0	45.5	46.2	46.7	51.1	52.3	5.7	5.6	6.1	5.8
Mathematics (with cwk)	36.4	41.3	42.9	32.4	36.8	38.0	−4.0	−4.5	−4.9	−4.5
Mathematics (no cwk)	42.5	41.9	43.2	32.8	35.6	37.9	−9.7	−6.3	−5.3	−7.1
Physics	43.5	48.6	52.3	47.5	52.7	56.3	4.0	4.1	4.0	4.0

Source: 1988, 1989 and 1990 GCSE Inter-Group Statistics. Reproduced with permission from Stobart *et al.* (1992a: 267).
cwk, course-work which was optional in GCSE mathematics until 1991.

Table 8.2   All GCSE groups entries, 1988–90

Subject	Male % of entry			Female % of entry		
	1988	1989	1990	1988	1989	1990
Biology	36.9	37.5	38.9	63.1	62.5	61.1
Chemistry	55.6	55.3	55.1	44.4	44.7	44.9
Economics	60.5	63.8	61.4	39.5	36.2	38.6
English	49.0	49.4	49.7	51.0	50.6	50.3
English literature	44.6	49.4	45.9	55.4	50.6	54.1
French	40.2	41.0	41.8	59.8	59.0	58.2
Geography	58.7	58.3	57.9	41.3	41.7	42.1
History	48.8	49.1	48.8	51.2	50.9	51.2
Mathematics (with cwk)	48.2	48.2	48.3	51.8	51.8	51.7
Mathematics (no cwk)	47.8	48.9	48.6	52.2	51.1	51.4
Physics	72.5	71.6	70.8	27.5	28.4	29.2

Source: 1988, 1989 and 1990 Inter-Group Statistics. Reproduced with permission from Stobart *et al.* (1992a: 265).
cwk, course-work which was optional in GCSE mathematics until 1991.

Following up these findings, Stobart *et al.* (1992a) compared male and female exam performance for 1985 GCE and CSE and for 1988 GCSE, in mathematics, physics, religious studies, history, French and English. Their results supported Quinlan's hypothesis but there were exceptions. For example, in French, which is a subject without course-work (although there is an oral examination), girls made significant gains over O Level performance and the girl–boy performance gap remained similar to that in 1985. Stobart *et al.* explained this finding in terms of the radical change in the tasks and style of communication that accompanied the introduction of GCSE French, a change which girls appeared to have handled more successfully than boys. Patrick's (1990) analysis of gender differences within the GCSE provides further evidence questioning the effect of course-work on the overall pattern of results. Patrick's findings showed typical patterns of gender differences in subject exam success irrespective of a course-work element. Furthermore, an overall difference in favour of one gender for a subject could mask syllabus-specific performance where the overall gender differences could even be reversed.

Cresswell's investigation of gender in the GCSE provided further insights into the nature of sub-group performance. He found that 'girls' average coursework marks are higher than the boys in every case . . . [however] as far as the variances are concerned . . . in every case the girls' coursework marks are more bunched than the boys' (Cresswell 1990: 5). In Cresswell's view, some of the variation was due to the coursework tasks set to candidates by the centres responsible for the GCSE. Cresswell also found that the magnitude of the gender effect varied between schools. At three centres where the gap between girls' and boys' performance on course-work was the largest, the boys' lead on the written exam paper was small. The centre where the boys out-performed the girls on the written paper to the greatest extent was where the boys overall had achieved a higher mean than girls on course-work.

The bunching of girls' marks is an interesting phenomenon. Does it, for example, reflect the quality of the girls' work, markers' expectations of them or is it a consequence of the types of tasks they choose? In Stobart and co-workers' review, they identified various factors that might be contributing to the differential performance of girls and boys. These included: the weighting and type of course-work required; the ability and socio-economic background of the population that take course-work-based GCSE; the influence of moderators' views about the appropriateness of course-work tasks on the marks given; the specific tasks set and their contexts both in the course-work component and the written exam; and the relative experience and expectations of girls and boys in terms of their abilities and familiarity with the method of assessment. In the authors' opinion, the GCSE 'provided important evidence that to vary the type of performance required, accompanied by assessment methods which show fitness-for-purpose [i.e. course-work], can significantly change the pattern of results' (Stobart *et al.* 1992a: 274).

A research project conducted jointly by members of the University of London Examinations and Assessment Council (ULEAC) and the National Foundation for Educational Research (NFER) studied two issues: the contribution of the GCSE examination to differential performance at 16+, and the contribution of schools in their preparation of pupils for the GCSE (Stobart *et al.* 1992b). The project was short-term (10 months), hence was limited in what methods it could use to research these two issues. First, statistics were reviewed alongside evidence from other assessments. The national criteria, upon which the GCSE was based, were also analysed along with the content and skill requirements of the various syllabuses and the form of the specific assessments used. Of particular interest to the researchers were the constructs being assessed, the style of response required and the emphases of the marking schemes used. As part of the analysis, the project team used classifications developed in the APU mathematics and English survey research. To explore the contribution of schools, the project carried out questionnaire surveys and case studies. These targeted the teaching arrangements for GCSE and the way in which these impinged on decisions made about which pupils were selected for entry into GCSE. Finally, teachers' perceptions of pupils' abilities were considered and the influence of these on entry policies and teaching styles.

We will briefly summarize the main findings of the project, then explore these in terms of the hypotheses we have identified about possible sources of gender differences. Before discussing the findings, it is important to consider the researchers' conceptualization of the problem. They describe their view of a 'fair' examination as one which does 'justice to the subject' and gives pupils 'opportunities to show what they "know, understand and can do". In practical terms, this is likely to mean offering content and skill requirements and a range of assessment techniques which allow both boys and girls to demonstrate their attainments which may not necessarily be the same' (Stobart *et al.* 1992b: 2). Therefore, fairness is *not* equated with equal outcomes necessarily, although neither is the discrepancy in girls' and boys' results assumed to be unproblematic.

Stobart *et al.* (1992b) noted that gender differences in GCSE English were large and not in decline with girls currently achieving 14 per cent more grades A–C than boys. The gender gap in performance was greatest for those English syllabuses with examination components. However, the test population for these syllabuses had a higher proportion of pupils from selective and independent schools. The gender differences in GCSE mathematics which used to favour boys were found to have narrowed, with boys achieving only 3 per cent more A–C grades than girls. This reflects the more recent evidence commented on in Chapters 2 and 4, where differences in mathematical ability before adolescence are minimal and after adolescence the phenomenon appears restricted to the more gifted students, i.e. that the overall group difference is caused only by a proportion of the population sample – the more able. To set these results in context, in 1991, 54 per cent of all candidates achieved grades A–C in English compared to 44 per cent in mathematics. In addition, there remains a substantial proportion of pupils who are not entered for the exams (approximately 13 per cent in English, 19 per cent in maths). The trend over time in GCSE has been to see an improvement in the overall performance of the population, thus sparking recent complaints by the government about falling standards of the examination.

To help explore the sources of this differential performance at GCSE level, the project report provides some additional informa-tion about gender differences in performance from the APU final surveys. For example, in English, overall gender differences for APU tasks are displayed allowing comparisons between tasks and across tasks to be made. These reveal for both reading and writing the influence of the task and response mode and format on pupils' performance. With regard to the results for the 1988 APU survey of writing, the project authors comment that where tasks draw directly on pupils' recent experiences or offer support in the form of materials or guidance, the performance gap between boys and girls decreases. Whereas tasks for which pupils have the respon-sibility 'to devise and shape subject matter, as well as to define the readership, proved to be ones on which girls did considerably better than boys' (Stobart *et al.* 1992b: 17).

APU findings such as these were used to predict which exam-ination syllabuses might differentially favour boys or girls. The characteristics of tasks identified as favouring girls included: responses demanding extended writing; assessment from multiple perspectives; and use of stimulus material that was predominantly literary. Boys' performance was predicted to improve where tasks required short or right/wrong responses and where *overall* writing competence was not required. Other boy-friendly factors included: using topics in tasks involving technical knowledge; responses requiring expository prose; and providing guidance in tasks. The project found that syllabuses tended to emphasize those aspects of English where girls typically do better than boys and that this was true for both examination and course-work components.

The project conducted a historical review of exam performance in English, which indicated that the gender gap in performance had existed for a long time and that it had been larger before the introduction of the GCSE. Indeed, girls out-performed boys on earlier exams which included a variety of response formats. The more open style of the GCSE method of measurement, the authors argue, cannot therefore explain why girls do better than boys in English.

GCSE mathematics and English have different entry policies. In English grade differentiation is achieved by outcome, whereas for maths there is a differentiated entry scheme with three tiers of entry: the foundation tier has grades E–G; the intermediate tier has grades C–F; and the higher tier has grades A–D. Those pupils entered for a particular tier but falling below the lowest grade in that tier are ungraded. The research identified two aspects of this differentiated entry policy in mathematics that might influence or even create differential performance. More girls than boys are entered for GCSE at age 16 (88 *vs* 79 per cent in 1991) but fewer girls than boys are entered for the higher tier, while substantially more are entered for the intermediate tier (29 *vs* 23 per cent – a difference of 30 443 females in 1991).

More girls than boys are entered for the foundation tier but the evidence available does not indicate whether pupil achievement is being underestimated by this. Evidence from questionnaires and case studies suggested that boys rather than girls are demotivated if placed in a tier they feel is not appropriate to their ability. As research shows that boys tend to rate their mathematical abilities more highly than girls, this could influence their performance in this tier. It might also influence teachers' judgement, as more boys than girls were not entered for GCSE mathematics in 1991 (21 *vs* 12 per cent).

The researchers were particularly concerned about the potential underestimation of girls' abilities evidenced by their over-representation in the intermediate tier. The questionnaire and case study data revealed that both girls and their teachers share a belief in girls' lack of confidence in mathematics. In addition, both girls and teachers agreed that boys were less anxious about failure than girls. Teachers were of the view that boys were more advantaged by a final examination but girls were less certain of this. There is evidence that some 1 per cent of pupils (approximately 5000) entered for the intermediate tier could have achieved a higher grade and that this affects more girls than boys. This 'misclassification' restricts their ability to continue their study of mathematics to A Level.

The maths papers, like the English ones, were analysed on the basis of APU findings to explore whether bias existed within them. The analysis of GCSE performance showed that only on topics where the APU had earlier identified substantial differences did gender-related differences remain (for example, rate and ratio, visualizing 3-D shapes, but not measurement of angle or geometrical transformation). Boys still do better on items concerned with shape and space and unit measures and girls continue to outperform boys on algebraic questions. While girls performed better than boys on mathematics course-work, this did not contribute disproportionately to their final grade; it is improved performance on examination papers that is the critical factor. (Similarly, there was no evidence in English that course-work contributed disproportionately to pupils' overall grades.) It was found to be the harder exam paper of the two at each tier which acted as the most powerful discriminator at subject level. A comparison of the statistical evidence of girls' and boys' performance on examinations did not reveal any particular difficulties for girls in contrast to teachers' views that examinations disadvantaged girls.

The analysis of the GCSE examination questions in mathematics did not indicate any bias. To determine bias, the researchers attempted to identify which attributes of items affected pupil performance. [The categories of attributes used in this analysis were a sub-set of the APU classification: see Foxman *et al.* (1985) for details.] The process of applying the categories was a hierarchical one, with each category linked to the one before (apart from context). The authors recognize that such a process does not allow interactions between categories to be revealed. What emerged from the classification was the dominant features within questions, which 'can only be used as an approximate measure of which features affect boy/girl performance' (Stobart *et al.* 1992b: 49).

There was some evidence from the comparison of predicted scores (based on APU data) and actual scores that contextualized questions gave a slight advantage to boys, whereas questions which favoured girls tended to be non-contextualized. This corresponds to the APU findings reported in Chapter 5. We were cautious about the selection of contexts and it is clear that there are instances where contexts are overtly masculine, involving sport, DIY, etc. The authors report that the context of the task was not perceived by the pupils to be acting as a barrier to them responding. However, other research (Murphy 1989) has shown that the context of a task, rather than acting as a barrier to the construction of meaning, plays a critical role in determining what task pupils perceive and what response they consider appropriate. How contexts are defined by assessors and interpreted by pupils does require more thorough consideration.

In summarizing the project findings, the authors comment on the need to raise the issue of boys' relative underachievement in English. The generality of national criteria and the way these are put into practice in GCSE syllabuses by offering a wide range and choice of content to both teachers and pupils is considered to be problematic. Schools, it is argued, need to be informed of the implications of their choices for potential discrimination between groups of pupils. Schools would benefit, therefore, from gender-related data – at question level – as would examiners. As the authors comment: 'Without such information the task of identifying and building upon the more limited range of boys' skills is rendered more difficult for both examiners and teachers' (Stobart *et al.* 1992b: 3).

In English, teaching practices such as setting led to 'top' groups in which girls predominated and 'middle/low' groups where boys outnumbered girls. Yet despite this, boys seemed relatively unperturbed by their lack of success in English, which may indicate their view of the status of the subject in terms of future careers, etc., hence boys' awareness as well as that of teachers and examiners needs to be addressed.

Teachers were of the view that in English 100 per cent course-work would enable most pupils to demonstrate their achievements. This was in marked contrast to their views about mathematics, where a 20 per cent course-work/80 per cent examination was considered the best assessment structure for both boys and girls. This indicates something about teachers' views of the nature of achievements in different domains and some mismatch between beliefs about pupil performance and actual performance.

The authors recommend that in mathematics, schools should seek to raise both girls' and boys' expectations in relation to differentiated entry. Girls' anxieties about failing and lack of confidence generally were highlighted as particular causes for concern. Beliefs about girls' mathematical ability and examination performance need to be challenged in the authors' views by dissemination of evidence of their improving performance. School setting policy in mathematics may be reinforcing misconceptions about girls' achievements and potential.

The project started from the stance that differential performance could not be explained by biological factors. The focus of the research is very much on the affective aspects of pupils' interactions with subjects and assessments of them, particular attention being paid to pupils' and teachers' expectations and beliefs. The project had limited success in identifying characteristics of tasks which might reveal how psychosocial variables differentially affect subgroup interactions with them. The time-scale for the research was clearly an inhibiting factor as regards further exploration of such issues.

Of particular importance are the project's findings about the influence of method of measurement. Simplistic perceptions of these effects (i.e. that standards have dropped in GCSE as a result of the introduction of course-work) have dominated recent policy decisions about GCSE. The project findings, however, indicate that these decisions have no basis in fact. The project's concern was to establish whether course-work did favour girls or boys differentially and there was no evidence of this. However, further exploration of the effects of course-work and method of measurement on the constructs being assessed in mathematics was not carried out.

The research into teachers' and examiners' awareness of gender differences was also significant. The findings reveal a limited awareness of the issues for both parties and a corresponding mismatch between beliefs about performance and actual performance. It is in the discussions of the English assessment that teachers' understanding of the constructs being assessed is seen as problematic. The authors note the influential role of the teacher in interpreting syllabuses and in presenting and responding to writing assignments. They suggest that a broader perspective on achievement is needed which includes a focus on expository writing (a form of response boys tend to favour). They also caution against the dominance of certain values, such as that placed on overtly personal writing (a response typically favoured by girls), which might lead to the underestimation by teachers of many boys' achievements whose style is often overtly impersonal but involves 'strongly personal undertones' (Stobart *et al.* 1992b: 69). Again this is a crucial issue which the project could only begin to address. The findings indicate that where the constructs are not clearly emphasized in marking schemes, then the potential for misrepresentation of pupils' achievements and the dominance of assessors' beliefs is increased. However, it is interesting that at no point is the issue of assessor bias considered directly. Yet this has been raised in various publications of assessment research findings and it must be remembered that GCSE scripts and course-work are identifiable by gender and carry the names of candidates. This would appear to be a significant omission in the research of the project.

Differential performance by ethnic and racial group

An early study looking at multiracial schools found that relatively few students were entered for public exams and, when they were, it was for the lower status CSE rather than O Level (Townsend and Brittan 1972). The Rampton Report found that, in six LEAs with high proportions of ethnic minority children, pupils from West Indian families achieved fewer high grades in O Level and CSE English and maths than either Asian or indigenous white children (Rampton 1981). Asian children performed slightly better than both other groups in maths and in overall number of passes at both O Level/CSE and A Level.

The Swann Report, which followed on from the Rampton Report, found that again West Indian children performed less well than the other two groups at O Level/CSE, but that their performance had improved since publication of the Rampton Report (Swann 1985). Six per cent of West Indians gained five or more higher passes in O Level and CSE compared with 17 per cent of 'Asians' and 19 per cent of 'all other leavers'.

A later study looking at the performance of pupils of white, South Asian and Afro-Caribbean origin in 23 comprehensive schools in six LEAs (Eggleston *et al.* 1986) found that white students were still more likely to be entered for O Level than ethnic minority students. As for exam performance, the picture varied across and within LEAs, but overall the performance of white and South Asian pupils was similar, with Afro-Caribbean boys gaining significantly fewer high-grade passes.

A study by Smith and Tomlinson (1989), which followed the secondary school careers of pupils in urban multiracial schools in four LEAs, found that patterns of performance were very different in different schools. The longitudinal study was able to look at the progress children made and relate this to measure of academic performance on entry to secondary school, using the multi-level modelling statistical technique which allows analysis of individual pupil results rather than a crude analysis of overall group results. Overall, the Asian and 'West Indian' children were behind at 11 and 13 but were catching up with white pupils by the time they sat O Level/CSE exams at 16. Specifically, Muslim children of Bangladeshi and Pakistani origin scored substantially below average on reading and maths at 11, while Sikhs and Hindus scored average or above. West Indian children scored below average but higher than the low-scoring South Asian group. After 2 years this gap widened; at this point, allocation to exam classes was made and white children were allocated to more, higher level exams. Over the next 3 years, the ethnic minority students caught up, although West Indian performance in maths remained poor. However, these children's exam results in English were rather better than those of white British children.

A point which Smith and Tomlinson made was that while the West Indian, Bangladeshi and Pakistani groups had entered the schools with lower than average scores in reading and maths, by the time they took their public exams they had narrowed the gap and achieved higher results than would have been predicted on the basis of their earlier attainment levels. Thus although they had poorer exam results than white pupils, they had made relatively greater progress during the last 3 years of compulsory schooling.

Smith and Tomlinson found that the ethnic minority pupils tended to appear in option subjects of lower academic status. Their statistical modelling, however, indicated that this was due to social class and attainment factors and not that ethnic group *per se* was being used as a criterion in the allocation to course levels (Smith and Tomlinson 1989: 216). More importantly, Smith and Tomlinson demonstrated that schools achieved very different results with children of similar backgrounds and earlier attainments:

. . . the differences in exam results attributable to ethnic group are very much smaller than those attributable to the school level. In other words, what school a child goes to makes far more difference than which ethnic group he or she belongs to.

(Smith and Tomlinson 1989: 281)

There were some criticisms of this study by other researchers, in particular Nuttall and Goldstein (Nuttall *et al.* 1989), who criticize the sample and the measure of school effectiveness used. Nevertheless, it was an important study, since it was the first to look at differential school effectiveness.

Nuttall, Goldstein and colleagues have themselves analysed ILEA public examination results by ethnic group and school. They employ a much more detailed breakdown of ethnic group. The very different achievement levels of Pakistani, Bangladeshi and Indian pupils (17.7, 4.2 and 26.4 per cent gaining five or more O Levels in 1985, respectively) shows the problem caused by using gross categories of ethnic group such as 'Asian' (ILEA 1987). Indeed, both the highest and lowest achieving groups in this study would have been classified as 'Asian' in earlier studies (Kysel 1988). After taking into account differences in verbal reasoning ability and sex, the performance of students of Pakistani, Indian, Greek and South-East Asian origin was better than that of students of English, Scottish or Welsh (ESW) background in 1985, 1986 and 1987 (ILEA 1987; Nuttall *et al.* 1989). As with the gender differences in the ILEA analysis and the ethnic group differences referred to in the above study, there was considerable variation from school to school. For example, the average difference in performance between Pakistani and ESW students was equivalent to an O Level grade A pass, but this varied from almost no difference in some schools to the equivalent of about two B grades in others.

One limitation of the early ILEA analyses is that they do not take account of social class at the pupil level and this is known to affect achievement and most probably accounts for the poor performance of the ESW and Irish (ESWI) group in the ILEA study. More recently, Nuttall and Goldstein have analysed the 1990 GCSE results for four London boroughs using the multi-level modelling approach and with information about free school meals

(FSM) as an indicator of social class. Thus analyses in relation to ethnic group, sex, social class, verbal reasoning level (VR) at age 11, and school were carried out looking at pupils within schools within LEAs (Nuttall *et al.* 1992).

The results were similar to the previous analyses (ILEA 1987; Nuttall *et al.* 1989) at the overall level of examination performance, with girls performing better than boys and students of Asian origin scoring substantially better than students from most other ethnic groups. The FSM effect was relatively small once other differences had been taken into account, specifically VR band and ethnicity, which are known to correlate with socio-economic status. Thus there appears to be no evidence here for the low social class of the ESW group explaining their poor performance. The analysis also looked at English and maths performance separately; girls did better than boys on English and vice versa with maths. The ethnic group performance was such that Indian and Pakistani pupils scored higher than ESW pupils and Caribbean pupils lower than ESW in both subjects although the Caribbean pupils' lower performance in English was not significant.

A third study, the Youth Cohort Study (Drew and Gray 1990), used a nationally representative sample, following successive cohorts between the ages of 16 and 19. It also collected data on social class, thus allowing comparison between pupils on the basis of ethnic origin, social class and gender. However, it collapses Indian, Pakistani and Bangladeshi pupils into an overall 'Asian' category. The 1985 data showed that pupils from professional/managerial backgrounds scored highest within each ethnic group; similarly, pupils from 'intermediate' category social backgrounds (including junior non-manual workers, personal service workers and some self-employed) scored higher than those from manual backgrounds. However, the size of some of these groups in the sample is small (e.g. only 12 professional/managerial Afro-Caribbeans and 17 Asians compared to 2118 whites in this category) and the results must be interpreted with caution, although the authors claim that the consistency of the effect lends some weight to the findings. Comparing across ethnic group, the Afro-Caribbean pupils had a lower average exam score than their Asian and white peers of similar social backgrounds. (Interestingly, it is only in the white group that there is a consistent gender difference with girls out-performing boys in all social groups.)

This study shows the complex interrelationship among gender, social class and ethnic group in explaining exam performance. Each of these three factors was found to be related to exam scores. Unlike the ILEA research, these researchers found that social class explained more of the variance than either ethnic group or gender; but that these three factors still left the larger part of the variance in exam performance unexplained.

Explanations for differential performance

Overall these researchers tend to look to environmental factors to explain differential group performance – social class and school attended as well as attainment on entry at age 11 – rather than factors within the assessments or curriculum. The picture revealed by the range of studies described here is a complex one, with social class *and* school attended having a mediating effect on performance by gender and ethnic group. The picture that emerges is one of overall differences in performance across broad ethnic divisions, with Afro-Caribbean students achieving at lower levels than other groups.

However, a major problem, particularly with the earlier studies, is the way in which ethnic group is identified. We noted that in the national curriculum assessment studies, ethnic group was identified by the teacher rather than by self-report on behalf of the pupil. The categorization of pupils is a critical aspect of these studies, as interpretations of performance will be misinformed if the categories are too crude or inaccurately applied.

Brewer and Haslum (1986) used data from the 1970 birth cohort study (Child Health and Education Study, CHES) to demonstrate a statistically significant relationship between each of ten indicators of social conditions and reading test scores for white UK children aged 10, but found none of the indicators to be related to the reading scores of 'West Indian' children of the same age. They found the same results when the samples were matched for intelligence test scores. In Plewis' (1987) critical review of Brewer and Haslum's study, he challenges the categories used to define ethnic groups. The categories used in Brewer and Haslum's study were white, black and Asian; children of mixed black and white union were excluded from the black group and 'Asians' was a blanket term used to cover a wide range of ethnic differences. He argues that if we are to 'better understand the relationship between attainment and ethnicity then this is more likely to come from at the least keeping separate Bangladeshis, Pakistanis, Indians and East African Asians' (Plewis 1987: 79).

Plewis also criticizes the treatment of the social indicators used to determine sub-groups. The influence of mothers' education on childen's attainment is confounded when 'education' includes anything from 'one low grade CSE to mothers with degrees' (Plewis 1987: 80). Plewis refers to another study where maternal education level was differentiated to some extent to demonstrate how significant interactions can he 'created' by crude categorizations applied to large samples (Blatchford *et al.* 1985). In this study of infant school children attending multiracial schools in inner London, attainments in reading and maths tests were related to maternal educational qualifications. The categorizations revealed a similar pattern of means for black and white children and for neither test is there a statistically significant interaction. However, when the categories of educational qualifications were collapsed, as in Brewer and Haslum's study, the association between mothers' education and attainment appeared stronger for white children than black children.

Reporting on the 1985 ILEA survey of ethnic group performance, Kysel (1988) notes that the achievement of some ethnic groups (i.e. African Asian and Indian pupils) was *well above average*; 'average' being defined in terms of the overall inner London population, where 40 per cent obtained at least one O Level grade A, B or C or CSE grade 1 and 10 per cent obtained five or more of these grades. Other groups whose performance was above average included Pakistani and South-East Asian pupils. In contrast, Bangladeshi pupils performed below the average; also, fewer Arab, Caribbean and Turkish pupils obtained five or more O Levels. Using the ILEA performance scores (i.e. 7 points for an O Level grade A, 1 point for a CSE grade 5, etc.), it was found that the average performance scores of Indian, African Asian, Pakistani, South-East Asian, Greek and African sub-groups were significantly higher than the overall average, whereas the performance scores of the Bangladeshi, Turkish, Caribbean and ESWI sub-groups were significantly lower. Kysel cites poverty, social class and lack of fluency in English as possible influences to explain the wide range of achievement across different ethnic groups. She quotes the finding from the ILEA language census that only 22 per cent of 15-year-old Bengali-speaking pupils were rated as fully fluent in English by their teachers, and the high level of unemployment among parents of Bangladeshi pupils, established by the ILEA Educational Priority Survey of 1986, as evidence in support of this.

Kysel also reviewed the assessment information coming through from the primary schools. Within the ILEA secondary school transfer process, pupils were also allocated a V-R level in a manner which left it open to charges of unfairness due to teacher stereotype. Teachers allocated individual pupils in the final year of junior school to one of three bands: Level 1 being the top 25 per cent, Level 2 the middle 50 per cent and Level 3 the bottom 25 per cent. The pupils then took a V-R test anonymously; this was marked centrally and a score distribution sent to the school which then adjusted the *numbers* of pupils assigned to the three bands. Kysel found that a disappointingly low number of pupils from the Arab, Bangladeshi, Caribbean, Greek and Turkish sub-groups were assigned to the top band for verbal reasoning by teachers, whereas a disproportionately high number of South East Asian and ESWI pupils were located in this band. Conversely, over half of the Bangladeshi pupils (53 per cent) and nearly half of the Turkish pupils (47 per cent) were assessed as being in the bottom band for verbal reasoning. A predicted performance score was computed based on the sex of the sample and the verbal reasoning band assigned. This predicted score was then compared with the actual score achieved. This analysis revealed that the verbal reasoning assessment *underestimated* the performance of African, African Asian, Greek, Indian, Pakistani and South-East Asian pupils. This was not the case for Arab, Bangladeshi, Caribbean and Turkish pupils. The results for ESWI pupils were, however, *overestimated* when the verbal reasoning assessment was compared with actual exam achievements.

Kysel suggests that the strong relationship between assigned verbal reasoning band and exam performance could result from the influence of the primary school assessment of pupils' ability on the secondary teachers' expectations of the pupils: 'Pupils fail to achieve in examinations not because they necessarily enter secondary school with any fewer skills than others but because they have been labelled "below average" in ability, and are expected to fail'

(Kysel 1988: 88). This is perhaps to overestimate the influence of primary assessment records on secondary practice. The 'starting fresh' syndrome of secondary schools is a well-known phenomenon. Teachers' judgements are also determined by a more complex array of influences than this explanation suggests; for example, you may recall the findings of the APU design and technology team concerning male and female markers' behaviour.

To counter the challenge that primary teachers' judgements of pupils' verbal ability is biased, Kysel herself quotes the results of the ILEA Junior School Project (Mortimore *et al.* 1988). This showed that teachers' judgements corresponded well with results on standardized tests. However, where disagreements arose, there was a tendency for Caribbean pupils to be placed in a lower verbal reasoning band, in contrast with ESWI pupils who were more likely to be placed in a higher band than their test scores would indicate. Kysel concludes that though allocation to verbal reasoning band is a crude measure open to some 'slight bias', it provides a 'useful measure of primary attainment against which examination results can be asessed'. However, Nuttall and Goldstein's more recent studies of exam results in London use a less problematic reading test score at age 11 rather than a V-R band.

The underestimation by teachers of pupils' potential and achievements when English is not their mother tongue continues, however, to be a major problem for assessment. It is a problem that has not been addressed adequately even with the introduction of external national assessments across the phases of schooling. Nor is the provision of interpreters providing solutions to the problem (Wick 1991).

Kysel points to the need to explore further the performance of those groups who are low attainers in the primary phase but overcome this in secondary schools and achieve examination results which are much better than predicted, for example some of the Asian sub-groups. The seeds of a possible solution to minority groups' low achievement may emerge if the process and sources of this improved performance are understood.

Drew and Gray carried out a review of ten British studies (including their own) into the black and white gap in examination results (Drew and Gray 1991). In this review, they challenge the explanation that socio-economic factors contribute to the examination gap between black and white students. In their study, although socio-economic group accounted for the largest part of the variance resulting from the three factors identified (i.e. gender, ethnic origin and socio-economic group), these factors together only accounted for about 10 per cent of the total variance.

They argue, in a similar vein to Plewis, against the use of simple and crude descriptions of social class in attempting to explain performance differences. However, they use the categorization 'black' to cover a wide range of ethnic groups, which has its own problems. Several of the studies found gender differences among ethnic groups; however, these differences are often small, with girls tending to do better than boys. Drew and Gray (1990) found little evidence of gender differences in the examination performance of their sample.

In their review, Drew and Gray (1991) are also critical of the ILEA studies that look at progress. In their opinion, the evidence does not support the view that pupils from ethnic minority groups (and from Afro-Caribbean ones in particular) make less progress in secondary schools than their white peers. They consider that the most plausible explanation for the greater 'progress' of some groups (e.g. the Afro Caribbean students), is, as we described above, the inaccuracy of teachers' V-R assessment at age 11 rather than any factors coming into play in secondary school [see Kysel's (1988) discussions]. Drew and Gray go on to consider the multi-level studies to see if these support their view about ethnicity and progress in secondary schools.

They identify two studies of school effectiveness (Smith and Tomlinson 1989; Nuttall *et al.* 1989) as germane to the debate. The fact that they involve multi-level modelling which allows school effectiveness to be considered for particular sub-groups is seen as a major advantage. The studies attempt to establish the degree to which attainment of particular groups is associated with ethnicity and the influence of the school on this attainment. Smith and Tomlinson's study concluded that 'some schools [were] much better than others and the ones that [were] good for white pupils tended to be about equally good for black pupils as well' (Smith and Tomlinson 1989: 305). Drew and Gray, however, are critical of the coverage of schools in the study, which limited what could be said about differential effectiveness with regard to black pupils. Drew and Gray's secondary analysis of the data indicated that probably more black pupils went to *less effective* schools.

Nuttall *et al.*'s (1989) study of 30 000 pupils in 140 ILEA secondary schools between 1985 and 1987 concluded that, in general, the progress of pupils from ethnic minority backgrounds was as good as that of white pupils, if not better. The exception to the trend was Afro-Caribbean pupils, who made slightly less progress than other sub-groups. They also reported on the differential effectiveness of schools by sub-group but argued for considering effectiveness as a multidimensional construct. They concluded that it was unhelpful to consider schools as being 'universally effective or ineffective'.

In reviewing these studies, Drew and Gray (1991: 170) comment that 'the average differences in school effects reported could be sufficiently large to account for the reported differences in the average exam performances of black and white pupils', i.e. the differential performance may be nothing to do with ethnicity *per se* but with the school attended. This is a fairly radical suggestion and we shall return to it in our final chapter. However, given that the dimensions of effectiveness have not been explored, these studies are not able to probe the question of the extent to which pupils from ethnic minority backgrounds attend less effective schools than their white peers. Without this information about the schools' contribution, a review of the 'fairness' of assessment procedures for ethnic sub-groups is severely limited.

Underachievement

Underachievement is a term that was widely used in the 1970s and 1980s, often in relation to ethnic minority pupils and their performance in public examinations. The definition of underachievement is problematic, since without a measure of 'expected achievement' for the individual, it is not possible to say whether underachievement exists. In addition, we have to be clear about ability and achievement: ability in an individual relates to some notion of potential, while achievement relates to the actual demonstration of performance. Measured IQ has traditionally had a role in the identification of 'underachievement' relating in this case to the discrepancy between IQ score and performance, the latter usually measured through formal tests and examinations (Plewis 1991). For example, the combination of an above average IQ score and a below average reading age is traditionally seen as denoting underachievement due to a specific reading difficulty. IQ is used in this case as a surrogate, or indicator for, potential achievement or intellectual ability.

The work of the APU (Chapter 5) was originally aimed at investigating underachievement, its terms of reference being: 'To promote the development of methods of assessing and monitoring the achievement of children at school, and to seek to identify the incidence of underachievement'. The background was that in the late 1960s and early 1970s there had been concern within the DES to monitor the performance of the educational system and at the same time there was concern about the 'underachievement' of particular groups, especially ethnic minorities (Gipps and Goldstein 1983). In 1974, the White Paper 'Educational Disadvantage and the Educational Needs of Immigrants' announced the setting up of two DES units: the Educational Disadvantage Unit (EDU) and the APU. The concept of underachievement in relation to the APU was thus directly linked to the performance of ethnic minority pupils. The APU defined underachievement in two ways:

- an individual achieving "less than some measure of his [*sic*] potential (however measured) suggests he ought to be able to achieve";
- an identifiable group e.g. pupils of one ethnic origin performing lower than the range achieved by other pupils in otherwise similar circumstances.

(Gipps and Goldstein 1983: 28)

The APU could not, however, identify underachievement in relation to the first definition because their national surveys were not designed to collect information about individuals, and even if IQ tests were used, there 'were many doubts about these as measures of potential'. The APU instead favoured focusing on the second definition: this in effect means low achievement of one group in relation to another, and for all intents and purposes the APU's use of the term underachievement meant *relatively low achievement*.

Evidence about ethnic minority groups' relatively low achievement continued to be presented in the 1980s: both the Rampton Report and the Swann Report from the Committee of Inquiry into the Education of Children from Minority Ethnic Groups concluded, on the basis of their examination results, that Afro-Caribbean children as a group were underachieving in the English educational system (Rampton 1981; Swann 1985). The surveys described in the previous section produced the same overall types of finding and the relative underachievement of ethnic minority groups became widely reported in the UK in the 1980s.

Troyna (1984), however, challenges conventional wisdom in this area. Interpreting the concept of underachievement in terms of relatively low achievement between groups implies that the groups are comparable. Troyna argues that ethnic minority and majority groups' experiences are so different that direct comparison between them is invalid: racism is for black pupils such a pervasive influence in their lives that intergroup comparison is not a valid measure. Furthermore, these comparisons reinforce stereotyped views of black children as underachieving; this reinforcement of stereotype tends to act against curriculum and pedagogical change.

More recently, Troyna (1991) continues to critique the focus on ethnic minority pupils' performance in terms of outcome (by comparing exam results) and urges that the processes by which ethnic minority pupils get these results be studied. Troyna illustrates his argument by writing about ethnic minority pupils' allocation to low sets in secondary school, which limits their access to GCSE courses. He gives evidence (building on Cecile Wright's case-study research) to show that Asian pupils were more likely to be allocated to lower ability sets than white pupils with 'comparable assessment profiles' [this is similar to the point Stobart *et al.* (1992a) make about girls in GCSE maths]. Furthermore, once allocated to lower sets they are unlikely to move out of them. The end result was that, by the fourth and fifth year in the school in question, they were not eligible to take GCSE. Troyna argues that this allocation is based on past achievement and perceived potential to succeed. The latter is based on 'a range of subjective, informal and less easy to codify set of (professional) judgements about the pupils' capacity to succeed in a given ability group or examination track' (Troyna 1991: 374). This is the reason for ethnic minority pupils being 'misallocated' and Troyna suggests that underachievement in this case should actually be called under-rating.

We do not know, of course, whether the pupils would have done better if they had been in the higher sets, but we suspect that they could have done, and indeed they should have had the opportunity. This relates to our earlier discussion of *actual* equality of opportunity in terms of access. This same argument lies behind criticisms of streaming and ability grouping; such grouping, though it might have pedagogical justification, limits actual equality of opportunity and is therefore inequitable.

Examinations at 18+

A Level in the UK

There has been no major study of Advanced or A Level entries by gender since Murphy's (1980) review, which covered the years 1951–77 (and there is certainly no analysis by ethnic group). We can, therefore, only report on what (little) research there is in relation to gender. We comment on the need to develop this aspect of assessment research in the final chapter. As we pointed out earlier in this chapter, Murphy found that entries for males and females in English and French were similar in 1951, but by 1977 the number of females entered was almost double that of males. In line with this increased entry rate for females came an increased pass rate.

Our analysis of entries by gender for the years 1988–92 shows that for English and French the total entry increased each year (see Table 8.3) and that the entry of females is now nearer to two and a half times that of males for French and almost that for English. However, an analysis of results shows that in 1990 and 1991, males were getting more higher grade passes in French: 35.7 per cent of males got grades A and B in 1990 and 35.5 per cent in 1991, 38.2 per cent in 1992 compared with 31.6, 32.7 and 33.6 per cent of females. For English, the figures are 30.2, 28.5 and 30 per cent for males and 26.7, 25.4 and 28.3 per cent for females over the two years (Inter Board Statistics, AEB, 1991, 1992 and 1993).

In maths, overall entry increased from 1988 to 1990 but declined over the last two years; in 1990 and 1991, twice as many males as females entered. Again a higher proportion of males gained grade A and B passes: 33.1, 34.2 and 35.6 per cent in 1990, 1991 and 1992 while 29.9, 31.5 and 33.5 per cent of females did so.

For chemistry and physics, the overall entry pattern from 1988 to 1992 was similar to maths with a decline in 1991 and 1992,

Table 8.3 A Level entries by gender

	1988	1989	1990	1991	1992
Biology					
M	x	15 860	17 940	17 570	18 611
F	x	22 257	28 525	29 037	29 663
Total	36 705	38 117	46 465	46 607	48 275
Chemistry					
M	x	26 357	27 429	26 187	24 735
F	x	18 236	18 769	18 253	17 719
Total	44 338	44 593	46 197	44 440	42 454
Physics					
M	x	36 815	35 300	33 642	31 948
F	x	10 135	10 029	9 773	9 125
Total	46 600	46 950	45 334	43 416	41 073
Maths					
M	x	x	52 078	48 878	47 064
F	x	x	25 984	24 592	23 859
Total	66 250	x	78 087	73 472	70 923
English (Lang. & Lit.)					
M	18 215	19 717	22 158	23 880	26 139
F	42 002	45 749	52 024	55 307	60 332
Total	60 217	65 466	74 182	79 187	86 473
French					
M	5 775	6 283	7 445	8 816	8 901
F	14 845	16 101	19 799	21 977	22 127
Total	20 629	22 384	27 245	30 794	31 028

Note: F + M does not add up to the *total* if some candidates have not specified their sex.
Source: Inter-Board Statistics (ULSEB 1989, 1990/AEB, 1991, 1992, 1993).
x, data not complete

but there were over three times as many males taking physics as females, while in chemistry it was around one and a half times as many. In chemistry, 35.0, 34.6 and 35.5 per cent of males gained either an A or B grade in 1990, 1991 and 1992 compared with 32.4, 33.1 and 33 per cent of females. In physics, the difference is less marked, with 29.5, 29.7 and 30.8 per cent of males gaining an A or B grade while 27.3, 27.2 and 29.8 per cent of females do so in the three years.

Table 8.4   A Level grades A–C by gender (percentages)

	1990	1991	1992
Biology			
M	43.7	40.6	45.5
F	41.4	38.8	43.1
Chemistry			
M	49.6	49.3	51.5
F	47.6	48.0	49.5
Physics			
M	44.6	44.7	46.2
F	44.2	43.7	47.3
Maths			
M	46.8	47.9	49.3
F	45.0	46.7	48.4
English (Lang. & Lit.)			
M	50.5	47.9	49.6
F	47.8	45.2	48.6
French			
M	54.5	54.9	57.7
F	50.5	51.4	52.5

Note: Includes all results for GCSE A Level in E, W + I.
Source: Inter-Board Statistics (AEB 1991, 1992, 1993).

Biology, which is seen as the classic 'female' science, was the only one of the three sciences to maintain a steady increase in entry over the years 1988–92, with around one and a half times more females entering than males (see Table 8.3). Again, even in biology more males than females attained a grade A or B: 28.3, 25.5 and 29 per cent of males compared with 25.9, 24.2 and 26.7 per cent of females.

It is much more usual to look at the overall A–C performance than A and B performance, as we have done here. If we do look at the overall A–C performance (Table 8.4), we find that the differences reduce between the two sexes, but that males are still ahead on all six subjects over the 3 years. The largest gap is in French, with 3.5 to 5.2 per cent more males gaining A–C than females in the 3 years; the smallest gap is in physics, with 0.4 and 1.0 per cent in favour of males in 1990 and 1991 which changes to 1.1 per cent in favour of girls in 1992. Thus the overall picture looks fairly equitable, but what it masks is males' better performance at grades A and B, in particular grade A, which are important for university entrance.

Preliminary analyses of the 1992 results by gender using a points system (10 points for grade A, 8 for B, 6 for C, etc.) show that one in eight males had the equivalent of three A grades compared with one in eleven females. Almost 3 per cent more males than females achieved the 30-point maximum at state schools (*The Times*, 10 November 1992: 'Boys turn the tables on girls in latest A-level examinations'). What these A Level results show is a quite dramatic reversal of the trend at GCSE (and national assessment at 7 and 14 years thus far). Explanations offered for these differences are: that the males who stay on for A Level are more able than the females; the emphasis is on timed exams in which females do less well; maturation patterns mean males catch up with females by 18; and possibly more top grades are awarded in science subjects which males tend to take.

The unexpected narrower gap between males' and females' performance in physics is generally thought to be due to 'ability' factors, i.e. females who take physics A Level tend to be particularly bright and, therefore, do well, as well as being highly motivated. A similar explanation is offered to account for females' superior performance in physics at GCSE, in which girls achieved 4.0 per cent more grades A–C than boys in 1989–90 (see the SISS discussion in Chapter 4). These factors would explain the performance patterns of girls in the prestigious selective independent girls' schools: in 1992, 39 per cent of the girls who took maths (20 per cent of the cohort) gained an A grade, while in physics (taken by 15 per cent of the cohort) the figure was 25 per cent (*Times Educational Supplement*, 13 November 1992: 'A-level triumph for girls' schools'). (The figures for *all* candidates in 1991 were 20 per cent of boys and 16 per cent of girls gaining an A grade in maths, with 15 per cent of boys and 12 per cent of girls gaining this grade in physics.)

What are we to make of these entry patterns and pass rates? First, despite criticisms of A Level as narrow, overly academic, etc., it is increasingly 'popular'; this is, of course, because it is the route into higher education. The choice of subjects is particularly interesting, since it gives an insight into potential career choices. The reduction of entries for physics, chemistry and maths can be viewed with concern because of their significance in science and engineering (*Education*, 21 August 1992, p. 144: 'More students take A-levels but shun science'). More students are opting for arts subjects and looking at careers in areas such as retail management, a trend which is causing concern among scientists and engineers.

As well as factors causing differential performance such as ability, maturity and the nature of the timed examination, we need also to consider the extent to which these differences are to do with the nature of the subject studied and the way in which it is assessed, boys' increased motivation at this stage, and society's views about the relative unimportance of girls' careers leading to lower expectations and self-perceptions for the girls.

A Level entries are seriously under-studied compared with GCSE/O Level, as we pointed out at the beginning of this section. Studies of gender differences do not go beyond looking at pass rates and grades achieved, while there appear to be no such breakdowns by ethnic group. Neither are there any studies of effect of question content and format in the examination. This is unfortunate given that the exam is highly significant to the pupils who take it and the changing patterns of gender performance suggest that a detailed comparison between GCSE and A Level could be very fruitful.

College entrance tests in the USA

We have presented a review of A Level patterns of entry and success using UK data. We report here on the outcomes of tests used in the admission procedures for entry into tertiary education in the USA. Research into the admissions process in the USA has considered whether bias in testing procedures and measures limits the educational opportunities of one group or other in a way that has not happened in the UK. The hypothesis most commonly explored is that women more than men are disadvantaged by the assessment procedures employed.

Educational Testing Services (ETS) is responsible for the development of the Scholastic Aptitude Test (SAT), taken each year by a large number of high school juniors and seniors seeking admission to college. The SAT produces separate scores for verbal and mathematical achievement and for a standard English test of writing. Males have been found consistently to out-perform females on the mathematical sub-section of the SAT. Women's average SAT verbal scores were slightly higher than men's up until the late 1960s; since then, the trend has been for a steady decline in female scores until 1980 when males out-performed females on average by 12 points. One factor for this shift in performance is the attempt that has been made to make the SAT-Verbal more 'sex-neutral' (AAUW 1992: 54). The amount of science content in the reading comprehension packages has jumped from 20 per cent before 1978 to 33 per cent afterwards. By 1980, 2 years after the increase in science content, reading sub-scores favouring males had climbed from 3 to 12 points. From what we know about gendered responses to different types of reading material, we could have predicted such a shift in scores. As the authors of the AAUW Report comment wryly: 'It is interesting to note that no efforts have been made to balance the SAT-Math, on which males outscore females by about one-half of a standard deviation, or about 50 points' (AAUW 1992: 54).

ETS uses the differential item functioning statistic (DIF: see Chapter 1) for checking whether items in the SAT are differentially difficult for various sub-groups. The DIF scale includes three categories to indicate the magnitude of the difficulty of the item for either the reference group or the 'focal' group, e.g. male/female, white/black, white/Asian, etc. The assumption underlying the DIF statistic is that people of the same background knowledge and skill should perform in the same way on test items irrespective of sex, race or ethnicity. ETS are at pains to point out that DIF is not a synonym for *bias*, 'Professional judgement' being required 'to determine whether or not the difference in difficulty shown by the DIF index is unfairly related to group membership'. Access to DIF values for various SAT items would provide useful evidence to illuminate potential sources of differences between sub-groups, but it seems that little of this data has been published.

Stanley (1987) examined gender differences in performance on the College Board achievement tests between 1982 and 1985 and Advanced Placement (AP) Examinations between 1984 and 1986. Significant effects were found in favour of males on the physics and European history tests. Small effects favouring males were found on the tests of American history, chemistry, mathematics levels I and II, biology and Latin. Other differences in favour of males or females were negligible. The data showed that the highest effect sizes favouring males occurred for tests where there was a high proportion of male students taking them. For example, 81 per cent of the physics test population were male and 65 per cent of the European history population were also male. The AP data revealed five large effects in favour of males on tests of physics, chemistry and computer science. Five other tests showed males ahead of females but the effect sizes were considered small. Similarly, the seven main effects in favour of females were also considered to be small. Stanley's analysis of the effects for both assessments led him to conclude that the gender disproportions among test-takers combined with the difference in performance between males and females placed women at a disadvantage where undergraduate admission and advanced placement and credit were concerned, especially in science, mathematics and history.

Validity studies typically focus on prediction and compare the performance of students on admission tests with their first year grade point average. Ramist (1984) reported that women's grade point average was better predicted than men's. Linn (1982) reported a tendency for the entrance test scores of females to correlate more strongly than males with performance measures and therefore to predict subsequent academic performance more accurately. Linn confirmed earlier findings that college entrance test scores have systematically under-predicted the performance of females. A more recent analysis by Wainer and Steinberg (1990), quoted by Chipman *et al.* (1991), revealed that when men and women are matched by college mathematics course taken and grade received, the women are found to have had a SAT-M score 30–40 points lower. The case for possible bias in the SAT seems strong in the face of evidence of this kind.

The AAUW (1992) report concludes that SAT scores under-predict women's grades at college and over-predict men's; furthermore, in maths, this effect is not a result of women taking easier courses. The report finds that there is evidence of unfairness to women on the SAT which, they say, has serious implications for their ability to gain college admission and to win scholarships.

In New South Wales, Australia, access to university is via a tertiary entrance exam – the HSC – which is then statistically scaled in such a way that candidates who take more 'difficult' subjects such as maths and sciences get higher (scaled) marks than candidates who take 'easier' humanities. This is done in order to make 'fair' comparisons of performance on tests of different levels of difficulty. But since boys are more likely to take maths and science, they have an advantage over the girls and get higher scaled marks. When it comes to admission to university, students are ranked across the State on the basis of their overall HSC score, and boys have a better chance of scoring high and being in the top section of the list which is then admitted to university. As a strategy to overcome this, more girls are taking maths and science at a higher level, but in many cases it is only in order to beat the system. For a career in law, for example, humanities would be a more appropriate background than sciences. (*Sunday Telegraph*, Sydney, 11 October 1992: 'Absurd "HSC mark shuns our best girls" ').

Sternberg (1987) documents case studies of students to demonstrate the way subjective views of 'intelligent behaviours' change as students progress through the education systems. These value-laden perspectives will be influenced by the subjects pursued and the dominance of males and females within that subject. Remember how female assessors in the APU design and technology assessment valued girls' work more than that of boys and how this value corresponded to the values within their own subject specialism. This was reversed for male assessors whose subject background and hence value perspective corresponded to that to which boys had more access. Such issues need to be borne in mind when comparing any across-age measures of achievement. It is also important to remember that the test populations post-16 are highly selective and not representative of the whole population.

We go on now to consider graduate performance in the UK as evidenced by the class of degree achieved by males and females for different subjects and in different institutions. There is again some evidence of an overlap in findings, which helps to identify what might be at issue when considering the fairness of assessment measures and procedures.

University degree results

In the review of differentiated performance at GCSE level, we noted the possible influence of stereotypes on teacher expectations of pupils. In earlier chapters, we also discussed the way achievements become valued in different domains or aspects of domains. These values correspond in differing degrees to 'masculine' or 'feminine' ways of looking at the world and are reflected in students' preferred ways of working and styles of expression. Various research studies have identified the 'typical' traits that teachers associate with girls as a group and boys as a group and which influence their perception of girls and boys as students. These traits in combination with domain stereotypes help determine teachers' views of characteristic girls' work and characteristic boys' work. Depending on the domain to which the work relates, girls' responses may be valued or devalued and the same is true for boys as a group. Consequently, when assessing pupils' work, teachers' preconceptions may determine their judgements irrespective of what a pupil has actually produced. We have quoted evidence for this from Goddard-Spear's (1983) research and the findings of the APU design and technology research (see Chapter 5). We suggested that these effects might also explain the gendered pattern of marking in GCSE course-work observed by Cresswell (1990) and the trend in admission patterns for the different tiers of GCSE mathematics commented on by Stobart *et al.* (1992b). We consider now whether the findings at tertiary level provide any further illumination of gender differences in performance at 16 + and indeed 18 +.

There is very little documented research into exam practice at degree level in terms of the types of questions set or the procedures used. There has, however, been a recent review of differential degree performance at Cambridge and Oxford Universities. Goodhart (1988a), responding to a debate about the under-representation of women on the staff at Cambridge at all levels, suggested that this may be due to the failure of female graduates to achieve as many firsts as their male counterparts (8.5 *vs* 17.9 per cent in 1987). He noted that while women achieved slightly more Class II(1) degrees, this did not match the deficiency in Class 1. More women than men achieve a Class II(2) and fewer women than men gain Class III or Class 0 degrees.

Goodhart considered the possible influence of subjects on this pattern of degree performance. Fewer women, for example, read mathematics, natural sciences and engineering subjects, which typically award more firsts and more Class III and Class 0 degrees. This could account for some of the differential performance, but in Goodhart's view it could not be the whole explanation 'since for all of the 12 major subjects (i.e. those with more than 50 candidates of each sex) the percentage of women in class I were below those for men'. It should be noted that the differences between males and females in Classics was negligible and women were found to do well in both medicine and modern and medieval languages. However, for all other subjects they achieved approximately half as many firsts as did the men.

In his discussion of these findings, Goodhart (1988a: 39) comments that given that twice as many males as females enter Cambridge, 'one might have supposed that the girls were being subjected to an even more rigorous process of selection so that those who were successful ought to be rather better than their male colleagues'. No information concerning the entry qualifications for students is provided, so the validity of this assertion cannot be judged. The possibility that examiner bias might operate to the disadvantage of women students, given that the large majority of examiners are male, is rejected by Goodhart on the grounds that scripts are not identifiable as male or female. An anecdote from one such examiners' meeting might, however, indicate that the possibility of examiners' differential expectations of female and male students is an issue. The meeting included a discussion of how to refer to candidates given that scripts bear numbers and not surnames. The suggestion that 'she' be used was commented on as 'unnatural'. Hence each candidate was referred to as 'he' until the Class III degrees were discussed. At this point, about half of the examiners (predominantly male, i.e. 9: 1) began to refer to certain candidates as 'she' without any apparent grounds for this in terms of the style or content of the scripts – a point we return to later.

In a later article, Goodhart (1988b) reviewed degree performance for the year 1988 and reported a similar pattern of male and female performance. In this article, Goodhart considered the possible influence of the college on students' achievements. A league table of colleges based on exam performance for males and females separately revealed that for men the range of firsts achieved from the top to the bottom of the league was 24 and 9 per cent, respectively, whereas for women these figures were 16.7 and 3.4 per cent, respectively. The figures for II(1)'s were 48.1 and to 32.1 per cent for men and 53.3 and 34.1 per cent for women. Hence overall the proportion of males and females achieving 'good' degrees is quite similar (57.7 *vs* 54.3 per cent).

Goodhart goes on to compare the performance of males and females in two colleges which were originally women's colleges (i.e. Girton and Newnham). Female students at both colleges used to achieve similar rates of success; however, since Girton became a mixed college in 1979, this is no longer the case. In 1988, Girton men achieved twice as many firsts as the women and slightly fewer II(1)'s; the performance of Girton women now being considerably worse than pre-1979. Women students at Newnham College, which has remained single-sex, now markedly out-perform those at Girton. Goodhart suggests that while Newnham must be losing 'a lot of good applicants to the former men's colleges', it continues to attract clever girls unlike Girton, which 'would not now seem to be especially attractive to many of those whose first choice is for a mixed college'. Hence it would seem that in Goodhart's view differential outcomes reflect the differing quality of the students entering the colleges.

Stewart (1988), in a letter responding to Goodhart's articles, looks at exam performance in Oxford for two 3-year periods, 1963–65 and 1983–85. He notes that in the earlier years, males and females achieved a similar proportion of firsts (9.6 *vs* 8.8 per cent). However, female students gained more second-class degrees (72.9 *vs* 57.1 per cent) and fewer thirds (18.3 *vs* 33.4 per cent) than males. In the 1980s, this changed, with males achieving nearly twice as many firsts as females (16.1 *vs* 8.9 per cent), and while women achieved more second-class degrees than men (81.3 *vs* 73 per cent), the proportions achieving third-class degrees were very similar (9.8 and 10.9 per cent for females and males, respectively). Stewart suggests that the reduction in the proportion of male students compared to female students in the Oxbridge intake from the 1960s through the 1980s made entry standards more comparable for men and women. This, in his view, would account for the decline in the number of male students achieving third-class degrees.

The change in the proportion of males achieving firsts Stewart finds baffling (note the similarity in the proportion of female firsts across the years). He speculates about several possible contributory factors to explain this phenomenon. These include: a differential intake (i.e. that the cleverest girls are not attracted to Oxford unlike clever boys); differential effectiveness of the attempt to broaden the base of entry to Oxford; differential response to exams (women students being less adept at exams than their male counterparts because of their preferred approach to study); and the possible deleterious effect on women students of the rapid onset of co-residence. On the last point, Stewart suggests that tutors used to dealing with undergraduates of one sex found that 'differences of tone and approach were sometimes required with the other sex'. Stewart speculates that these differences in tutorial style may take time to acquire and until then existing practice may be affecting female students adversely. Both Goodhart and Stewart agree about how little is known about the issues and call for further research (on the first one that is).

McCrum (1991) picks up the debate when he looks at the fairness of the admissions system for Oxford. In his review of intake patterns, he highlights the problem for women in achieving first-class results. He is attracted to Davies and Harré's hypothesis to account for this anomaly. Davies and Harré suggest that there is a compatibility between the 'socially constructed masculinity of male students and success in the education system' and an incompatibility between 'the corresponding femininity of female students and the way performances are valued in schools and colleges including Oxbridge' (Davies and Harré 1989). McCrum suggests, along with Stewart, that another factor to be considered is whether or not the Oxford tutorial system is incompatible with females' preferred style of learning. He characterizes the Oxford approach as 'combative' and a female learning style as 'collaborative'. In his view, while Oxford has opened its doors to women, it is the women who have to adapt to a system that has not changed.

To tackle the problem, he recommends an examination of existing assessment procedures followed by the introduction of carefully monitored changes to the university's approach to assessment. The key change that McCrum advocates is extending the time-scale of assessment and thus reducing the pressure on students. By implication, a pressurized approach is seen to enable male students, while disallowing females, to demonstrate their achievements in their preferred way. This is interesting considering GCSE course-work and the suggestion that this mode advantages girls and disadvantages boys and by contrast that the emphasis on a timed exam at A Level disadvantages girls. The relationship between anxiety, types of tests and academic achievement are complex, however (Saranson 1980), and there appears to be a negative relationship between anxiety and achievement.

Zoller and Ben-Chaim (1989) looked at this relationship and preferred examination types in a study of college science students in Israel. They found that females significantly more than males prefer the 'take-home' exam where any supporting material can be used and in unlimited time. Female students also have significantly more negative attitudes to oral exams than male students. Written exams with no supporting material allowed and with a restricted time allowance were the least desirable type for all students. A written exam with no time limit and access to any supporting material was popular with both males and females. Zoller and Ben-Chaim found that the test anxiety of female students was higher than that of males in traditional written exam conditions but dropped substantially in 'take-home' examinations. This reduction in anxiety was also found to correlate with better academic performance significantly more for females than males. Zoller and Ben-Chaim suggest that gender differences in science achievement are 'a possible testing artifact explained in terms of sociological perspectives and assessment practices'. Cross-cultural results such as these can be seen to add weight to McCrum's recommendations for changes in the examination procedures at Oxbridge. In the debate at university level, there seems to have been little inclination to examine either how the procedures used influence the constructs purported to be assessed or whether a review of scripts would reveal examiner bias in expectations.

Hannabus (1991, 1992) enters the debate to counter McCrum's view that women are disadvantaged by the examination system in Oxford. He rejects Davies and Harré's hypothesis on the grounds that up until 1976 the exam performance of males and females was remarkably alike, in that similar proportions achieved first-class degrees. Hannabus finds more compelling the evidence concerning the timing of the divergence in performance between male and female students.

Over a 4-year period from 1976 to 1980, males achieved more firsts while female performance remained relatively stable, leading to a 7 per cent gap in performance in favour of male students, this performance gap being maintained throughout the 1980s. The spurt in the performance of men corresponds to the introduction of mixed colleges at Oxford. For Hannabus, the performance effects are a by-product of the mixing of colleges. He offers no explanation about how the change in intake brought about an elevation in male degree success but he does reject the following explanations: erosion of standards; changes in recruitment policy; differential changes in the competition for admission of males and females; and differential responses to mixing. While this latter explanation is supported to an extent by research into girls' and boys' performance in schools, it remains the case that men's degree performance, in terms of the number of first-class degrees obtained, improved across both single-sex and mixed colleges.

Goodhart (1992) reports a similar phenomenon at Cambridge, i.e. a big improvement in men's results over the period 1983–89 without any large decline in women's performance for the same period. He likewise is unable to explain the phenomenon. Furthermore, he returns to the contentious issue of the ratio of male to female academics and reiterates that until more females achieve firsts the situation is unlikely to change. Consequently, one is left wondering which is the chicken and which is the egg.

Rowell (1991), prompted by Goodhart's findings, carried out a review of male and female performance at her own university, Berkeley. The intake pattern for Berkeley is very different to that of Oxford and Cambridge. Almost equal numbers of males and females enter, selected on merit and slightly more women than men graduate. The ethnic and cultural diversity of Berkeley students is also considerably greater than that of the student populations of Oxford and Cambridge. Rowell found no significant differences in the final grades achieved by male and female students at Berkeley for the academic year 1989–90. She does, however, point out that the examination system at Berkeley is very different to that of Oxford and Cambridge and that direct comparisons are invalid. At Berkeley, students take examinations at the end of each semester and accumulate a grade point average.

Rowell challenges Goodhart's assumption that examiner bias is eradicated by the use of initials and not names and suggests that at various points in the assessment procedure it would be easy for an examiner to get to know who students were despite numerical identifiers. She goes on to consider the mode of assessments used and suggests that bias in judgement of essay responses is bound to 'creep in' when both style and content influence examiners. She also gives credit to the view that there are differences in approach in female scholarship and traditional male scholarship and comments that this may lead 'to some of the best women students being under-appreciated by male examiners'. Consequently, she hypothesizes that the 'less elegant examinations set at Berkeley might also be less biased'. By 'less elegant' Rowell is referring to the use of exams without essay-type responses, a response mode she prefers to short answers or multiple-choice formats and one which is common to Cambridge exams. This is an interesting point, which focuses on bias in assessors' responses to students rather than bias in the assessment itself.

Bradley's (1984) study was based on the hypothesis that personal supervisors' familiarity with students decreased the potential for bias in their assessment of their projects. Hence she predicted that second markers furnished only with the names of students would mark males more extremely than their supervisors, i.e. males would be awarded more firsts and thirds. The results from four university departments did produce more extreme marks for males than females from second markers. Belsey (1988) looked at degree performance in the Art Faculty at University College Cardiff in the UK before and after 1985, which was the time blind marking was introduced. The figures for English showed that women achieved a significantly higher proportion of 'good' degrees (i.e. firsts and upper seconds) relative to men after 1985, resulting in a narrowing of the performance gap that had existed previously. Whether these findings can be attributed to marker bias remains debatable.

The need to consider institutional assessment practice is further supported by Mason's (1985) study of Open University (UK) students' degree success. Here again we have a very different student population and the distance learning mode does negate the possibility of examiners 'knowing' the students, which is not to say that examiner bias at a more global level can be ruled out. Mason again found no significant differences in the overall achievements of male and female students.

Standing back from this debate, there are several avenues that warrant further exploration. The institutional influence clearly needs to be explored by looking at male and female degree success across other institutions by subjects studied. Alongside this it would be necessary to investigate institutional practices in terms of the types of examinations used, the nature of examiners' meetings, the contribution of continuous assessment and the potential for differential examiner expectations within these procedures. These two latter avenues should also be considered in light of findings and hypotheses emerging from research into assessment practice and pupil performance at the secondary and primary levels of education.

Another problem that cannot be disregarded when looking across institutions relates to the very different characteristics of the student populations involved. Clearly entry qualifications should be considered, but research reviewed in previous chapters indicates that this is not always a good predictor of future success, and again may vary according to the gender, race and ethnic background of the student.

As with any consideration of the 'fairness' of assessment procedures, the research questions to be addressed are complex and multivariable. Bearing in mind the complex interaction already revealed between pupil and task and the influence of self-image and gender stereotypes on this interaction, the research at tertiary level would have to take seriously the potential alienating influence on groups of students of certain institutional approaches to learning as well as assessment. With this in mind, it would be important to consider the changes in student population from entry to graduation. For example, since mixed colleges were introduced at Cambridge and Oxbridge, what effect has there been on the drop-out rate of male and female students? How does this vary from subject to subject and what characterizes the females who drop out and the females who stay the course?

Questions such as these have been the subject of research in the domains of science and technology where explanations have been sought to account for the under-representation of women. For example, Linden *et al.* (1985) compared the male and female undergraduates who persisted successfully in their engineering programme with those students who left. Her study was part of the National Engineering Career Development Study at Purdue University. She found that entry qualifications were the most important predictors of success for both males and females; however, other variables were also significant for female students. In particular, female students' *self-perceived abilities* helped determine whether or not they persisted in the programme. Those females

who graduated tended to have higher entry grades than successful males but somewhat lower self-perceived abilities. Linden
highlights the need for institutions to support females in developing
a positive view of their talents if they are to achieve their entry
potential. Matyas (1987) reported similar findings in her study
of retention rates for biology majors in a large mid-western US
university.

Gardner (1975) looked at the drop-out rate for male and female
engineering students and found that equal numbers of males and
females drop out but that their reasons for doing so vary. For
example, the attrition rate for men due to their academic performance was five times greater than for females. Women transferred
in the main because of the restrictions imposed by the curriculum
and the atmosphere of the university. Findings such as these are
not replicated in other countries. Rom (1987), for example, looked
at undergraduate performance in Israel for the year 1977 and found
that more female students graduated, fewer dropped out and overall they achieved higher grades than male students. These statistics
were true for the whole population and more pronounced when
considered for each faculty separately.

Discussion

What this chapter illustrates is a complex and changing pattern of
measured performance in examinations between males and females
from 16+ through to degree level. At GCSE, girls' performance
is steadily improving over boys. By 1992, 42 per cent of girls
achieved five passes at grades A–C compared with only 34 per cent
of boys; 14 per cent more girls than boys attained grades A–C in
English and 11 per cent more in modern languages; and in maths
and science girls were attaining almost as many A–C grades as
boys, compared with 10 per cent fewer in the early 1980s. In 1992
for the first time, girls were 'leaving school with a greater overall
proportion of grades A to C in Mathematics, Science and English,
regarded as critical qualifications for students who wish to take A
levels' (*Times Educational Supplement*, 8 November 1992: 'Girls
outshine boys in school exams').

At advanced level, however, the trend is reversed. Despite more
girls staying on and taking A Levels than boys, male candidates

achieved higher average grades overall and were much more likely to achieve the maximum points score used for university entrance than girls. One in eight boys compared with one in eleven girls gained the equivalent of three A grade A Levels in 1992. At university level, the male advantage over females seems to increase at Oxford and Cambridge with men from state schools more than twice as likely to gain a first-class degree than women. The same findings are not the case for other universities which have different types of intake, teaching style and examination mode from Oxford and Cambridge.

Studies of differential performance by ethnic and racial group reveal that Asian pupils in the UK out-perform their white peers in London schools at 16 +, and that Afro-Caribbean pupils achieve lower average exam scores than either white pupils or pupils from other ethnic or racial backgrounds. The studies typically identify social class, ethnic group and gender as the factors which account, to differing extents, for the variation in the exam performance of sub-groups at 16 +. More recent studies of this performance effect have, however, tended to focus on the school's contribution to differential exam performance and consider that it is the school rather than the pupils' ethnicity which is the critical factor in determining the level of exam success.

Considered overall, these studies suggest that social class and the school attended mediate the exam performance of ethnic sub-groups. However, how this arises is not yet understood and there remain problems with defining the social indicators used to determine sub-groups and how best to represent a multidimensional construct such as school effectiveness. Furthermore, the studies do not consider how the assessment instruments and processes used in examinations at 16 + contribute to differential sub-group performance.

To some extent, these changing patterns of performance have been linked to the changing nature of the particular test population. Hence girls' success in physics at GCSE and A Level is explained by their being a more highly selected sample. At times, however, links have been made between the *proportion* of male and females entering for exams and their subsequent success in them. The implication is that the greater the representation of the sub-group, the greater the level of success achieved by it in grade terms; alternatively, where a subject has a large entry from one gender only, relatively high attainers from the other gender enter it. Discussion of possible patterns in undergraduate performance has, however, suggested that females' achievements have decreased in relation to males as the proportion of females in the total undergraduate sample has increased. These wide-ranging speculations indicate our limited understanding of the factors causing these shifting, differential patterns in sub-group performance.

It is widely accepted that affective factors mediate students' performance in assessments. There is evidence presented in this chapter that these factors may interact with gender and method of measurement. If the learnt behaviours and expectations of sub-groups alter their reaction to different methods of measurement, this may lead to misrepresentation of sub-group achievement. For example, a task with a particular mode of response rather than measuring the construct assumed may for some students only measure their level of confidence in themselves with regard to the domain being assessed. Nor can we assume that non-responses, or 'I don't knows', in these instances mean that pupils have not achieved the construct. For both males and females, there is a need to explore *characteristic* responses to assessment tasks. Without further evidence of this kind, assessment outcomes cannot be interpreted, nor can fair assessments be developed, or steps taken to tackle the limiting effects of certain domain-related psycho-social factors on students' progress.

As well as finding out how students react to tasks and a range of measurement methods, it is necessary to establish how, or if, these influence teachers' judgements of achievements. There is some indication of these influences in the course-work review by Stobart *et al.* (1992b), but further exploration of the distribution of course-work marks for males and females in relation to the constructs being assessed would be valuable. Account also needs to be taken of moderators' perceptions of achievements within domains and how these might lead to differential school and centre effects at GCSE.

Across the phases discussed in this chapter, the problem of teacher/assessor beliefs has been raised. There are numerous research studies which consider how attributes of students (e.g. physical attraction, compliance, race, gender, etc.) affect teachers' beliefs about their intelligence and potential educational achievement (Ritts *et al.* 1992). The measures used in these studies are often questionable, as they tend to focus on extremes in the case of physical or behavioural attributes. It is also rare to find studies of this kind which look at the interaction between potential sources of personal bias. It should be noted that there is evidence that teachers' expectations accurately predict student performance. The issue, then, is perhaps not so much about assessor bias but self-fulfilling prophecies, which may be initiated in the wider society but compounded in schools and other education institutions. Although blind marking is becoming more widely advocated, as much to ensure that equal opportunities are *seen* to be being provided (British Psychological Society 1989), recent studies at the tertiary level have failed to replicate the finding that females are marked less extremely than males (Newstead and Dennis 1990). Clearly there is again not enough empirical evidence to indicate whether non-blind marking does indeed lead to the misrepresentation of student achievement.

What this chapter does indicate is that we cannot be complacent about our lack of awareness of the effects of assessment method and practices on the validity of judgements about student performance. It also suggests that any further exploration of potential sources of assessment invalidity must include a consideration of racial and ethnic group responses to a range of different assessment items and circumstances. The factors identified in the research discussed here which might be influential sources of invalidity include: factors within the assessment itself (e.g. item format and response mode); the effect of the gender and specialism of the marker; examiners' constructions of the subject and what counts as achievement in it; maturational differences between the genders; school effects (especially for minority ethnic groups); ability level of selected 18 + samples; racism in schools and outside it; tutorial style and pressure of examinations; motivation and self-esteem; expectations from self and society. The list is long and probably not complete; it covers *all* the hypotheses and most of the factors we listed in the Introduction as causing differential performance – biological, environmental and assessment-based hypotheses. It is, of course, impossible to say which set of hypotheses is most relevant and in any case the water is murky. As we pointed out at the beginning of this chapter, changes in assessment practice, which contribute to differential performance, also reflect changes in approach to how subjects are defined and what constitutes 'success' in them. We hope to tie up some of these many threads in the final chapter.

9

CONCLUSIONS: BEYOND THE CONCEPT OF A FAIR TEST

We start this chapter by reviewing the purpose of assessment; we need to consider what assessment is before we can evaluate whether it is fair, valid or sound. 'Fitness for purpose' is a crucial aspect of the discussion about tests and testing but it is all too often forgotten or relegated.

Assessment can be used to identify what pupils have learned, what they have not learned and where they are having difficulty. In this way, it supports the teaching–learning process and this form of assessment is described as *formative*; this category includes diagnostic assessment, which is a specific form of formative assessment. Assessment can also be used for managerial purposes – to select and certificate students – and as an accountability tool – to provide evaluative information about teachers, schools or age groups at a national level. Assessment used for these purposes is *summative*, i.e. the assessment tends to be a one-off taken at the end of a course or period of schooling and involves collating and reporting results for third parties (for a more detailed discussion, see Gipps and Stobart 1993). Formative and summative assessments have different properties; for example, for summative assessment, consistency across tasks and markers is important, since we need some confidence that it can be used to make comparisons between individuals, schools, LEAs, etc. For formative assessment, consistency is less significant, informality tends to be a feature and content and construct validity are much more important than reliability (see Harlen *et al.* 1992).

Whether assessment is for formative or summative purposes has a bearing on how we consider bias or slant in the assessment. First, bearing in mind different uses, there may be an equity argument for reducing differential group performance in summative assessment (although we would maintain that this should be done only in cases when not to do so would misrepresent student achievement), while for formative assessment we might wish to explore such differences for what they can tell us about pupils' learning and understanding of particular tasks/constructs. Second, focusing on consequential validity – whether an assessment is valid for the uses to which it is put – we would say that the more significant the use of the assessment for any individual, the more important it is to consider the equity issues, which might influence how we interpret performance in terms of achievement; these would include access to learning as well as any unfairness in the assessment or assessment process itself.

Our view is that the main purpose of assessment should be for professional rather than managerial or accountability purposes. But we recognize that, as we pointed out in the Introduction, the high profile of assessment in this decade is in relation to managerial and accountability purposes, so we must address these in this review and conclusion. The need to reconsider the purpose of assessment relates to our critique of psychometrics. Assessment as originally developed had a very particular and specific function – to identify and classify individuals' specific skills and abilities. Psychometrics thus developed in a particular way to support a particular assessment purpose. Assessment now has many more uses and the appropriate model for assessment to support learning is an educational assessment model.

Educational assessment has a constructive focus where the aim is to help rather than sentence the individual; thus it emphasizes the individual's achievement relative to him or herself rather than to others, or in relation to defined criteria. It is most effective when standardized procedures are relaxed and consequently does not produce well-behaved data (after Wood 1986). Performance assessment, which is currently much discussed in the USA, is a sub-set of educational assessment, and emphasizes best rather than typical performance based on assessment tasks which emulate the kind of process-based higher-order tasks thought to represent good practice (Shepard 1991). This form of assessment is most suitable for formative purposes, although both in the UK (with SATs and course-work in GCSE) and in the USA, attempts are being used to develop their role in summative assessment for accountability purposes, because of the impact which high-stakes tests have on the curriculum and pedagogy (Linn 1993; Gipps 1993).

We have critiqued the psychometric approach in a number of chapters and our conclusion is that using statistical techniques to select the items in a test in order to produce particular performance patterns is misguided and misleading. What this does is to confound the construct being assessed and consequently the scores cannot be interpreted adequately; the test may in fact be assessing a different attribute. The emphasis on gaining reliable results through statistical means (e.g. in NAEP) has meant that issues of construct validity are ignored and yet this is crucial in any consideration of performance and achievement. The notion of general ability, which stems from factor analysis models of intelligence testing, is also an unhelpful legacy as it allows a focus on performance in narrow aspects of achievement related to numeracy and literacy which are considered predictive of all other aspects of achievement and hence can be used to make judgements about individuals.

Psychometrics and educational assessment are based on different concepts of the nature of learning and learners. Critiques of the psychometric model therefore dispute that a narrow definition of achievement along single traits like verbal and quantitative ability adequately represent human achievement and potential. Educational assessment reflects the view that achievement in domains is far more complex than that represented in typical psychometric models, hence the need to consider construct validity from both the subject perspective and the learner's perspective. Assessment that is concerned with identifying what pupils have learned must be based on a conception of the nature of learning and learners; when considering fairness (or 'soundness') of assessments, we need to be clear about the conceptions underlying the specific assessments. However, educational assessment is still in its infancy, and within it definitions of achievement and learning vary.

As Goldstein (1993) points out, 'bias' is built into the test developers' construct of the subject and their expectations of differential performance. As we noted in Chapter 6 in relation to science testing, more effort has gone into exploring cognitive deficits in girls to explain their poor performance than into asking whether the reliance on tasks and apparatus associated with upper middle-class white males could possibly have something to do with it. Similarly, we feel that focusing on 'bias' in tests, which suggests that there is such a thing as a fair test, has distracted attention from wider equity issues, such as actual equality of access, inhibiting classroom practices and the like.

Furthermore, a number of the statistical techniques used in psychometrics assume a single latent trait in the construct being assessed, e.g. Item Response Theory (IRT) methods and the NAEP proficiency scales. What this does is to ignore the obvious (we would say) dimensionality of domains; the process is therefore artificial and casts doubt on the validity of a single 'score' to indicate performance in a complex domain. One interesting development is that performance assessment cannot be developed using traditional psychometric techniques, because far fewer items are involved. This means that the Differential Item Functioning (DIF) procedure for detecting item bias (Linn *et al.* 1991) cannot be used. This may force a shift towards other ways of reviewing and evaluating items based on qualitative approaches (e.g. sensitivity review), consideration of the construct and how the task might interact with experience. It may also require us to be far more circumspect in our interpretations of assessment outcomes in terms of what they tell us about individual achievement.

Hypotheses relating to sources of group differences

A review of the evidence presented in Chapters 4–8 can help us to comment on the status of these hypotheses. As we point out, research evidence indicates that biological explanations of differences in performance between racial and ethnic groups are not tenable, and this argument is no longer used, in the UK at any rate. We believe, however, that the data from international surveys and the changing patterns of performance in O Level/GCSE exams in the UK shows that biological factors do not account for gender differences either. Girls in certain social settings can outperform boys in the same and other social settings and variation within groups is greater than variation between groups (in the school subjects), so gender differences cannot be argued on the basis of genetic, hormonal or brain structure difference between the sexes.

Environmental, or psycho-social, factors are much more likely to be the cause of differences in performance, particularly, as Halpern points out, for the vast majority of the population, the value of the environmental hypotheses over biological ones is that they imply the possibility of change. However, as Chapter 2 shows, the issues are enormously complex and we could not possibly offer a definitive review of each of these hypotheses.

Differences in achievement, the APU, NAEP and international surveys show, are related to differences in opportunity to learn to a large extent: when differences in curriculum background are controlled or out-of-school experiences taken into account, group differences are reduced. This differential learning experience can advantage or disadvantage one group because of their different experience of context, content, task demand, mode of assessment and style of response. Attitudes, APU studies have shown, also have an important effect on achievement via students' level of confidence and more subtle effects such as what is seen as significant in the task(s). In terms of gender, the psycho-social variables affect how boys and girls come to view themselves, how they become viewed by others, how the subject is 'constructed' and how achievement within it is defined. These effects alter how students perceive assessment tasks, the solutions they consider appropriate and their perceptions of their potential success or failure in regard to them.

We have to recognize that views of what constitutes achievement both in terms of how it is defined and revealed will reflect the value judgements of powerful groups in society. Hence people outside of those groups who are subject to different values by choice or otherwise will be affected by assessments based on such perspectives. Nor indeed is it tenable to see a time in the future when these differential values and power positions will be removed.

They will no doubt change but differences and barriers to equality will continue. Hence to achieve justice in assessment, interpretations of students' performance should be set in the explicit context of what is or is not being valued and on the basis of what evidence or prejudice. We have at present a classic example of this in the assessment of English achievement in the UK: achievement in this domain now reflects the values of a minority group which has great power. By defining achievement in this way, large numbers of individuals will appear deficient (from this perspective). This is 'unfair' if one does not accept the minority view, but within the paradigm that the minority is working in, it is valid and hence 'fair'. In exploring issues of equity and fairness in assessment we are essentially exploring perspectives on the nature of learners and views of human learning. The book reveals insights that provide a basis for further research enquiry, which we take up later in this chapter.

In relation to the research reviewed, we can see that international surveys are based on relatively narrow definitions of subject achievement and rely on single and similarly narrow systems of measurement, i.e. objective standardized test formats. As such, these reflect the traditions of the psychometric paradigm. We can consider differential performance outcomes, not to determine if there are ability differences between groups, but what messages they convey about the groups' educational experience which leads to the achievement or non-achievement of the qualities valued in international assessment instruments. The performance differences in maths and science are explained in terms of environmental factors, largely in terms of the way girls and boys relate to subjects and how affective responses mediate their cognitive response. However, there is the issue of differential access raised by these samples, so that performance outcomes may indeed reflect differences in actual achievement because the opportunities to learn are not equal across sub-groups.

Support for the hypothesis of differential access is strengthened by the measured differences in performance between cultures where curriculum values vary. Hence, for example, while boys outperform girls on physics in Japan, Japanese girls out-perform American boys. This finding is explained by some researchers in terms of the greater value placed on mathematics for all pupils in Japan, which affects performance in physics.

The other significant issue to emerge from these surveys relates to the definition of achievement. There is some suggestion that the content validity of the maths tests is questionable and a strong case put by Kelly that the subject of science itself is a masculine activity reflecting masculine values which are not accessible to girls, hence the definition of the subject is biased. To explore these points further it would be necessary to focus on the content validity and construct validity of the test instruments. However, as these surveys are generally reported within the psychometric tradition', such questions are obviously (and legitimately) not asked by the assessors themselves.

The NAEP national surveys reflect similar narrow definitions of achievement which are considered in equally narrow ways, i.e. multiple-choice tests, small numbers of tasks per trait. In the psychometric model, equality of outcome is assumed; where it does not emerge, it is assumed that real differences in achievement are being measured. The correspondence between NAEP results and many of the trends in the international surveys does indicate that significant differences in sub-group performance in relation to how achievement is defined do arise across countries for maths, science and English for males and females; and across the board for ethnic and racial groups compared with white students. This lends support to environmental hypotheses because of (1) their consistency and (2) the differences that emerge are for a sub-group overall, but individuals within each sub-group achieve the highest and lowest levels for the population as a whole, hence refuting the possibility of biological explanations for 'innate' differences between groups.

Patterns of performance

There do seem to be clear changes in patterns of performance between black and white pupils in the USA, boys and girls in the UK and USA, and some minority groups and ethnic majority pupils in the UK. NAEP data show that the black–white achievement gap has narrowed, although significant differences continue in each content area tested; the improvements by blacks have been in the lower proficiency levels in reading, maths and science (Linn 1992). Gender differences in maths in the USA show a consistent decline, although this trend has been more gradual at the level of college admission tests (Linn 1992). International surveys appear to show that the gender gap in maths has narrowed, even reversed. The pattern of performance in the UK now shows girls performing better than boys in English, maths and science in the Standard Assessment Tasks at ages 7 and 14. At GCSE (age 16), girls' performance is improving compared with boys: in 1992, girls gained significantly more good grades (A–C) in GCSE overall than boys. However, the 7–16 pattern is reversed at 18 + and the same appears to be the case in the USA.

In the UK, Asian pupils are performing better than white pupils in London schools, while Afro-Caribbean pupils are performing least well generally. The interaction between social class and ethnic group in the UK has not been well-enough studied, however, to disentangle its effect.

What we have to ask, however, is whether these trends reflect *actual* changes in achievement or whether they are the result of changes in the make-up of the sample tested, the type of test item used or changes in the definition of the subject? The answer to these questions is not straightforward. For example, the piece about declining SAT results in the Introduction is quite misleading because it does not make the point about the sample sufficiently clear. The overall mean has dropped if you look at the total (test-taking) population:

> However, although the mean of the total population has dropped, the mean of every major racial and ethnic group within the main population has *risen* over the last 15 years. It is the increased involvement of the lower scoring groups that has led to the overall drop.
>
> (Jaegar 1992, quoted by Linn 1993)

Thus once account is taken of the larger overall test-taking population, by any logical interpretation of the notion of 'standards' these have risen on the SAT despite publicity to the contrary.

Our review of the APU data suggests that there is a relatively stable pattern of performance within subjects and that where this changes it is due to alteration in the definition of the subject, e.g. by extending the range of achievements monitored and the way in which these are elicited. It is also actually quite difficult to evaluate the changing patterns of performance in O Level/CSE and GCSE because of the changes in style of assessment and the constructs assessed. There is also the pervasive difficulty of evaluating changes in performance over time; to measure change accurately, we need to use the same test items from one test survey to the next, but the problem with this is that these items will over time either date (and become harder) or be over-prepared for (and become easier) (see Nuttall 1986).

In the UK, it is apparent that changes to the 16+ public exam with the introduction of GCSEs have affected patterns of differential performance, in particular the introduction of course-work assessment so that the final grade is not totally derived from a timed examination. This is thought to be a main contributing factor to girls' improved performance; there is evidence that females do less well in timed examinations due to higher levels of anxiety. However, we believe it is fair to say that course-work is *not* the sole cause of improved performance among girls in this examination. In maths, where there was little course-work until 1991, girls' performance has also improved compared with that of boys and the particularly well-established gap between them at this age has narrowed. This pattern of improving girls' scores in mathematics is matched by similar findings in international studies, the APU and national curriculum assessment at Key Stage Three. The work of women maths educators in curriculum development and teacher education should not be underestimated here: girls are enjoying and participating in maths more, and they see the subject less in functional terms and less as a male subject (Stobart *et al.* 1992).

There was a direct relationship between the improvement in girls' grades between 1985 and 1988 and the type and weighting of course-work in the GCSE syllabuses (Quinlan 1991). However, as we pointed out in Chapter 8, the picture is far from clear-cut and it is important not to make simplistic judgements. A common belief is that girls' success in course-work can be accounted for in terms of better organizational and presentation skills, but a qualitative review of course-work in English and maths (ULEAC/ NFER 1992) indicates that this is not the case.

For maths, the finding of this research on the 1991 GCSE was that girls showed a small but consistent mark advantage on course-work which tended to offset similar small mark advantages for boys on the examinations. Cresswell (1990) also found that girls' course-work marks tended to be more bunched than boys; if course-work marks are bunched and the examination marks spread widely, then it is the examination that is likely to play the main role in determining pupils' rank order. Thus it would seem from the evaluations carried out so far that girls' improved performance compared with that of boys in GCSE is not simply a course-work effect.

It is, of course, possible that course-work is affecting performance in some other way; for example, that doing well-structured course-work results in deeper engagement with the subject which, and particularly so in the case of girls in mathematics, leads to a generally improved performance in the subject. The APU science team found that when girls were able to establish tasks for themselves, rather than working with established tasks which were to them less relevant, their performance was better than that of boys. Similar findings emerged from Thailand and Australia where 'girl-friendly' science is seen as being based on open novel tasks (Murphy 1991). It may be that the scope for defining and controlling the task in course-work assessment does *actually* enhance the performance of girls. More research on other cohorts and papers would be appropriate, as would similar analyses by ethnic group.

There is still much to be understood about the effect of course-work on performance and this is important to our understanding of assessment (not just to gender differences in performance), since course-work is a school-based performance assessment and represents a more valid and less artificial assessment in the educational assessment paradigm than timed examinations.

Psycho-social factors can also affect pupil performance. Within-school experience is clearly a major contributing factor to differential group performance and there is a considerable amount of research in this area. However, in our view it is not generally particularly well conceptualized and we hope that the contribution of this book will be as much to the re-conceptualization of the issues as to the general raising of awareness. Furthermore, the large-scale studies tend not to look at the interactions of gender, ethnic group and social background when looking at differential performance, although as Plewis (1988) points out, multi-level modelling techniques now make this feasible.

Studies of performance which do look at a range of factors and use multi-level modelling techniques, offer a focus on the effect of the school (although the conclusions on this are not clear-cut). There is increasing evidence that some schools are more effective for one group than another; for example, the ILEA Junior School Study found that there were some schools which were more effective in teaching reading for boys than girls (Mortimore *et al.* 1988). Later more sophisticated re-analysis of the data also indicated that some schools were more effective for pupils who were higher or lower attainers on entry (Sammons *et al.* 1993). The ILEA analysis of examination results revealed that some schools were particularly effective for Pakistani pupils, or Caribbean pupils or boys/girls, i.e. that school effectiveness varies in terms of the relative performance of different sub-groups (Nuttall *et al.* 1989). In Drew and Gray's (1991) view, the case is not proven that the school is a *major* contributing factor to the differences in performance among ethnic groups, although they accept that schools certainly differ in their effectiveness.

A main 'linking' factor seems to be social class. Although the ILEA analysis did not show what Cuttance (1988) refers to as a 'true compositional effect' i.e. that a concentration of low socio-economic status (SES) pupils depresses the performance of a school (because there was no measure of SES for individual pupils), there was an indication of it in that as the percentage of free school meals in a school increased, performance levels decreased. In his own work, Cuttance found that attainment in schools in deprived neighbourhoods is depressed even after pupil ability and family background have been taken into account (i.e. that there is a compound or compositional effect). This would suggest that for some ethnic minority pupils who are disadvantaged (e.g. Bangladeshi pupils in London), there may be a school effect on achievement if they are concentrated together. This was a finding of the Coleman Report in the USA: the one school characteristic that showed a consistent relationship with test performance was the one characteristic to which poor black children were denied access – classmates from affluent homes (Jencks 1972).

A recent study in California suggests that 'racial and ethnic segregation' can, but does not always, lead to achievement differences across schools and among ethnic groups (Rumberger and Willms 1992). Their results suggest that there can be a school effect in that 'students, in general, achieve better results when they attend a school with higher average parental background. Because minority students are less likely to attend schools with favourable school contexts, they are less able to capitalise on contextual effects.' The authors conclude that de-segregating students *and* changing the distribution of resources would reduce the white/minority achievement gap. They found that context (i.e. proportion of black/white pupils and proportion of pupils with advantaged home backgrounds as measured by level of parental education) was correlated with level of teaching and non-teaching resources. This is not surprising, since in the USA funding is largely locally determined so that 'poor' areas spend less on education and disadvantaged children are likely to be in disadvantaged, poorly resourced schools. In the UK, the situation is different and many inner-cities and/or disadvantaged areas spend more per pupil on education than do more privileged areas.

We have a number of times referred to teacher stereotype as having an effect on differential performance. The mechanism through which the effect operates is expectation: teacher expectation has for a number of years been understood (although imperfectly) to have a self-fulfilling effect on performance through determining the range of curriculum experiences offered to different individuals, and the type of feedback.

With regard to gender, the position seems to depend on the subject context in which judgements are made and the curriculum background of the teachers. For example, in maths GCSE there appears to be a tendency to restrict certain boys' entry to the foundation level; more girls are assumed to be 'average' rather than above average in their achievements in this area and are entered for the intermediate level; however, more boys than girls are entered for the highest level. These findings reinforce research in the area which suggests that boys' approach to learning is often viewed as indicative of high intelligence. Their approach typically is labelled as more ebullient, aggressive, confident and risk-taking, all of which are values associated with a greater cognitive understanding of subjects (see Walden and Walkerdine 1985). Girls' tendency to conform, work hard and to prioritize neatness are seen, on the other hand, to reflect a mediocrity of mind. Consequently, teachers expect less of girls as a group, which results in the 'learned helplessness' syndrome quoted by Licht and Dweck

(1983). Yet these approaches to school work are learnt behaviours related to differential socialization patterns of boys and girls and are not fair indicators of achievement.

The overall picture, put crudely, is that more girls than boys will be considered average; consequently, some girls' achievement will be underestimated whereas others may be overestimated. Conversely, there is more likelihood that boys rather than girls will be considered either to be high achievers or low achievers and their actual achievements will also be misrepresented. What is not clear in this picture is the influence of the perceived value of the subject on the distribution of the genders in teacher judgements of performance.

It has been suggested that in the UK many teachers have negative attitudes towards Afro-Caribbean pupils and low expectation of their academic performance; that as a result, they treat them less favourably in the classroom and in wider school processes, denying them the educational opportunities enjoyed by their white peers; and that many therefore experience alienation, low academic achievement and consequently restricted life chances (Foster 1990). This is less likely to be the case for Asian pupils whose families are perceived as valuing education, whose approach to schooling is more similar to that of the white middle class, and for whom any early problems may be seen to be related to lack of English proficiency.

Teacher–student interaction is both caused and determined by teacher stereotypes of various groups of pupils. Gillborn (1992) points out that a number of studies indicate a more positive 'caricature' of Asian students where they are in schools which have high proportions of both South Asian and Afro-Caribbean students. By contrast, the few studies that have looked at Asian pupils in schools where they are in the majority, and the minority is mainly white, suggests that teachers have more negative stereotypes of Asian pupils in such a setting.

The influence of teacher expectation in an assessment context is crucial. With the introduction in the UK in 1994 of differentiated exam entry based on teacher judgements in *all* subjects in GCSE *and* in national assessment at Key Stages Two and Three, the issue of differential teacher expectations must be of central concern in any debate about equity and assessment.

A factor which contributes to performance is confidence – this is intimately related to both past achievement and motivation. Lack of confidence has frequently been cited as a reason for inhibiting the success of girls and women. This is not, however, necessarily related to low ability, since even when girls achieve as well or better than boys, they tend to underestimate themselves compared with boys (Lundeberg 1992). However, this is not a general effect: it is domain-specific. Similarly, sex differences in causal attributions are dependent on the context and task. Thus we can see that content assessed, confidence, achievement and attributions interact. For our theme, the important point is that when looking at achievement we must also look at the task-in-context in order to interpret the outcomes.

The shift in the pattern of gender performance that occurs around the age of 16 points up the significance of attitudes. Society's attitudes to male and female sex roles and appropriate careers may be changing, but they are still different for the two genders. A major factor behind this shift seems to be what society at large, and therefore girls themselves, think it is appropriate and acceptable for girls to do. Girls may get turned off the status, style and connotations of some high-status subjects and of careers altogether, in a similar way to that in which some Afro-Caribbean and other ethnic minority boys can get turned off school. Nelson-Le Gall (1992) points out that white girls' academic and personal self-esteem plummets between elementary and high school in the USA, a phenomenon referred to as 'going underground'.

It seems that the affective traits acquired by certain groups of pupils concerning their abilities and roles in life are reinforced in school (and by society) as they come towards the end of compulsory schooling and the effect is to control their cognitive potential. This results in the underachievement of girls and some ethnic minority groups in relation to boys and the majority group.

Towards equity: An agenda

By now it should be clear that there is no such thing as a fair test, nor could there be: the situation is too complex and the notion simplistic. However, by paying attention to what we know about factors in assessment and their administration and scoring, we can begin to work towards tests that are more fair to all the groups likely to be taking them, and this is particularly important for assessment used for summative and accountability purposes. Context is a particular example: developers are told that they should avoid domains which may be more familiar to males than females or to the dominant culture. But there are problems inherent in trying to *remove* context effects by removing passages that advantage males or females, because it reduces the amount of items/contexts available. Decontextualized assessment is anyway not possible, and complex reasoning processes require drawing on complex domain knowledge (Linn 1992). In an assessment which looks for best rather than typical performance, the context of the item should be the one which allows the pupil to perform well; this would suggest different contexts for different pupils or groups, an awesome development task.

One reason why we cannot look for fair tests is that we cannot assume identical experiences for all. This is also why we do not look for equal outcomes; for this we would need assessment tailored to different groups. However, studies of exam performance in the UK tend to operate on the (unstated) hypothesis of equal outcomes. One can see why this is so: an equity argument can be sustained here, since one might look for equal outcomes in public exams in order to put, say, ethnic minority students in as good a position as ethnic majority students for gaining jobs and access to higher education. The fact is that despite the influence of racism on employment (Brown 1984), exam results are important, since the possession of higher grade passes is associated with lower levels of unemployment for all ethnic groups (Clough and Drew 1985, quoted in Gillborn 1990), and they tend to be a necessary, if not sufficient, condition of access to high-status employment. We do argue, therefore, that on the grounds of equity, all groups be offered actual equality of access to the curriculum and that the exams and assessments are as fair as possible to all groups.

So how do we ensure that assessment practice and interpretation of results is as fair as possible for all groups? It is likely that a wide-ranging review of syllabus content, teacher attitudes to both boys and girls, assessment mode and item format is required if we wish to make public exams as fair as possible to both genders (and remember that boys are seriously under-performing in English in relation to girls, which must be of concern). Although this is a major task, it is one which must be addressed in the developing context of national standards, national curricula and national assessment. As an example that it is possible, we cite the case of the Physics Higher School Certificate in South Australia; girls' performance in physics has improved since 1988 when a female chief examiner was appointed. This examiner has deliberately worked within a particular model of physics (which takes a 'whole view' of the subject); simplified the language of the questions; included contexts only that are integral to particular physics problems; offered a range of different ways of answering questions which does not privilege one form of answer over another; provided a list of key instruction words and how students would go about answering questions which include these words (ESSSA 1992).

Given what we have said about marking – in which the perceived gender of the student can have a powerful effect on the mark ascribed – we suggest also that names of candidates are replaced by numbers in public exams; this would be more fair to different ethnic groups as well as to girls and boys. There are signs that this is beginning to happen within the university sector (*Times Higher Education Supplement*, 16 April 1993).

We also need to instil into the public's consciousness that tests and assessments have their limitations: 'Tests are not mysterious sources of information, miraculously perfect and fair' (ETS 1991: 3). They can give us some information about what pupils were able and willing to do at one particular point in time in relation to what the test was designed to measure *and* depending on how efficient it is at this.

We need to encourage clearer articulation of the test/exam developers' construct on which the assessment is based, so that the construct validity may be examined by test-takers and -users. Test developers need to justify the inclusion of context and types of response mode in relation to the evidence we have about how these interact with gender and curriculum experience. We must encourage the use of a range of modes and task style; we need also to expand the range of indicators used: 'Multiple indicators are essential so that those who are disadvantaged on one assessment have an opportunity to offer alternative evidence of their expertise' (Linn 1992: 44).

Although we do not look for equality of outcome, we must continue to seek genuine equality of access; this means that all courses, subjects studied, examinations, etc., are actually equally available to all groups *and* are run/presented in such a way that all groups feel able to participate fully. One suggestion from the USA is that, since opportunity to learn is a key factor in performance, schools may have to 'certify delivery standards' as part of a system for monitoring instructional experiences (Linn 1993). How realistic it is to do this remains to be seen, but it does put the onus on schools to address the issue of equal access, at an actual rather than formal level.

Achievement, in both its definition and assessment, is heavily context- and culture-dependent. As yet, we have a naive understanding of these issues and we must develop a programme of research in this area.

Our research and monitoring agenda includes work on: continuing to monitor patterns of performance in GCSE and national assessment; ethnic monitoring in these exams should be a priority; A Level is hardly researched at all and yet it is a highly significant examination; we must monitor the placement of girls and ethnic minority groups on the basis of national assessment in the wake of the pressure towards more streaming/setting; we must press for continued technical evaluations of national assessment, as the examination boards do routinely for public exams. More information must also be made available on item-writing panels, sensitivity review details, etc. In the UK, large sums are being spent on the developing programme of National Curriculum assessment without anything like appropriate monitoring and scrutiny of these issues. Alongside detailed quantitative studies, we also need careful analytic case studies on a much wider scale than is currently the case, in order to illuminate statistical trends through in-depth study and to help us identify and understand the processes which are operating. As Plewis is at pains to point out:

> statistical analyses of the educational progress of ethnic minority pupils cannot be kept separate from the evidence on racism. Therefore, any statistical explanations that might be found need to be set in that context, even though they may not be directly attributable to racism.
>
> (Plewis 1988: 325)

One of the problems is that professional understanding of the issues is still at a low level for teachers, examiners, test developers and policy makers. Those to whom our recommendations are addressed do not necessarily have the knowledge to carry them out. The first task, then, is one of dissemination of information: about sub-group differences; interaction of mode of assessment with construct assessed and pupil experience; society's views about, and expectations of, the abilities of different groups of pupils; and how this impacts on expectation, teaching and curriculum offered. A programme of professional development based on the available research evidence needs to be made a priority (and most of the research evidence is reviewed in this book). Moderation among groups of teachers focusing on construct issues would also raise awareness of how meaning in tasks is construed by teachers and students alike.

The information on equality of access is even more limited. However, a concerted effort to explore and develop equity in assessment practice will, we feel, inform and feed progress on the equal access front. In the process of an integrated exploration of learning, teaching and assessment, equity may be approached, and possibly attained one day.

Finally, at all costs we must avoid the 'disadvantage' model described in Chapter 1, which sees girls as deficient boys (and ethnic minorities similarly as deficient majorities), who can be encouraged to compete by becoming more like boys and furthermore which sees their superior performance as indicative of invalidity in the assessment. We need to make it clear that this is a view of the world which accepts white middle-class males as 'normal' and all other groups as 'other'; we need to encourage the questioning of this world view to challenge traditional attitudes and to value other groups' perspectives, achievements and concerns. There is no question of achieving equity without this.

REFERENCES

AEB (1991) *Inter-Board Statistics: GCE A Level for 1990.* Guildford: AEB.

AEB (1992) *Inter-Board Statistics: GCE A Level for 1991.* Guildford: AEB.

AEB (1993) *Inter-Board Statistics: GCE 'A' Level for 1992.* Guildford: AEB.

Adams, R. (1986) Some contributions to sex differences in scholastic aptitude score. *Studies in Educational Evaluation*, 12: 267–74.

Adey, P. and Shayer, M. (in press) An exploration of long-term transfer effects following an extended intervention programme in the high school science curriculum. *Cognition and Instruction*.

Adey, P. S., Shayer, M. and Yates, C. (1989) *Thinking Science: The Curriculum Material of the CASE Project.* Basingstoke: Macmillan.

Aiken, L. (1986–87) Sex differences in mathematical ability: A review of the literature. *Educational Research Quarterly*, 10: 25–35.

American Association of University Women. (1992) *How Schools Shortchange Girls.* Washington, DC: AAUW.

Anastasi, A. (1958) *Differential Psychology*, 3rd edn. New York: Macmillan.

Anderson, J. (1989) Sex-related differences on objective tests among undergraduates. *Educational Studies in Mathematics*, 20: 165–77.

Anderson, L., Jenkins, L. B., Leming, J., Macdonald, W. B., Mullis, I. V. S., Turner, M. J. and Wooster, J. S. (1990) *The Civics Report Card: Trends in Achievement from 1976–1988 at Ages 13 and 17; Achievement in 1988 at Grades 4, 8 and 12*. Princeton, NJ: Educational Testing Service.

Andrew, R. J. and Rogers, L. (1972) Testosterone, search behaviour and persistence. *Nature*, 237: 343–6.

Apple, M. W. (1989) How equality has been redefined in the conservative restoration. In Secada, W. (ed.) *Equity and Education*. New York: Falmer Press.

Applebee, A. N., Langer, J. A. and Mullis, I. V. S. (1986) *Writing Trends Across the Decade 1974–1984*. Princeton, NJ: Educational Testing Service.

Applebee, A. N., Langer, J. A. and Mullis, I. V. S. (1989) *Crossroads in American Education: A Summary of Findings. The Nation's Report Card*. Princeton, NJ: Educational Testing Service.

Applebee, A. N., Langer, J. A., Mullis, I. V. S. and Jenkins, L. B. (1990a) *The Writing Report Card 1984–1988: Findings from the Nation's Report Card*. Princeton, NJ: Educational Testing Service.

Applebee, A. N., Langer, J. A., Jenkins, L. B., Mullis, I. V. S. and Foertsch, M. A. (1990b) *Learning to Write in Our Nation's Schools: Instruction and Achievement in 1988 at Grades 4, 8 and 12*. Princeton, NJ: Educational Testing Service.

Archer, J. (1971) Sex differences in emotional behaviour: A reply to Gray and Buffery. *Acta Psychologia*, 35: 415–29.

Archer, J. (1976) Biological explanations of psychological sex difference. In Lloyd, B. B. and Archer, J. (eds) *Exploring Sex Differences*. London: Academic Press.

Archer, J. (1978) Biological explanations of sex-role stereotypes. In Chetwynd, J. and Hartnett, O. (eds) *The Sex Role System*. London: Routledge and Kegan Paul.

Asher, S. R. and Gottman, J. M. (1973) Sex of teachers and student reading achievement. *Journal of Educational Psychology*, 65: 168–71.

Asher, S. R. and Markell, R. A. (1974) Sex differences in comprehension of high- and low-interest reading materials. *Journal of Educational Psychology*, 66: 680–87.

Ashworth, K. (1990) Maths and science: A nation still at risk. *Principal*, January, pp. 15–17.

Backman, M. E. (1972) Patterns of mental abilities: Ethnic, socioeconomic and sex differences. *American Educational Research Journal*, 9: 1–12.

Banikiotes, F. G., Montgomery, A. A. and Banikiotes, P. G. (1972) Male and female auditory reinforcement of infant vocalizations. *Developmental Psychology*, 6: 476–81.

Barnsley, R. H. and Rabinovitch, M. S. (1970) Handedness: Proficiency versus stated preference. *Perceptual Motor Skills*, 30: 343–62.

Baumeister, R. F. (1988) Should we stop studying sex differences altogether? *American Psychologist*, 42: 756–7.

Bayley, N. (1956) Individual patterns of development. *Child Development*, 27: 45–74.

Becker, B. J. and Hedges, L. V. (1984) Meta analysis of cognitive gender differences: A comment on an analysis by Rosenthal and Rubin. *Journal of Educational Psychology*, 76: 583–7.

Bejar, I. I. (1983) Introduction to item response models and their assumptions. In Hambleton, R. K. (ed.) *Applications of Item Response Theory*. Vancouver, BC: Educational Research Institute of British Columbia.

Belsey, C. (1988) Marking by number. *AUT Women*, 15: 1–2.

Benbow, C. P. (1988) Sex differences in mathematical reasoning ability in intellectually talented preadolescents: their nature, effects, and possible causes. *Behavioural and Brain Sciences*, 11: 169–232.

Benbow, C. P. and Stanley, J. C. (1980) Sex differences in mathematical ability: Fact or artifact? *Science*, 210: 1262–4.

Benbow, C. P. and Stanley, J. C. (1981) Mathematical ability: Is sex a factor? (Letter). *Science*, 212: 118–21.

Benbow, C. P. and Stanley, J. C. (1983) Sex differences in mathematical reasoning ability: More facts. *Science*, 222: 1029–31.

Bennett, G. K., Seashore, H. G. and Wesman, A. G. (1959) *Differential Aptitude Tests*, 3rd edn. New York: The Psychological Corporation.

Bennett, G. K., Seashore, H. G. and Wesman, A. G. (1966) *Differential Aptitude Tests*. New York: The Psychological Corporation.

Berry, J. W. (1966) Temne and Eskimo perceptual skills. *International Journal of Psychology*, 1: 207–229.

Blatchford, P., Burke, J., Farquhar, C., Plewis, I. and Traid, B. (1985) Educational achievement in the infant school: The influence of ethnic origin, gender and home on entry skills. *Educational Research*, 27: 52–60.

Block, R. A., Arnott, D. P., Quigley, B. and Lynch, W. C. (1989) Unilateral nostril breathing influences lateralized cognitive performance. *Brain and Cognition*, 9: 181–90.

Bock, R. D. (1967) A family study of spatial visualizing ability. Paper presented at the Meeting of the American Psychological Association, Washington, DC, September.

Bolger, N. and Kellaghan, T. (1990) Method of measurement and gender differences in scholastic achievement. *Journal of Educational Measurement*, 27(2): 165–74.

Bradley, C. (1984) Sex bias in the evaluation of students. *British Journal of Social Psychology*, 23: 147–63.

Brewer, R. I. and Haslum, M. N. (1986) Ethnicity: The experience of socio-economic disadvantage and educational attainment. *British Journal of Sociology of Education*, 7: 19–34.

Brimer, M. A. (1969) Sex differences in listening comprehension. *Journal of Research and Development in Education*, 3: 72–9.

British Psychological Society (1989) *Guidelines for External Examiners on Undergraduate Psychology Degrees*. Leicester: British Psychological Society.

Broadfoot, P. (1979) *Assessment, Schools and Society*. London: Methuen.

Broverman, D. M., Klaiber, E. L., Kobayashi, Y. and Vogel, W. (1968) Roles of activation and inhibition in sex differences in cognitive abilities. *Psychological Review*, 75: 23–50.

Brown, C. (1984) *Black and White in Britain*. The Third Policy Studies Institute Survey. Aldershot: Gower.

Buffery, A. W. H. and Gray, J. A. (1972) Sex differences in the development of spatial and linguistic skills. In Ounsted, C. and Taylor, D. C. (eds) *Gender Differences: Their Ontogeny and Significance*. London: Churchill.

Campaign for Racial Equality (1985) *Birmingham LEA and Schools, Referral and Suspension of Pupils*. London: CRE.

Caplan, P. J., Macpherson, G. M. and Tobin, P. (1985) Do sex-related differences in spatial abilities exist? *American Psychologist*, 40: 786–99.

Caron, A. J., Caron, R. F., Caldwell, R. C. and Weiss, S. J. (1973) Infant perception of the structural properties of the face. *Developmental Psychology*, 9: 385–99.

Chipman, S., Marshall, S. P. and Scott, P. A. (1991) Content effects on word problem performance: A possible source of test bias? *American Educational Research Journal*, 28(4): 897–915.

Clarke-Stewart, K. A. (1973) Interactions between mothers and their young children: characteristics and consequences. *Monographs of Society for Research in Child Development*, 38(153).

Coard, B. (1971) *How the West Indian Child is Made Educationally Sub-normal in the British School System*. London: New Beacon Books.

Coates, S. W. (1972) *Pre-school Embedded Figures Test*. Palo Alto, CA: Consulting Psychologists' Press.

Cohen, R. (1986) *Conceptual Styles and Social Change*. Acton, MA: Copley Publishing.

Cole, N. and Moss, P. (1989) Bias in test use. In Linn, R. (ed.) *Educational Measurement*, 3rd edn. New York: AERA/NCME, Macmillan.

Coleman, J. A. (1968) The concept of equality of educational opportunity. *Harvard Educational Review*, 38: 7–22.

Coleman, J., Campbell, E., Hobson, C., McPartland, J., Mood, A., Weinfeld, F. and York, R. (1966) *Equality of Educational Opportunity*. Washington, DC: National Centre for Educational Statistics.

Coltheart, M., Hull, E. and Slater, D. (1975) Sex differences in imagery and reading. *Nature*, 53: 430–40.

Comber, L. C. and Keeves, J. P. (1973) *Science Education in Nineteen Countries: An Empirical Study*. London: John Wiley.

Conel, J. L. (1963) *The Cortex of the Four-year-old Child*. Cambridge, MA: Harvard University Press.

Consortium for Assessment and Testing in Schools (1991a) *A Report on the Pilot Study of SATs for Key Stage One*. London: SEAC.

Consortium for Assessment and Testing in Schools (1991b) *Pilot Report 1991 Key Stage 3 Maths*. London: SEAC.

Consortium for Assessment and Testing in Schools (1991c) *Pilot Report 1991 Key Stage 3 English*. London: SEAC.

Consortium for Assessment and Testing in Schools (1991d) *Pilot Report 1991 Key Stage 3 Science*. London: SEAC.

Consortium for Assessment and Testing in Schools (1991e) *Pilot Report 1991 Key Stage 3 Technology*. London: SEAC.

Corah, N. L. (1965) Differentiation in children and their parents. *Journal of Personality*, 33: 300–308.

Cresswell, M. (1990) Gender effects in GCSE: Some initial analyses. Paper presented to a Nuffield Seminar at the University of London, Institute of Education, June.

Cresswell, M. and Gubb, J. (1987) *The Second International Maths Study in England and Wales*. Windsor: NFER-Nelson.

Cronbach, L. J. (1980) Validity on parole: How can we go straight? *New Directions for Testing and Measurement*, 5: 99–108.

Crook, J. H. (1970) Introduction: Social behaviour and ethology. In Crook, J. H. (ed.) *Social Behaviour in Birds and Mammals*. London: Academic Press.

Cuttance, P. (1988) Intra-system variation in the effectiveness of schooling. *Research Papers in Education*, 3: 180–216.

Darwin, C. (1871) *The Descent of Man, and Selection in Relation to Sex*. London: John Murray (1901 edn).

Davies, B. and Harré, R. (1989) Explaining the Oxbridge figures. *Oxford Review of Education*, 15(3): 221–8.

Dawson, J. L. M. (1967) Cultural and physiological influences upon spatial–perceptual processes in West Africa. *International Journal of Psychology*, 2: 115–28.

Denckla, M. B. (1973) Development of speed in repetitive and successive finger-movements in normal children. *Developmental Medicine of Child Neurology*, 15: 635–45.

Department of Education and Science (1974) *Educational Disadvantage and the Educational Needs of Immigrants (Cmnd5720)*. London: HMSO.

Department of Education and Science (1988a) *Science at Age 11: A Review of APU Survey Findings 1980–1984*. London: HMSO.

Department of Education and Science (1988b) *Science at Age 15: A Review of APU Survey Findings 1980–1984*. London: HMSO.

Department of Education and Science (1988c) *Task Group on Assessment and Testing: A Report*. London: HMSO.

Department of Education and Science (1989) *Science at Age 13: A Review of APU Survey Findings 1980–1984*. London: HMSO.

Department of Education and Science (1991) *Testing 7 year olds in 1991: Results of the National Curriculum Assessments in England*. London: HMSO.

Dore, R. (1976) *The Diploma Disease*. London: Unwin Educational.

Dossey, J. A., Mullis, I. V. S., Lindquist, M. M. and Chambers, D. L. (1988) *The Mathematics Report Card: Are We Measuring Up? Trends and Achievement Based on the 1986 National Assessment*. Princeton, NJ: Educational Testing Service.

Douglas, J. W. B. (1964) *The Home and the School*. London: MacGibbon and Kee.

Drew, D. and Gray, J. (1990) The fifth year examination achievements of black young people in England and Wales. *Educational Research*, 32(3): 107–17.

Drew, D. and Gray, J. (1991) The black–white gap in examination results: A statistical critique of a decade's research. *New Community*, 17(2): 159–72.

Droege, R. C. (1967) Sex differences in aptitude maturation during high school. *Journal of Counselling Psychology*, 14: 407–411.

Dwyer, C. A. (1974) Influence of children's sex role standards on reading and arithmetic achievement. *Journal of Educational Psychology*, 60: 811–16.

Educational Testing Service (1987) *Reading Objectives: 1986 and 1988 Assessment*. National Assessment of Educational Progress. Princeton, NJ: ETS.

Educational Testing Service (1991) *How Can We Judge the Fairness of Tests?* Public Accountability Report. Princeton, NJ: ETS.

Eggleston, J. (1988) The new education bill and assessment: Some implications for black children. *Multicultural Teaching*, 6(2): Spring.

Eggleston, J., Dunn, D., Anjali, M. and Wright, C. (1986) *Education for Some*. Stoke-on-Trent: Trentham Books.

Elliott, C. D. (1971) Noise tolerance and extraversion in children. *British Journal of Psychology*, 62, 375–80.

Elliott, C., Murray, D. and Pearson, L. (1978) *The British Ability Scales.* Windsor: NFER.

Elwood, J. (1992) *Making maths equal: Differential performance and equal opportunity in GCSE mathematics.* Unpublished MA dissertation, University of London, Institute of Education.

Equal Opportunities Commission (1982) *Do You Provide Equal Educational Opportunities?* London: EOC.

Equal Opportunities Commission (1988) Successful challenge to 11-plus sex discrimination, Press Notice, 1 July.

Equal Opportunities Commission (1991) *Equal Opportunities in Schools: A Guide for School Governors.* London: EOC.

Equal Opportunities Commission (1992) Draft Judgment, *R. v Birmingham City Council*, Ex Parte The EOC, CO/1163/91.

ESSSA (1992) *Gender Equity in Senior Secondary School Assessment Project: Third Progress Report*, September 1992. Senior Secondary Assessment Board of South Australia.

Evans, B. and Waites, B. (1981) *IQ and Mental Testing: An Unnatural Science and Its Social History.* London: Macmillan.

Faggen, J. (1987) Golden Rule revisited: Introduction. *Educational Measurement: Issues and Practice*, 6(2): Summer.

Fairweather, H. (1976) Sex differences in cognition. *Cognition*, 4: 231–80.

Fawcett Society (1987) *Exams for the Boys.* Hemel Hempstead: The Fawcett Society.

Feingold, A. (1988) Cognitive gender differences are disappearing. *American Psychologist*, 43: 95–103.

Feingold, A. (1991a) Are cognitive gender differences really diminishing? A life span perspective. Unpublished manuscript, Yale University.

Feingold, A. (1991b) Sex differences in variability in intellectual abilities: A cross-cultural perspective. Unpublished manuscript, Yale University.

Feingold, A. (1992) Sex differences in variability in intellectual abilities: A new look at an old controversy. *Review of Educational Research*, 62: 61–84.

Fennema, E. (1990) Justice, equity and mathematics education. In Fennema, E. and Leder, G. C. (eds) *Mathematics and Gender.* New York: Teachers College Press, Columbia University.

Ferguson, C. (1977) GCE 'O' level Biology. Internal Report: London: University of London, School Examinations Department.

Flanagan, J. C., Dailey, J. T., Shaycoft, M. F., Gorham, W. A., Orr, D. B., Goldberg, I. and Neyman, C. A. Jr (1961) *Counsellor's Technical Manual for Interpreting Test Scores.* Palo Alto, CA: Project Talent.

Floud, J. and Halsey, A. H. (1957) Intelligence tests, social class and selection for secondary schools. *British Journal of Sociology*, 8: 33–9.

Ford, J. (1969) *Social Class and the Comprehensive School.* London: RKP.

Ford, J., Mongon, D. and Whelan, M. (1982) *Special Education and Social Control.* London: RKP.

Foster, P. (1990) Case not proven: An evaluation of two studies of teacher racism. *British Educational Research Journal,* 16(4): 335–49.

Foxman, D. (1992) *Learning Mathematics and Science: The Second IAEP in England.* Windsor: NFER.

Foxman, D., Ruddock, G., Joffe, L., Mason, K., Mitchell, P. and Sexton, B. (1985) *A Review of Monitoring in Mathematics 1978 to 1982, Part 1 and Part 2.* London: DES.

Foxman, D., Ruddock, G. and McCallum, I. (1990) *Assessment Matters: No. 3 APU Mathematics Monitoring 1984–1988 (Phase 2).* London: SEAC.

Foxman, D., Ruddock, G., McCallum, I. and Schagen, I. (1991) *APU Mathematics Monitoring (Phase 2).* London: SEAC.

Fulton, C. D. and Hubbard, A. W. (1975) Effect of puberty on reaction and movement times. *Research Quarterly American Alliance for Health, Physical Education and Recreation,* 46: 335–44.

Garai, J. E. and Scheinfeld, A. (1968) Sex differences in mental and behavioural traits. *Genetic Psychology Monographs,* 77: 169–299.

Gardner, R. (1975) Women in engineering: The impact of attitudinal differences on educational institution. *Engineering Education,* February.

Gates, A. I. (1961) Sex differences in reading ability. *Elementary School Journal,* 61: 431–4.

Gillborn, D. (1990) *'Race', Ethnicity and Education.* London: Unwin Hyman.

Gillborn, D. (1992) Racism and education: Issues for research and practice. In Brown, S. and Riddell, S. (eds) *Class, Race and Gender in Schools.* SCRE/EIS Practitioner Mini Paper 12. Edinburgh: Scottish Council for Research in Education.

Gipps, C. (1992a) Equal opportunities and the SATS for 7 year olds. *The Curriculum Journal,* 3(2): 171–83.

Gipps, C. (ed.) (1992b) *Developing Assessment for the National Curriculum.* University of London, Institute of Education Bedford Way Series. London: Kogan Page/ULIE.

Gipps, C. (1993) Reliability, manageability and validity in large scale performance assessment. Paper given at AERA, Atlanta, April.

Gipps, C. and Goldstein, H. (1983) *Monitoring Children: An Evaluation of the Assessment of Performance Unit.* London: Heinemann Educational.

Gipps, C. and Stobart, G. (1993) *Assessment. A Teacher's Guide to the Issues,* 2nd edn. Sevenoaks: Hodder and Stoughton.

Goddard-Spear, M. (1983) Sex bias in science teachers' ratings of work. Paper given to the Second GASAT Conference, Oslo, September.

Goldstein, A. G. and Chance, J. E. (1965) Effects of practice on sex-related differences in performance on embedded figures. *Psychonomic Science*, 3: 361–2.

Goldstein, H. (1986) Gender bias and test norms in educational selection. *Research Intelligence*, May: 2–4.

Goldstein, H. (1991) More thoughts on testing. *Education Canada*, Spring: 44–7.

Goldstein, H. (1993a) Assessing group differences. *Oxford Review*, 19(2): 141–50.

Goldstein, H. (1993b) Interpreting international comparisons of student achievement. Paper presented for UNESCO, June.

Goldstein, H. and Wood, R. (1989) Five decades of item response modelling. *British Journal of Mathematical and Statistical Psychology*, 42: 139–67.

Goodhart, C. B. (1988a) Women's examination results. *The Cambridge Review*, 109: 38–40.

Goodhart, C. B. (1988b) Examination results in single sex and mixed colleges at Cambridge. *The Cambridge Review*, 109: 139–41.

Goodhart, C. B. (1992) Sex and class in examinations. *The Cambridge Review*, 113: 43–4.

Gorman, T. (1987) *Pupils' Attitudes to Reading*. Windsor: NFER-Nelson.

Gorman, T. P., White, J., Brooks, G., Maclure, M. and Kispal, A. (1988) *Language Performance in Schools: Review of APU Language Monitoring 1979–1983*. London: HMSO.

Gorman, T., Whyte, J., Brooks, G. and English, F. (1991) *Assessment Matters No. 4: Language for Learning*. London: SEAC.

Goslin, D. A. (1963) *The Search for Ability*. New York: Russell Sage Foundation.

Gould, S. J. (1981) *The Mismeasure of Man*. New York: W.W. Norton.

Gray, J. A. (1971) Sex differences in emotional behaviour in mammals including man: Endocrine bases. *Acta Psychologia*, 35: 29–46.

Great Britain Board of Education (1926) *The Education of the Adolescent*, Consultative Committee Chair Sir W. H. Hadow. London: HMSO.

Great Britain Board of Education (1938) *Secondary Education with Special Reference to Grammar Schools and Technical High Schools*, Consultative Committee Chair W. Spens. London: HMSO.

Gubb, J., Gorman, T. and Price, E. (1987) *The Study of Written Composition in England and Wales*. Windsor: NFER-Nelson.

Guetzkow, H. (1951) An analysis of the operation of set in problem-solving behaviour. *Journal of General Psychology*, 45: 219–44.

Guilford, J. P. (1967) *The Nature of Human Intelligence*. New York: McGraw-Hill.

Halpern, D. F. (1988) Sex differences in mathematical reasoning ability: Let me count the ways. *Behavioural and Brain Sciences*, 11: 191–2.

Halpern, D. F. (1992) *Sex Differences in Cognitive Abilities*. Hillsdale, NJ: Lawrence Erlbaum Associates Inc.

Halsey, A. H., Heath, A. F. and Ridge, J. M. (1980) *Origins and Destinations: Family, Class, and Education in Modern Britain*. Oxford: Clarendon Press.

Hammack, D. C., Hartoonian, M., Howe, J., Jenkins, L. B., Levstik, L. S., MacDonald, W. B., Mullis, I. V. S. and Owen, E. (1990) *The U.S. History Report Card: The Achievement of Fourth, Eighth and Twelfth Grade Students in 1988 and Trends from 1986 to 1988 in the Factual Knowledge of High School Juniors*. Princeton, NJ: Educational Testing Service.

Hammersley, M. and Gomm, R. (1993) A response to Gillborn and Drew on 'race', class and school effects. *New Community*, 19(2): 348–53.

Hanna, G. (1986) Sex differences in mathematics achievement of eighth graders in Ontario. *Journal for Research in Mathematics Education*, 17: 231–7.

Hannabus, K. C. (1991) Mixed results. *Oxford Magazine*, 74: 4–5.

Hannabus, K. C. (1992) Mixed results. *The Cambridge Review*, 113: 40–42.

Harding, J. (1979) Sex differences in examination performance at 16. *Physics Education*, 14: 280–84.

Harding, J. and Craig, J. (1978) *Girls and Science Education Project Report*. London: Chelsea College Centre for Science Education.

Harlen, W., Gipps, C., Broadfoot, P. and Nuttall, D. (1992) Assessment and the improvement of education. *The Curriculum Journal*, 3(3): 215–30.

Harris, J. W. (1971) Aspects of the guessing behaviour of young Irish subjects on multiple choice items. Unpublished master's thesis, University College, Cork.

Hartlage, L. C. (1970) Sex-linked inheritance of spatial ability. *Perceptual Motor Skills*, 31: 610.

Heim, A. (1970) *Intelligence and Personality: Their Assessment and Relationship*. Harmondsworth: Penguin.

Hier, D. B. and Crowley, W. F., Jr (1982) Spatial ability in androgen-deficient men. *New England Journal of Medicine*, 306: 1202–1205.

Hilton, T. L. and Berglund, G. W. (1971) *Sex Differences in Mathematics Achievement: A Longitudinal Study*. Princeton, NJ: Educational Testing Service.

Hines, M. (1990) Gonadal hormones and human cognitive development. In Balthazart, J. (ed.) *Hormones, Brain and Behaviour in Vertebrates.* Vol. 1. *Sexual Differentiation, Neuroanatomical Aspects, Neurotransmitters and Neuropeptides.* Basel: Karger.

Horner, M. S. (1969) Femininity and successful achievement: A basic inconsistency. In Bardinck, J. M. *et al.* (eds) *Feminine Personality and Conflict.* Monterey, CA: Brooks/Cole.

Hoste, R. (1981) Sex differences and similarities in performance in a CSE biology examination. Paper presented at the 1981 BERA Conference, September.

Hudson, L. (1986) Item-level analysis of sex differences in mathematics achievement test performance. Dissertation, *Abstracts International,* 47(2).

Husen, T. (ed.) (1967) *International Study of Achievement in Mathematics,* Vol. 2. London: John Wiley.

Husen, T. and Tuijnman, A. (1991) The contribution of formal schooling to the increase in intellectual capital. *Educational Researcher,* 20, October: 10–25.

Hutt, C. (1972a) *Males and Females.* Harmondsworth: Penguin.

Hutt, C. (1972b) Sex differences in human development. *Human Development,* 15: 153–70.

Hutt, C. (1972c) Sexual differentiation in human development. In Ounstead, C. and Taylor, D. C. (eds) *Gender Differences: Their Ontogeny and Significance.* London: Churchill.

Hyde, J. S. and Linn, M. C. (eds) (1986) *The Psychology of Gender: Advances Through Meta-Analysis.* Baltimore, MD: Johns Hopkins University Press.

Hyde, J. S. and Linn, M. C. (1988) Gender differences in verbal ability: A meta analysis. *Psychological Bulletin,* 104: 53–69.

Hyde, J. S., Fennema, E. and Lamon, S. J. (1990) Gender differences in mathematics performance: A meta analysis. *Psychological Bulletin,* 107: 139–53.

Ingram, D. (1975) Motor asymmetries in young children. *Neuropsychologia,* 13: 95–102.

Inner London Education Authority (1968) *The Education of Immigrant Pupils in Special Schools for ESN children.* Report No. 657, 10 September 1968. London: ILEA.

Inner London Education Authority (1983) *Race, Sex and Class: Achievement in Schools.* London: ILEA.

Inner London Education Authority (1987) *Ethnic Background and Examination Results 1985 and 1986.* Report No. RS 1120/87, ILEA Research and Statistics Branch. London: ILEA.

Inner London Education Authority (1988) *Characteristics of Pupils in Special Schools and Units*. Report No. RS 1198/88. London: ILEA.

Inner London Education Authority (1990) *Suspensions and Expulsions from School 1987–88*. Report No. RS 1270/90. London: ILEA.

Jacklin, C. N. (1989) Female and male: Issues of gender. *American Psychologist*, 44: 127–33.

Jencks, C. (1972) *Inequality: A Reassessment of the Effects of Family and Schooling in America*. New York: Basic Books.

Jensen, A. R. (1969) How much can we boost IQ and scholastic achievement? *Harvard Educational Review*, 39(1): 1–123.

Joffe, L. and Foxman, D. (1988) *Attitudes and Gender Differences: Mathematics at Age 11 and 15*. Windsor: NFER-Nelson.

Johnson, S. (1989) *National Assessment: The APU Science Approach*. London: HMSO.

Johnson, S. and Murphy, P. (1986) *Girls and Physics: Reflections on APU Survey Findings*. APU Occasional Paper No. 4. London: DES.

Joint Committee on Testing Practice (JCTP) (1988) *Code of Fair Testing Practices in Education*. Washington, DC: American Psychological Association.

Kagan, J. and Kogan, N. (1970) Individuality and cognitive performance. In Mussen, P. H. (ed.) *Carmichael's Manual of Child Psychology*. New York: John Wiley.

Kail, R., Carter, P. and Pellegrino, J. (1979) The locus of sex differences in spatial ability. *Perception and Psychophysics*, 26: 182–6.

Kamin, L. J. (1974) *The Science and Politics of IQ*. Harmondsworth: Penguin.

Katzman, S. and Alliger, G. M. (1992) Averaging untransformed variance ratios can be misleading: a comment on Feingold. *Review of Educational Research*, Winter, 62(4): 427–8.

Kaufman, A. S. and Doppelt, J. E. (1976) Analysis of WISC-R standardization data in terms of the stratification variables. *Child Development*, 47: 165–71.

Keating, D. P. (1972) The study of mathematically precocious youth. Paper presented at the American Association for the Advancement of Science, Washington, DC, April.

Keating, D. P. and Stanley, J. C. (1972) *Extreme Measures for the Exceptionally Gifted in Mathematics and Science: Study of the Mathematically and Scientifically Precocious Youth*. Baltimore, MD: Johns Hopkins University, Department of Psychology.

Kelly, A. (1978) *Girls and Science: An International Study of Sex Differences in School Science Achievement*. Stockholm: Almqvist and Wiksell International.

Kelly, A. (1981) Sex differences in science achievement. In Kelly, A. (ed.) *The Missing Half.* Manchester: Manchester University Press.

Keogh, B. K. (1971) Pattern copying under three conditions of an expanded spatial field. *Developmental Psychology*, 4: 25–31.

Keogh, B. K. and Ryan, S. R. (1971) Use of three measures and field organization with young children. *Perceptual Motor Skills*, 33: 466.

Keys, W. (1987) *Aspects of Science Education in English Schools.* Windsor: NFER-Nelson.

Keys, W. and Foxman, D. (1989) *A World of Differences: A UK Perspective on an International Assessment of Maths and Science.* Windsor: NFER-Nelson.

Kimball, M. M. (1989) A new perspective on women's math achievement. *Psychological Bulletin*, 105: 198–214.

Kimbell, R., Stables, K., Wheeler, T., Wosmak, A. and Kelly, V. (1991) *The Assessment of Performance in Design and Technology.* London: SEAC.

Kinsbourne, M. and McMurray, J. (1975) The effect of cerebral dominance on time sharing between speaking and tapping by pre-school children. *Child Development*, 46: 240–42.

Kipinis, D. (1976) Intelligence, occupational status and achievement orientation. In Lloyd, B. B. and Archer, J. A. (eds) *Exploring Sex Differences.* London: Academic Press.

Kysel, F. (1988) Ethnic background and examination results. *Educational Research*, 30(2): 83–9.

Langer, J. A., Applebee, A. N., Mullis, I. V. and Foerthsch, A. (1990) *Learning to Read in our Nation's Schools: Instruction and Achievement in 1988 at Grades 4, 8 and 12.* Princeton, NJ: Educational Testing Service.

Laosa, L. M. and Brophy, J. E. (1972) Effects of sex and birth order on sex-role development and intelligence among kindergarten children. *Developmental Psychology*, 6: 409–415.

Lapointe, A., Mead, N. and Phillips, G. (1989) *A World of Differences: An International Assessment of Mathematics and Science.* Princeton, NJ: Educational Testing Service.

Lapointe, A., Mead, N. and Askew, J. (1992) *Learning Mathematics: An International Assessment of Educational Progress.* Princeton, NJ: Educational Testing Service.

Levine, D. (1975) 'Inequality' and the analysis of educational policy. In Levine, D. and Bane, M. (eds) *The 'Inequality' Controversy: Schooling and Distributive Justice.* New York: Basic Books.

Lewis, M. and Freedle, R. (1972) Mother–infant dyad: The cradle of meaning. Paper presented at a symposium on Language and Thought:

Communication and Affect, Erindale College, University of Toronto, March.

Licht, B. G. and Dweck, C. S. (1983) Sex differences in achievement orientations: Consequences for academic choices and attainments. In Marland, M. (ed.) *Sex Differentiation and Schooling*. London: Heinemann.

Linden, K. W., Jagacinski, C. M., Le Bold, W. K. and Shell, K. D. (1985) Predicting persistence in engineering for undergraduate women. Paper presented to the Third GASAT Conference, London, April.

Linn, M. C. (1992) Gender differences in educational achievement. In *Sex Equity in Educational Opportunity, Achievement, and Testing*. Princeton, NJ: Educational Testing Service.

Linn, M. C. and Hyde, J. S. (1989) Gender, mathematics and science. *Educational Researcher*, 18(8): 17–27.

Linn, M. C. and Peterson, A. C. (1986) A meta analysis of gender differences in spatial ability: Implications for mathematics and science achievement. In Hyde, J. S. and Linn, M. C. (eds) *The Psychology of Gender: Advances Through Meta-analysis*, pp. 62–101. Baltimore, MD: Johns Hopkins University Press.

Linn, R. L. (1982) Ability testing: Individual differences, predictions and differential prediction. In Wigdor, A. and Garner, W. (eds) *Ability Testing: Uses, Consequences and Controversies*, pp. 335–8. Washington, DC: National Academy Press.

Linn, R. L. (1989) Current perspectives and future directions. In Linn, R. (ed.) *Educational Measurement*, 3rd edn. New York: ACE/NCME, Macmillan.

Linn, R. L. (1993) Educational assessment: Expanded expectations and challenges. *Educational Evaluation and Policy Analysis*, 15(1): 1–16.

Linn, R. L. and Dunbar, B. S. (1990) The nation's report card goes home: Good news and bad news about trends in achievement. *Phi Delta Kappa*, October: 127–33.

Linn, R., Baker, E. and Dunbar, S. (1991) Complex performance-based assessment: Expectations and validation criteria. *Educational Researcher*, 15–21.

Lockheed, M. E., Thorpe, M., Brooks-Gunn, J., Casserly, P., and McAloon, A. (1985) *Sex and Ethnic Differences in Middle School Mathematics, Science and Computer Science. What Do We Know?* Princeton, NJ: Educational Testing Service.

Lundeberg, M. (1992) Highly confident, but wrong: Gender differences and similarities in confidence judgements. Paper presented to AERA Conference, San Francisco, April.

Maccoby, E. E. and Jacklin, C. N. (1974) *The Psychology of Sex Differences*. Stanford, CA: Stanford University Press.

Mallow, J. V. (1987) *Science Anxiety: College Physics.* New York: Worth Publications.

Marshall, S. P. (1983) Sex differences in mathematical errors: An analysis of distractor choices. *Journal for Research in Mathematics Education,* 14(4): 325–36.

Marshall, S. P. and Smith, J. D. (1987) Sex differences in learning mathematics: A longitudinal study with item and error analyses. *Journal of Educational Psychology,* 79: 372–83.

Mason, J. (1985) Changing attitudes to women in science and technology in Great Britain: the Open University experience. In Vamos Uvesco, E. (ed.) *Women in Science: Options and Access.* Budapest: UNESCO.

Matyas, M. L. (1987) Keeping undergraduate women in science and engineering: Contributing factors and recommendations for action. Contributions to the Fourth GASAT Conference, Vol. III, Michigan.

McCrum, N. G. (1991) A fair admissions system. *Oxford Magazine,* 72: 16–17.

McGuinness, D. (1972) Hearing: Individual differences in perceiving. *Perception,* 1: 465–73.

McGuinness, D. (1976) Perception and cognition. In Lloyd, B. and Archer, J. (eds) *Exploring Sex Differences.* London: Academic Press.

McHugh, M. C., Koeske, R. D. and Frieze, I. H. (1986) Issues to consider in conducting non-sexist research: A guide for researchers. *American Psychologist,* 41: 879–90.

McLean, L. D. and Goldstein, H. (1988) The US national assessments in reading: reading too much into the findings. *Phi Delta Kappa,* January: 369–72.

McKitrick, K. G. (1965) Bodily activity and perceptual activity. *Perceptual Motor Skills,* 20: 1109–1112.

Meece, J. L., Eccles-Parsons, J., Kaczala, C. M., Goff, S. B. and Futterman, R. (1982) Sex differences in math achievement: Towards a model of academic choice. *Psychological Bulletin,* 91: 324–448.

Messick, S. (1989) Validity. In Linn, R. L. (ed.) *Educational Measurement,* 3rd edn. New York: ACE/NCME, Macmillan.

Meyer, W. J. and Bendig, A. W. (1961) A longitudinal study of the Primary Mental Abilities Test. *Journal of Educational Psychology,* 52: 50–60.

Miles, C. (1954) Gifted children. In Carmichael, L. (ed.) *Manual of Child Psychology,* 2nd edn. New York: John Wiley.

Milton, G. A. (1959) Sex differences in problem solving as a function of role appropriateness of the problem content. *Psychological Review,* 5: 705–708.

Miner, J. B. (1957) *Intelligence in the United States.* New York: Springer-Verlag.

Moore, T. (1967) Language and intelligence: A longitudinal study of the first eight years. Part 1: Patterns of development in boys and girls. *Human Development*, 10: 88–106.

Mortimore, P., Sammons, P., Stoll, L., Lewis, D. and Ecob, R. (1988) *School Matters: The Junior Years*. Hove: Lawrence Erlbaum Associates Ltd.

Moss, P. (1992) Shifting conceptions of validity in educational measurement. *Review of Educational Research*, 62(3): 229–58.

Mullis, I. V. S. and Jenkins, L. B. (1988) *The Science Report Card: Elements of Risk and Recovery, Trends and Achievement Based on the 1986 National Assessment*. Princeton, NJ: Educational Testing Service.

Mullis, I. V. S. and Jenkins, L. B. (1990) *The Reading Report Card 1971–1988: Trends from the Nation's Report Card*. Princeton, NJ: Educational Testing Service.

Mullis, I. V. S., Owen, E. H. and Phillips, G. W. (1990) *Accelerating Academic Achievement: A Summary of Findings from 20 Years of NAEP*. Princeton, NJ: Educational Testing Service.

Murphy, P. (1990) Gender differences: Implications for assessment and curriculum planning. Paper presented at the BERA Symposium on Social Justice and the National Curriculum, Roehampton, August.

Murphy, P. (1981) An investigation into mode of assessment and performance for girls and boys. Paper presented at the British Educational Research Conference, Manchester, September.

Murphy, P. (1989) Gender and assessment in science. In Murphy, P. and Moon, B. (eds) *Developments in Learning and Assessment*. London: Hodder and Stoughton.

Murphy, P. (1991) Gender and practical work. In Woolnough, D. (ed.) *Practical Work in Science*. Buckingham: Open University Press.

Murphy, R. J. L. (1980) Sex differences in GCE examination results and entry statistics. Paper presented at the International Conference on Sex Differentiation and Schooling, Cambridge, January.

Murphy, R. J. L. (1982) Sex differences in objective test performance. *British Journal of Educational Psychology*, 52: 213–19.

National Assessment of Educational Progress (1985) *The Reading Report Card: Progress Toward Excellence in our Schools*. Princeton, NJ: Educational Testing Service.

National Foundation for Educational Research/Bishop Grosseteste College (1991a) *A Report on the Pilot Study of SATs for Key Stage One*. London: SEAC.

National Foundation for Educational Research/Bishop Grosseteste College (1991b) *An Evaluation of the 1991 National Curriculum Assessment Report 3: Further Evidence on the SAT: Manageability and Relationships with Teacher Assessment*. Unpublished, June.

Nelson-Le Gall (1992) The condition of sex equity in education: Sex, race and ethnicity. In ETS (ed.) *Sex Equity in Educational Opportunity, Achievement and Testing*. Princeton, NJ: ETS.

Newbould, C. A. (1980) *Advanced Level Scientists and Their Measured Achievement*. Cambridge: Test Development and Research Unit.

Newbould, C. A. and Scanlon, L. A. J. (1981) *An Analysis of Interaction between Sex of Candidate and Other Factors*. Cambridge: Test Development and Research Unit.

Newstead, S. E. and Dennis, I. (1990) Blind marking. *Assessment and Evaluation in Higher Education*, 15(2): 132–9.

Noddings, N. (1992) Variability: A pernicious hypothesis: *Review of Educational Research*, 62: 85–8.

Nuttall, D. (1986) Problems in the measurement of change. In Nuttall, D. (ed.) *Assessing Educational Achievement*. London: Falmer.

Nuttall, D. L. (1987) The validity of assessments. *European Journal of Psychology of Education*, 11(2): 109–118.

Nuttall, D., Goldstein, H., Prosser, R. and Rasbash, H. (1989) Differential school effectiveness. *International Journal of Educational Research*, 13: 769–76.

Nuttall, D., Thomas, S. and Goldstein, H. (1992) *Report on Analysis of 1990 Examination Results*. Unpublished.

Nyborg, H. (1984) Performance and intelligence in hormonally different groups. In DeVries *et al.* (eds) *Progress in Brain Research*, 61: 491–508.

Nyborg, H. (1988) Mathematics, sex hormones and brain function. *Behavioural and Brain Sciences*, 11: 206–207.

Nyborg, H. (1990) Sex hormones, brain development and spatioperceptual strategies in Turner Syndrome. In Berch, D. B. and Bender, B. G. (eds) *Sex Chromosome Abnormalities and Human Behaviour*, pp. 100–128. Washington, DC: American Association for the Advancement of Science.

Orwin, R. G. and Cordray, R. S. (1985) Effects of deficient reporting on meta-analysis: A conceptual framework and reanalysis. *Psychological Bulletin*, 97: 134–47.

Patrick, H. (1990) Gender differences in public examination results. Paper presented at the British Educational Research Conference, London, August.

Petersen, A. C. (1976) Physical androgyny and cognitive functioning in adolescence. *Developmental Psychology*, 12: 524–33.

Petersen, A. C. and Crockett, L. (1985) Factors influencing sex-differences in spatial ability across the life span. Unpublished conference paper, presented at the 93rd Annual Convention of the American Psychological Association, Los Angeles, CA, August.

Plewis, I. (1987) Social disadvantage, educational attainment and ethnicity: A comment. *British Journal of Sociology of Education*, 8: 95–100.

Plewis, I. (1988) Assessing and understanding the educational progress of children from different ethnic groups. *Journal of the Royal Statistical Society*, 151(2): 316–26.

Plewis, I. (1991) Underachievement: A case of conceptual confusion. *British Educational Research Journal*, 17(4): 377–86.

Quinlan, M. (1991) Gender differences in examination performance. Unpublished paper, ULSEB/LEAG.

Ramist, L. (1984) Predictive validity of the ATP tests. In Doulon, T. (ed.) *The College Board Technical Handbook for the Scholastic Aptitude Test and Achievement Tests*. New York: College Board.

Rampton, A. (1981) *West Indian Children in Our Schools*, Cmnd 8273. London: HMSO.

Randall, G. J. (1987) Gender differences in pupil–teacher interactions in workshops and laboratories. In Weiner, G. and Arnot, M. (eds) *Gender Under Scrutiny*. Milton Keynes: Open University Press.

Richardson, K. (1991) *Understanding Intelligence*. Buckingham: Open University Press.

Ritts, V., Patterson, M. and Tubbs, M. (1992) Expectations, impressions and judgements of physically attractive students: A review. *Review of Educational Research*, 62(4): 413–26.

Robitaille, D. F. and Garden, R. A. (1989) *The IEA Study of Mathematics 11: Context and Outcomes of School Mathematics*. Oxford: Pergamon Press.

Rom, Y. (1987) Girls towards degrees in engineering: A national need. In Contributions to the Fourth GASAT Conference, Vol. II, Michigan, September.

Rosenthal, R. and Rubin, D. (1982) Further meta-analytic procedures for assessing cognitive gender differences. *Journal of Educational Psychology*, 74: 708–721.

Rowell, T. (1991) Women's examination results. *The Cambridge Review*, 100: 94–5.

Rumberger, R. and Willms, J. D. (1992) The impact of racial and ethnic segregation on the achievement gap in California high schools. *Educational Evaluation and Policy Analysis*, 14(4): 377–96.

Ryan, J. (1972) IQ: The illusion of objectivity. In Richardson, K. and Spears, D. (eds) *Race, Culture and Intelligence*. Harmondsworth: Penguin.

Sammons, P., Nuttall, D. and Cuttance, P. (1993) Differential school effectiveness: results from a reanalysis of the ILEA's junior school project data. *British Educational Research Journal*, 19(4): 381–405.

Sanders, B., Soares, M. P., and D'Aquila, J. M. (1982) The sex difference on one test of spatial visualization: A nontrivial difference. *Child Development*, 53: 1106–1110.

Saraga, E. (1975) *Girls and Boys: Are There Differences in Ability in Girls and Science Education Cause for Concern?* London: Centre for Science Education, Chelsea College.

Scarr, S. (1984) *Race, Social Class, and Individual Differences in IQ.* London: Lawrence Erlbaum Associates Ltd.

Schiff, W. and Oldak, R. (1990) Accuracy of judging time to arrival: Effects of modality, trajectory and gender. *Journal of Experimental Psychology: Human Perception and Performance*, 16: 303–316.

Schools Examination and Assessment Council (1990a) *Assessment Matters No. 1: Graph Work in School Science.* London: SEAC.

Schools Examination and Assessment Council (1990b) *Assessment Matters No. 2: Measurement in School Science.* London: SEAC.

Schools Examination and Assessment Council (1991a) *Assessment Matters No. 5: Profiles and Progression in Science Exploration.* London: SEAC.

Schools Examination and Assessment Council (1991b) *Assessment Matters No. 6: Planning and Carrying Out Investigations.* London: SEAC.

Schools Examination and Assessment Council (1991c) *Assessment Matters No. 7: Patterns and Relationships in School Science.* London: SEAC.

Schools Examination and Assessment Council (1991d) *Assessment Matters No. 8: Observation in School Science.* London: SEAC.

Schools Examination and Assessment Council (1991e) *Key Stage One Pilot 1990: A Report from the Evaluation and Monitoring Unit.* London: SEAC.

Schools Examination and Assessment Council (1991f) *National Curriculum Assessment: A Report on TA by the NFER/BGC Consortium.* London: SEAC.

Schools Examination and Assessment Council (1991g) *NC Assessment at Key Stage 3: A Review of the 1991 Pilots with Implications for 1992.* London: SEAC.

Schools Examination and Assessment Council (1992a) *An Evaluation of the 1991 National Curriculum Assessment Report 4.* NFER/BGC. London: SEAC.

Schools Examination and Assessment Council (1992b) *ENCA 1 Project: The Evaluation of National Curriculum Assessment at Key Stage 1.* Leeds: Leeds University, School of Education.

Scottish Council for Research in Education (1967) *The Scottish Standardisation of WISC.* London: University of London Press.

Secada, W. (1989) Educational equity versus equality of education. In Secada, W. (ed.) *Equity and Education.* New York: Falmer Press.

Shepard, L. (1983) The role of measurement in educational policy: Lessons from the identification of learning disabilities. *Educational Measurement: Issues and Practice*, Fall: 4–8.

Shepard, L. (1991) Psychometricians' beliefs about learning. *Educational Researcher*, 20(7): 2–16.

Shepard, L., Camilli, G. and Averill, M. (1981) Comparison of procedures for detecting test item bias with both internal and external ability criteria. *Journal of Educational Statistics*, 6: 317–75.

Sherman, J. A. (1967) Problem of sex differences in space perception and aspects of intellectual functioning. *Psychological Review*, 72: 290–99.

Sherman, S. W. (1974) *Multiple Choice Test Bias Uncovered by Use of an 'I Don't Know' Alternative.* ERIC document ED 121824.

Sherman, J. A. (1977) Effect of biological factors on sex-related differences in mathematics achievement. In Fox, L. H., Fennema, E. and Sherman, J. (eds) *Women and Mathematics: Research Perspectives for Change*, pp. 137–206. Washington, DC: National Institute of Education.

Shields, S. (1978) Sex and the biased scientist. *New Scientist*, 7 December, 752–4.

Shipman, V. C. (1971) *Disadvantaged Children and Their First School Experiences.* Princeton, NJ: Educational Testing Service.

Simon, B. (1971) *Intelligence, Psychology and Education.* London: Lawrence and Wishart.

Sitkei, E. G. and Meyers, C. E. (1969) Comparative structure of intellect in middle- and lower-class four year olds of two ethnic groups. *Developmental Psychology*, 1: 592–600.

Smith, D. and Tomlinson, S. (1989) *The School Effect.* London: Policy Studies Institute.

Smith, G. A. and McPhee, K. A. (1987) Performance on a coincidence timing task correlates with intelligence. *Intelligence*, 11: 161–7.

Smith, P. and Whetton, C. (1988) Bias reduction in test development. *The Psychologist*, July, 257 and 258.

Stafford, R. E. (1961) Sex differences in spatial visualization as evidence of sex linked inheritance. *Perceptual Motor Skills*, 13: 428.

Stafford, R. E. (1963) *An Investigation of Similarities in Parent–Child Test Scores for Evidence of Hereditary Components.* Princeton, NJ: Educational Testing Service.

Standard Testing and Assessment Implementation Research Group (1991) *A Report on the Pilot Study SATs for Key Stage One.* London: SEAC.

Stanford Research Institute (1972) *Follow Through Pupil Tests, Parent Interviews, and Teacher Questionnaires*, Appendix C. Stanford, CA: SRI.

Stanley, J. (1987) Sex differences on the College Board Achievement Tests and the Advanced Placement Examinations. Paper presented at the

Annual Meeting of the American Educational Research Association, Washington, DC, April.

Stein, A. H. and Bailey, M. M. (1973) The socialization of achievement orientation in females. *Psychological Bulletin*, 80: 345–66.

Sternberg, R. (1987) Second game: A school's eye view of intelligence. In Langer, J. A. (ed.) *Language, Literacy and Culture: Issues of Society and Schooling*. Norwood, NJ: Ablex.

Stewart, D. (1988) Women and men. *Oxford Magazine*, 39: 16.

Stobart, G., Elwood, J. and Quinlan, M. (1992a) Gender bias in examinations: How equal are the opportunities? *British Educational Research Journal*, 18(3): 261–76.

Stobart, G., White, J., Elwood, J., Hayden, M. and Mason, K. (1992b) *Differential Performance at 16+: English and Mathematics*. London: SEAC.

Stones, I., Beckman, M. and Stephens, L. (1982) Sex differences in mathematical competencies of pre-calculus college students. *School Science and Mathematics*, 82: 295–9.

Strutl, G. F., Anderson, D. R. and Well, A. D. (1973) Developmental trends in the effects of irrelevant information on speeded classification. Paper presented to the Society for Research in Child Development, Philadelphia.

Sutherland, G. (1984) *Ability, Merit and Measurement*. Oxford: Oxford University Press.

Svensson, A. (1971) *Relative Achievement: School Performance in Relation to Intelligence, Sex and Home Environment*. Stockholm: Almquist and Wiksell.

Swann, M. (1985) *Education for All*, Cmnd 9453. London: HMSO.

Sweeney, E. J. (1953) Sex differences in problem solving. Unpublished PhD thesis, Stanford University, Stanford, CA.

Terman, L. M. and Tyler, L. E. (1954) Psychological sex differences. In Carmichael, L. (ed.) *Manual of Child Psychology*, 2nd edn. New York: John Wiley.

Terman, L. M. *et al.* (1925) Mental and Physical traits of a thousand gifted children. In Terman, L. (ed.) *Genetic Studies of Genius*, Vol. 1. Stanford, CA: Stanford University Press.

Thelin, A. A. (1990) Working towards equal opportunities: The Swedish context. In Weiner, G. (ed.) *The Primary School and Equal Opportunities: International Perspectives on Gender Issues*. London: Cassell.

Thom, D. (1986) The 1944 Education Act: The 'art of the possible'. In Smith, H. (ed.) *War and Social Change: British Society in the Second World War*. Manchester: Manchester University Press.

Thompson, G. B. (1975) Sex differences in reading attainments. *Educational Review*, 18: 16–23.

Thompson, G. B. and Sharp, S. (1988) History of mental testing. In Keeves, J. (ed.) *Educational Research Methodology and Measurement: An International Handbook.* Oxford: Pergamon Press.

Tierney, R. J. and Lapp, D. (eds) (1979) *National Assessment of Education Progress in Reading.* Delaware City, OK: International Reading Association.

Tizard, B., Blatchford, P., Burke, J., Farquar, C. and Plewis, I. (1988) *Young Children at School in the Inner City.* Hove: Lawrence Erlbaum Associates Ltd.

Tomlinson, S. (1982) *A Sociology of Special Education.* London: Routledge and Kegan Paul.

Tomlinson, S. (1983) *Ethnic Minorities in British Schools: A Review of the Literature 1960–82.* Aldershot: Gower.

Torrance, H. (1981) The origins and development of mental testing in England and the United States. *British Journal of Sociology of Education,* 2(1): 45–59.

Torrance, H. (1991) Evaluating SATs: The 1990 pilot. *Cambridge Journal of Education,* 21(2): 129–40.

Townsend, H. and Brittan, E. (1972) *Organisation in Multi-racial Schools.* Windsor: NFER.

Troyna, B. (1984) 'Fact or artefact? The educational underachievement of black pupils. *British Journal of Sociology of Education,* 5(2): 153–66.

Troyna, B. (1991) Underachievers or under-rated? The experience of pupils of South Asian origin in a secondary school. *British Educational Research Journal,* 17(4): 359–74.

Tyler, L. E. (1965) *The Psychology of Human Differences,* 3rd edn. New York: Appleton.

University of London Examinations and Assessment Council/National Foundation for Educational Research (1992) *Differential Performance in Examinations at 16+: English and Mathematics.* ULEAC/NFER Report. London: SEAC.

University of London Schools Examination Board (1989) *Inter-Board Statistics: GCE 'A' Level for 1988.* London: USLEB.

University of London Schools Examination Board (1990) *Inter-Board Statistics: GCE A Level for 1989.* London: ULSEB.

Vernon, P. (ed.) (1957) *Secondary School Selection.* London: Methuen.

Very, P. S. (1967) Differential factor structures in mathematical abilities. *Genetic Psychology Monographs,* 75: 169–207.

Vietze, P., Foster, M. and Friedman, S. (1974) Response differentiation in infants: A sex difference in learning. *Perceptual Motor Skills,* 38: 479–84.

Wainer, H. and Steinberg, L. S. (1990) *Sex Differences in Performance* on the *Mathematics Section of the Scholastic Aptitude Test: A Bi-directional Validity Study.*

Walden, R. and Walkerdine, V. (1985) *Girls and Mathematics: From Primary to Secondary Schooling.* Bedford Way Paper No. 24. London: University of London, Institute of Education.

Wapner, S. (1968) Age changes in perception of verticality and of the longitudinal body axis under body tilt. *Journal of Experimental Child Psychology,* 6: 543–55.

Watson, P. (1972) Can racial discrimination affect IQ? In Richardson, K. and Spears, D. (eds) *Race, Culture and Intelligence.* Harmondsworth: Penguin.

Weiner, G. (1990) Developing educational policy on gender. In Weiner, G. (ed.) *The Primary School and Equal Opportunities: International Perspectives on Gender Issues.* London: Cassell.

Weiss, J. (1987) The Golden Rule Bias Reduction Principle: A practical reform. *Educational Measurement: Issues and Practice,* 6(2): 23–5.

Whitley, B. E. Jr and Frieze, I. H. (1985) The effect of question wording style and research context on attributions for success and failure: A meta analysis. Paper presented at the Annual Meeting of the Easter Psychological Association, Boston.

White, J. (1986) *Girls into Science and Technology: The Story of a Project.* London: Routledge and Kegan Paul.

White, J. (1988) *The Assessment of Writing: Pupils Aged 11 and 15.* Windsor: NFER-Nelson.

Wick, T. (1991) Assessment and bilingual children. In Murphy, P. (ed.) *Assessment and the Primary Curriculum.* Milton Keynes: Open University Press.

Wigdor, A. and Garner, W. (eds) (1982) *Ability Testing: Uses, Consequences and Controversies,* Part 1. Washington, DC: National Academy Press.

Wilder, G. Z. and Powell, K. (1989) *Sex Differences in Test Performance: A Survey of the Literature.* New York: College Board Publications.

Wilder, G. Z., Casserley, P. and Burton, N. (1988) *Young SAT-Takers: Two Surveys.* College Board Report No. 88–1. New York: College Entrance Examination Board.

Wilder, G. Z. and Powell, K. (1989) *Sex Differences in Test Performance: A Survey of the Literature.* College Board Report No. 89–3. New York: College Entrance Examination Board.

Witkin, H. (1967) A cognitive style approach to cross cultural research. *International Journal of Psychology,* 2: 233–50.

Witkin, H. A., Goodenough, D. R. and Karp, S. A. (1967) Stability of cognitive style from childhood to young adulthood. *Journal of Personality and Social Psychology,* 7: 291–300.

Witkin, H. A., Dyke, R. B., Faterson, H. E., Goodenough, D. R. and Karp, S. A. (1962) *Psychological Differentiation*. New York: John Wiley.

Witt, E. A., Yunttan, M. and Hoover, H. D. (1990) Recent trends in achievement test scores: which students are improving and on what levels of skill complexity? Paper presented at the Annual Meeting of the National Council on Measurement in Education, Boston, April.

Wolfe, R. (1989) An indifference to differences: Problems with the IAEP-88 study. Paper presented at the AERA Conference, April.

Wood, R. (1986) The agenda for educational measurement. In Nuttall, D. (ed.) *Assessing Educational Achievement*. Lewes: Falmer Press.

Wood, R. (1987) Assessment and equal opportunities. Text of public lecture at the University of London, Institute of Education, 11 November.

Wood, R. (ed.) (1991) *Assessment and Testing: A Survey of Research*. Cambridge: Cambridge University Press.

Wood Report (1929) *Report of the Mental Deficiency Committee*. Board of Education and Board of Control. London: HMSO.

Wright, C. (1986) School processes: An ethnographic study. In Eggleston, J., Dunn, D. and Anjali, M. (eds) *Education for Some: The Educational and Vocational Experience of 15–18 Year Old Members of Minority Ethnic Groups*. Stoke-on-Trent: Trentham Books.

Wright, C. (1987) Black students – white teachers. In Troyna, B. (ed.) *Racial Inequality in Education*. London: Tavistock.

Yates, A. and Pidgeon, D. A. (1957) *Admission to Grammar Schools*. Windsor: NFER/Newnes Educational.

Yates, L. (1985) Is 'girl friendly schooling' really what girls need? In Whyte, J., Deem, R., Kant, L. and Cruikshank, M. (eds) *Girl Friendly Schooling*. London: Methuen.

Yen, W. M. (1975) Sex-linked major-gene influence on selected types of spatial performance. *Behaviour Genetics*, 5: 281–98.

Zoller, U. and Ben-Chaim, D. (1989) Gender differences in examination type preferences, test anxiety, and academic achievements in college science education. In Contributions to the Fifth GASAT Conference, Vol. 2, Haifa, Israel.

INDEX

INNOVATION AND CHANGE
DEVELOPING INVOLVEMENT AND UNDERSTANDING

Jean Rudduck

Jean Rudduck argues that we must involve classroom teachers and students in the processes of innovation and change in our schools. It is the right of teachers and pupils as partners in the daily life of the classroom to understand what they are doing and why they are doing it; to recognize the areas where they can influence and improve the experience of learning and teaching; and to appreciate, each in their own ways, that the goal always is to extend the possibilities of control over one's own working environment and over one's life changes through deeper professional and personal understanding. Throughout she emphasizes the significance of co-operative work, of who 'owns' the new ideas and the innovations, and of the meaning as well as the management of change.

Contents
Part 1: Setting the scene – Getting hooked on change: an autobiographical note – Understanding the problems of innovation and change – Part 2: Challenging traditional values and assumptions – 'A majority ruled by knowledge'? – Cooperative group work: democracy or divisiveness? – Part 3: Pupil involvement and understanding – Introducing innovation to pupils – Helping pupils manage the transition to enquiry-based learning – The right to question and the right to understand the structures of learning – Part 4: Teacher involvement and understanding – Ownership as the basis of individual commitment to change – Understanding the world of the classroom: the importance of a research perspective – Partnerships for building understanding – Ownership as the basis of school commitment to change – Part 5: Taking stock – Building and sustaining alternative habits of thought and disposition – References – Name index – Subject index.

168pp   0 335 09580 1 (Paperback)   0 335 09581 X (Hardback)

'RACE', GENDER AND THE EDUCATION OF TEACHERS

Iram Siraj-Blatchford (ed.)

Despite growing concern over the level of racism and sexism in our schools, recruitment and retention of ethnic minority students into teacher education remains very low. Reports by the UK Commission for Racial Equality and the Equal Opportunities Commission continue to show the poor career prospects of women and ethnic minority groups in education. This timely book fills the gap in research and writing on the practical and theoretical approaches to achieving 'race' and gender equality at all levels of teacher education. It examines the central role of teacher educators in reconstructing and promoting equality.

The chapters analyse the effects and implications of continued racist and sexist practices in teacher education. They explore the extent, nature and outcomes of inequality practices in teacher education. They discuss how practitioners and policy makers can provide equal opportunities for students and staff through courses, admission procedures, recruitment, school practice, administration and management. They examine the need for schools, communities and higher education to form closer collaborations to promote equality and raise ethnic minority recruitment. This book is essential reading for all teacher educators and students interested in issues of 'race', gender and equality.

Contents

Contributors

Maud Blair, Pam Boulton, Leone Burton, Lynda Carr, John Clay, John Coldron, Gill Crozier, Pratap Deshpande, Anne Flintoff, Rosalyn George, Uvanney Maylor, Ian Menter, Nargis Rashid, Pat Sikes, Iram Siraj-Blatchford, Gaby Weiner.

192pp   0 335 19017 0 (Paperback)